T0074914

"This is a ground-breaking, rigorously researched volume that explores the intersection of language and translation technologies in healthcare settings, ultimately calling for more effective communication between providers and patients. Whether you are a healthcare professional, a language service provider, or a patient navigating the healthcare system, this book is an indispensable guide to breaking down barriers and promoting technological, linguistic and cultural competence in healthcare."

– Prof. Jorge Díaz-Cintas, University College London

"This book is an insightful deep dive into the multitude of ways that translation tools can be used to advance health communication. This is a must-read for any individual with an interest in developing or evaluating technologies to address gaps in translation access in the healthcare setting. The authors provide foundational knowledge about the types of technologies available, how they can be applied, and approaches to evaluations. Through case studies, the readers then learn about challenges and opportunities for translation technologies to advance health globally. These wide-ranging examples collated into a single volume demonstrate the potential of these tools to transform communication across language barriers."

– Elaine Khoong, MD, University of California, San Francisco

Translation Technology in Accessible Health Communication

Digital health translation is an important application of machine translation and multilingual technologies, and there is a growing need for accessibility in digital health translation design for disadvantaged communities. This book aims to address that need by highlighting state-of-the-art research on the design and evaluation of assistive translation tools, along with systems to facilitate cross-cultural and cross-lingual communications in health and medical settings. Using case studies as examples, the principles of designing assistive health communication tools are illustrated. These are (1) detectability of errors to boost user confidence by health professionals; (2) adaptability or customizability for health and medical domains; (3) inclusivity of translation modalities (written, speech, sign language) to serve people with disabilities; and (4) equality of accessibility standards for localized multilingual websites of health contents. This book will appeal to readers from natural language processing, computer science, linguistics, translation and interpreting studies, public health, media, and communication studies.

MENG JI is an Associate Professor of Translation Studies at The University of Sydney, where she specializes in empirical translation studies and multilingual communications. She received the first PhD in Translation Studies from Imperial College of Science, Technology and Medicine and has worked in London and Tokyo with competitive research fellowships from national research councils in the UK and Japan. The author and editor of more than two dozen books, Dr. Ji has published extensively on environmental and health translation, empirical multilingual translation methodologies, people-centered translation quality assessment, and inclusive translation services and technologies.

PIERRETTE BOUILLON is a professor and dean at the Faculty of Translation and Interpreting, University of Geneva, Switzerland. She is the author of numerous publications in natural language processing, particularly within speech-to-speech machine translation for medical domain and pre- and post-editing, and more recently accessibility. She currently co-leads the Swiss Research Centre Barrier-Free Communication with Zurich University of Applied Sciences, and is the lead investigator of multiple projects of translation studies from the Swiss National Science Foundation and the European Research Council.

MARK SELIGMAN is the founder and President of Spoken Translation, Inc. and the Chief Linguist of Speech Morphing, Inc. Since the 1990s, he has led the design, testing, and implementation of multiple speech translation systems for English, Spanish, Japanese, French, and German, with research associations in the USA, Japan, and Europe, and has contributed to artificial intelligence research and development since the 1980s. He received his PhD in Computational Linguistics from University of California–Berkeley in 1991.

STUDIES IN NATURAL LANGUAGE PROCESSING

Series Editor:
Chu-Ren Huang, The Hong Kong Polytechnic University

Associate Editor:
Qi Su, Peking University, School of Foreign Languages

Editorial Board Members:
Alessandro Lenci, University of Pisa
Lori Levin, Carnegie Mellon University
Yuji Matsumoto, Nara Institute of Technology
Nianwen Xue, Brandeis University

Volumes in the SNLP series provide comprehensive surveys of current research topics and applications in the field of natural language processing (NLP) that shed light on language technology, language cognition, language and society, and linguistics. The increased availability of language corpora and digital media, as well as advances in computer technology and data sciences, has led to important new findings in the field. Widespread applications include voice-activated interfaces, translation, search engine optimization, and affective computing. NLP also has applications in areas such as knowledge engineering, language learning, digital humanities, corpus linguistics, and textual analysis. These volumes will be of interest to researchers and graduate students working in NLP and other fields related to the processing of language and knowledge.

Also in the series

Douglas E. Appelt, *Planning English Sentences*
Madeleine Bates and Ralph M Weischedel (eds.), *Challenges in Natural Language Processing*
Steven Bird, *Computational Phonology*
Peter Bosch and Rob van der Sandt, *Focus*
Pierette Bouillon and Federica Busa (eds.), *Inheritance, Defaults and the Lexicon*
Ronald Cole, Joseph Mariani, Hans Uszkoreit, Giovanni Varile, Annie Zaenen, Antonio Zampolli, and Victor Zue (eds.), *Survey of the State of the Art in Human Language Technology*
David R. Dowty, Lauri Karttunen, and Arnold M Zwicky (eds.), *Natural Language Parsing*
Ralph Grishman, *Computational Linguistics*
Graeme Hirst, *Semantic Interpretation and the Resolution of Ambiguity*

András Kornai, *Extended Finite State Models of Language*
Kathleen R McKeown, *Text Generation*
Martha Stone Palmer, *Semantic Processing for Finite Domains*
Terry Patten, *Systemic Text Generation as Problem Solving*
Ehud Reiter and Robert Dale, *Building Natural Language Generation Systems*
Manny Rayner, David Carter, Pierette Bouillon, Vassilis Digalakis, and Matis
  Wiren (eds.), *The Spoken Language Translator*
Michael Rosner and Roderick Johnson (eds.), *Computational Lexical
  Semantics*
Richard Sproat, *A Computational Theory of Writing Systems*
George Anton Kiraz, *Computational Nonlinear Morphology*
Nicholas Asher and Alex Lascarides, *Logics of Conversation*
Margaret Masterman (edited by Yorick Wilks), *Language, Cohesion and Form*
Walter Daelemans and Antal van den Bosch, *Memory-based Language
  Processing*
Laurent Prévot (eds.), *Ontology and the Lexicon: A Natural Language
  Processing Perspective*
Chu-Ren Huang, Nicoletta Calzolari, Aldo Gangemi, Alessandro Lenci,
  Alessandro Oltramari, *Ontology and the Lexicon: A Natural Language
  Processing Perspective*
Thierry Poibeau and Aline Villavicencio (eds.), *Language, Cognition, and
  Computational Models*
Bing Liu, *Sentiment Analysis: Mining Opinions, Sentiments, and Emotions,
  Second Edition*
Marcos Zampieri and Preslav Nakov (eds.), *Similar Languages, Varieties, and
  Dialects: A Computational Perspective*
Tommaso Caselli, Eduard Hovy, Martha Palmer, Piek Vossen (eds.)
  Computational Analysis of Storylines: Making Sense of Events
Piek Vossen and Antske Fokkens (eds.) *Creating a More Transparent Internet*
Kiyong Lee, *Annotation-based Semantics for Space and Time in Language*
Alessandro Lenci and Magnus Sahlgren, *Distributional Semantics*
Meng Ji, Pierrette Bouillon and Mark Seligman, *Translation Technology in
  Accessible Health Communication*

Translation Technology in Accessible Health Communication

MENG JI
University of Sydney

PIERRETTE BOUILLON
University of Geneva

MARK SELIGMAN
Spoken Translation, Inc.
Speech Morphing, Inc.

With contributions from:

BASTIEN DAVID, MAGALI NORRÉ, IRENE STRASLY,
HERVÉ SPECHBACH, JOHANNA GERLACH, LUCIA
MORADO VAZQUEZ, SILVIA RODRIGUEZ VAZQUEZ

CAMBRIDGE
UNIVERSITY PRESS

Shaftesbury Road, Cambridge CB2 8EA, United Kingdom

One Liberty Plaza, 20th Floor, New York, NY 10006, USA

477 Williamstown Road, Port Melbourne, VIC 3207, Australia

314–321, 3rd Floor, Plot 3, Splendor Forum, Jasola District Centre,
New Delhi – 110025, India

103 Penang Road, #05–06/07, Visioncrest Commercial, Singapore 238467

Cambridge University Press is part of Cambridge University Press & Assessment,
a department of the University of Cambridge.

We share the University's mission to contribute to society through the pursuit of
education, learning and research at the highest international levels of excellence.

www.cambridge.org
Information on this title: www.cambridge.org/9781108837378

DOI: 10.1017/9781108938976

First published 2023

Printed in the United Kingdom by TJ Books Limited, Padstow Cornwall

A catalogue record for this publication is available from the British Library.

Library of Congress Cataloging-in-Publication Data
Names: Ji, Meng (Professor of translation studies), editor. | Bouillon, Pierrette, editor. | Seligman, Mark, editor.
Title: Translation technology in accessible health communication / Meng Ji, Pierrette Bouillon, Mark
Seligman ; with contributions from Bastien David, Magali Norré, Irene Strasly, Hervé Spechbach,
Johanna Gerlach, Lúcia Morado Vásquez, Silvia Rodríguez Vásquez.
Other titles: Studies in natural language processing.
Description: Cambridge : New York, NY : Cambridge University Press, 2023. | Series: Studies in natural
language processing | Includes bibliographical references and index.
Identifiers: LCCN 2023029455 | ISBN 9781108837378 (hardback) | ISBN 9781108938976 (ebook)
Subjects: MESH: Health Communication – methods | Translating | Informatics – methods | Software |
Communication Barriers
Classification: LCC R118 | NLM WA 590 | DDC 610.1/4–dc23/eng/20230720
LC record available at https://lccn.loc.gov/2023029455

ISBN 978-1-108-83737-8 Hardback

Contents

Contributors

Fabio Alessi, *Department of Mathematics and Computer Science, Udine University*

Marc Bezem, *Department of Informatics, Bergen University*

Felice Cardone, *Department of Informatics, Torino University*

Mario Coppo, *Department of Informatics, Torino University*

Mariangiola Dezani-Ciancaglini, *Department of Informatics, Torino University*

Gilles Dowek, *Department of Informatics, 'Ecole Polytechnique; and INRIA*

Silvia Ghilezan, *Center for Mathematics & Statistics, University of Novi Sad*

Furio Honsell, *Department of Mathematics and Computer Science, Udine University*

Michael Moortgat, *Department of Modern Languages, Utrecht University*

Paula Severi, *Department of Computer Science, University of Leicester*

Introduction

Accessible Health Translation Technology Matters

This book was conceived in 2018 when Pierrette and I were working together on a funded project that evaluated the performance of machine translation for migrant and minority languages. The project was co-funded by the University of Geneva and the University of Sydney as part of a strategic research partnership between the two universities. When visiting Geneva, I was fortunate to meet with the research team Pierrette leads, a group of talented multilingual researchers from around the world, passionate about improving access to translation technology for vulnerable communities: culturally and linguistically diverse refugees, migrants, and people with disabilities. Mark, meanwhile, is well known to both of us – as a long-time acquaintance of Pierrette and as a close research collaborator of mine in recent years. A seasoned developer and senior researcher of multilingual medical speech translation systems, he offers a unique perspective on the design and evaluation of health and medical translation systems that can serve multicultural communities. Together, we began to plan a volume focused upon uses of linguistic technology in healthcare, with special interest in service to widely diverse and underserved communities.

Multilingualism and multiculturalism have always been proud traditions in Europe, as these values compose the core of democracy, social equality, and sustainability. Thriving multilingualism has provided a fertile and favorable social environment for translation research and innovation in our changing world. Increasing populations of migrant minorities, refugees, and displaced people in Europe are broadening the definition of, and our traditional understanding of, this multilingual and multicultural continent. In response, translation research is developing to reflect and interact with this changing social environment. Pierrette's own agenda in speech translation research, for

1

instance, exemplifies European emphasis on enhancing the social benefits, inclusiveness, and humanitarian concerns of innovation in this area of technology. Facilitation of effective, accessible health communication with disadvantaged populations through use of enhanced translation technologies is seen as a practical, innovative, and cost-effective strategy for tackling health inequality in today's multilingual and multicultural Europe.

In modern Australia, too – my own research home – multiculturalism is widely recognized as a key to prosperity and social cohesion. In 2020, 29.8 percent of Australia's population was born overseas, while more than 200 languages are spoken in Australian homes. Accordingly, the chief function of translation and interpreting in Australia is provision of essential language assistance to people with limited English proficiency to improve their access to healthcare, medical treatments, and other essential social services. However, only professional translators – interpreters who have obtained their qualifications through the National Accreditation Authority for Translators and Interpreters (NAATI) process – may provide translation services. While in Europe systematic and conventionalized use of machine translation tools and curated multilingual databases are current, authorities in Australia only adopt translation technology in medical and health settings conservatively, despite increasing demands during the pandemic crisis for more timely, direct, and effective engagement with diverse communities. (To be sure, careful adoption is warranted – a point to which we will return at length.)

And of course, Mark's home base, the United States, is more than ever a melting pot. In a favorite San Francisco restaurant, bearing the Greek name Acropolis (a word that Mark's Korean-Japanese wife still struggles to pronounce), Russian food is prepared by Chinese staff. No healthcare facilities can avoid the consequent communication issues, though the specific linguistic and cultural demands and coping strategies (whether via professional interpreters in person or via video, intercession by family members or bilingual staff members, or available translation technology) vary considerably from state to state and region to region. In California, for instance, healthcare assistance in the patient's dominant language is mandated by law (though, too often, still absent in practice). Translation requirements at a major San Francisco facility are sketched in Chapter 2.

To linguistic and cultural challenges may be added physical and mental health challenges. And, in fact, the number of people with disabilities is increasing worldwide. Currently, according to the World Health Organization, over one billion or about 15 percent of the world's population is estimated to live with some impairment in mental, sensory, or mobility functions. This finding highlights another way in which speech and translation technology can serve: not only to narrow the gap between languages and cultures, but also to lower barriers to effective communications associated with hearing impairment, speech disorders, and related impairments.

A special case within the disabled population is the Deaf community, which can be served through sign language translation, which utilizes a repertoire of gestures, a sign language lexicon, to interpret verbal messages. Technology integrating such translation can significantly improve access to healthcare services among people with hearing loss or impairment.

A final group deserving special consideration with respect to health communication is the population with limited literacy or educational attainment. And indeed, in multicultural countries, lack of English proficiency is often associated with limited health literacy.

For all these diverse and often underserved multilingual and multicultural groups, studies of translation, whether by humans or machines, are clearly vital. And yet, until now, quality assessments have in our judgment focused too narrowly on the accuracy of linguistic details, thus overlooking the actual linguistic comprehensibility, cultural accessibility, and relevance of translations for multicultural people with limited literacy and health literacy.

Hence this volume. Here, for example, we illustrate the design of medical speech translation systems equipped with tools for increasing speech recognition and translation reliability and customization per use case; and we discuss inclusion of simplified visual aids such as health-themed pictograms for use in emergency departments to facilitate understanding of medical terms by patients with limited literacy or local-language proficiency. Overall, we stress *accessible* speech and translation technology.

Accessible translation technology can provide much-needed help in addressing and reducing healthcare inequalities due to language discordances, disabilities, and limited educational level and health literacy – inequalities often associated with entrenched socioeconomic disadvantages. However, rather than define such accessibility and inclusivity narrowly, we prefer an open, principled approach. The key principles highlighted and illustrated throughout this book are these: (1) detectability of errors to boost user confidence by health professionals; (2) adaptability or customizability for health and medical domains; (3) inclusivity of translation modalities (written, speech, sign language) to serve people with disabilities; and (4) equality of accessibility standards for localized multilingual websites of health contents. To summarize these key principles for promotion of accessible and reliable translation technology, we use the acronym I-D-E-A.

I-D-E-A: Principles of Accessible Health Translation Technology

Detectability of Machine Translation Errors to Boost User Confidence

No form of modern technology is error free, and machine translation systems are no exceptions, whether based on earlier rule-based models or the latest neural networks. Chapter 1 explains the principal types of speech and text translation systems, comparing their theoretical underpinnings and assessing their relative strengths and limitations. Chapter 2 goes on to examine their applications in the healthcare context, with emphasis on speech translation.

General-purpose translation systems are constantly improving in measurable translation accuracy, as compared to professional human translations. In specialized healthcare domains, however, lack of confidence persists: even when measurably accurate, the systems fall short in *reliability*, as this is partly a psychological matter. One reason is the difficulty of understanding these technologies, and thus the natural hesitation to trust them – an issue directly addressed in Chapter 1, where the technologies are explained. We share the view that adoption of speech and translation technology for healthcare must proceed conservatively and with *informed* caution.

Detection of errors, we believe, should be a vital element of that caution and confidence building. Mechanisms are needed to increasingly enable healthcare professionals to predict potential translation errors and to detect actual ones.

But what errors should be predicted and detected? In current machine translation performance evaluation for health and medical applications, consistent definitions and supporting systems for differentiation and classification of wide-ranging translation errors are still lacking.

For translation of general material, error assessment often draws upon experienced translators' human judgment and consensus concerning the acceptability of inherent lexical, semantic, syntactic, and pragmatic variations between the source text and the target translation. The assessment's level of granularity depends upon the purpose of the exercise. Higher granularity entails increases in breadth and scoring of details; so this approach is most suitable for interpreters at advanced skill levels, and for interpreter training. Further, for specialized text or speech translation in healthcare, assessment must also align with the evaluation of miscommunication risks and their severity levels, as judged by health professionals. Sensitivity to miscommunication on health issues entails a subtle, discreet, and risk-based approach to translation error detection. Such judgment calls can be challenging, even for skilled translators and interpreters without proper medical training or extensive practical experience: indeed, detection of *clinically relevant* errors in machine translation output can be handled effectively and efficiently *only* by highly experienced translators specializing in health and medicine, or by professionals with proven bilingual proficiency. These must demonstrate in-depth understanding of health concepts, health beliefs, and traditions in both source and target languages.

Our brief is that, if machine translation is to gain wide applicability in healthcare, professionals at all levels of expertise and experience need transparent systems providing instant expert feedback concerning the quality of translation output and risk levels of input. Reliable and consistent mechanisms and tools for error prediction and detection are required that can leverage the cross-lingual/cross-cultural sensitivity and keen awareness of highly experienced health translators regarding clinically significant miscommunication risks.

Chapter 2 will illustrate several tools for error *detection*, especially during translated conversations.

Prediction of clinically significant errors can boost user confidence by reducing the uncertainty and risks associated with machine translation tools. Prediction can be particularly useful for users without sufficient resources to make informed, safe decisions – that is, without linguistic proficiency, adequate health, medical knowledge, or some combination. Thus Chapters 3 and 4 illustrate a novel approach to estimating the likelihood of translation errors that could mislead users, or to estimating the danger of including expressions with negative connotations in the target language when translating sensitive content regarding mental health status. This approach to managing the risk of machine translation combines the strengths of humans and machines – the insights and sensitivity of experienced health translators on one hand, and the consistency and high prediction accuracy of machine learning algorithms on the other. We hope that its use can significantly increase users' confidence in machine translation systems.

Adaptability or Customizability

Chapter 5 introduces BabelDr, an automatic speech translation system for medical emergencies which has been piloted and evaluated with diverse end users, especially multicultural migrants and refugees admitted to University of Geneva Hospitals in Switzerland, with the goal of enabling interactions with French-speaking physicians. Chapters 1 and 2 detail the design of such phrase-based medical speech translation tools, which have significantly enhanced reliability and adaptability for specific health and medical domains when compared to general-purpose machine translation systems.

Since their translations are prepared in advance, phrase-based translation systems may be presented in various innovative media and formats. For example, BabelDr integrates graphical images of health messages, an innovation inspired by earlier studies on the effect of pictographs on user satisfaction in healthcare communication. Feedback from multicultural patients has verified the comprehensibility of pictographs and their potential for augmenting traditional text- or speech-based medical translation tools. For example, Chapter 5 discusses the adaptation of visual aids in BabelDr, selected from open sources and initially designed for Hispanic users, for use by multicultural patients speaking Albanian, Arabic, Dari, Farsi, and Tigrinya.

Because BabelDr's visual interface simplifies speech-based interpreting, it can ease logistic issues, for example, by facilitating recruitment of adequately trained health interpreters for minority languages. At the same time, visual aids can improve attention, recall, satisfaction, and adherence among patients, thus helping to reduce health communication barriers due to patients' limited health literacy or educational levels.

Chapter 5 also shows that pictograph usability depends on various factors – not only on the comprehensibility of the pictographs per se, but also on the manner of presentation (e.g., on the order and number of images).

Per Chapters 1 and 2, development of automated translation systems tends to favor languages for which copious data is available. The resulting machine translation tools thus often perform much better on these than on low-resource languages like those studied by Pierrette and her students. However, because phrase-based speech translation systems like BabelDr can be adapted to new health situations or demographics with relative ease, adaptation for low-resource languages likewise becomes more practical – a breakthrough in automatic health translation research. What's more, the benefits extend even further: technology-enhanced communications can be made accessible to a range of disadvantaged minorities; and breakthroughs based upon work with minorities can significantly benefit high-resource languages as well.

Thus the BabelDr project, having arisen from efforts to exploit pretranslated textual or spoken translations for their reliability, has led to recognition of the usefulness in those translations of images and visual aids, since these can be universally understandable by people of many languages, cultures, educational levels, health statuses, or disabilities. Pictogram-based approaches, whether replacing or augmenting text- or speech-based methods, hold great promise for technology-enhanced healthcare communication, just as universal emojis have become indispensable in everyday textual communications.

Meanwhile, research toward increased customization of text- and speech-based translation can continue in parallel. Chapter 2 illustrates a related facility in the Converser for Healthcare speech translation prototype – the Translation Shortcuts tool. Shortcuts are prepared translations for specific use cases like pharmacy consultations and in-hospital nursing, and thus are comparable to the pretranslated phrases of BabelDr. They differ, however, in that they're designed to operate in seamless cooperation with unrestricted automatic speech translation, rather than to replace it: If an input closely enough matches a source language utterance with a prepared translation, that translation will be used; and if not, the input will be subjected to full machine translation. Shortcuts, in other words, function as translation memory – as repositories for translations known to be correct and available for reuse – but can also be quickly added on demand and efficiently browsed and searched. Thus they, too, like strictly phrase-based translation systems, answer this volume's call for adaptability and customizability, showing that these criteria can be applied to many translation approaches.

Inclusivity to Serve People of Disability

Chapter 6 introduces a sign language version of the BableDr system expressly designed for people with hearing loss or impairment.

Globally, hearing impairment is on the rise. One in six adults is affected in the UK or Australia, and one in eight people in the United States. To improve communication between impaired patients and their healthcare providers, automatic translation tools can be crucial; and sign language is widely recognized as an important translation genre.

Each sign language has a unique vocabulary repertoire and an associated set of expressive bodily gestures and facial movements, while variations may be found across communities and cultures. Accordingly, Chapter 6 discusses the creation of a Swiss French Sign Language (LSF-CH) version of BabelDr, for which sign language interpreting by virtual interpreters (avatars) was derived from videos recorded by human sign interpreters. The research team then evaluated the reception of the avatar version among Deaf people on the BabelDr platform. It was determined that, at the present stage of avatar development, the subtle nuances of sign language interpreting were better conveyed by the facial expressions and bodily movements of humans than by the avatars' comparable actions. Nevertheless, the authors conclude that the use of virtual characters does interest the target audience and does appear promising in the medical context. They call for further research on the complex perception of sign language interpreting among Deaf people.

Equality of Accessibility Standards for Localized Multilingual Websites

Chapter 7 discusses the prevalent lack of high accessibility standards in the translation and localization of online health information websites. The level of accessibility is found to vary considerably across translated versions of original English websites. In particular, the authors studied localized Spanish versions of many English websites developed by health authorities and health-promotion organizations, finding that accessibility in the target language was often insufficient – for instance, in website titles when changing English to Spanish. The relevant suboptimal elements of major health websites following translation and localization were not recognized by existing systems for assessing accessibility but were identified only through the authors' labor-extensive manual assessment.

Unfortunately, low standards of accessibility in localized healthcare websites directly affect the target audiences – Hispanic populations worldwide – in many ways.

First, target language errors can hamper the automatic recognition of website texts by screen readers – programs that read onscreen text out loud – for users with visual loss or impairment, or by people with limited literacy and educational level who require audio versions of website information.

Second, target language errors can hinder the accessibility of website title pages, thus impeding users' searches. Numerous error types were identified: titles in Spanish (1) were too long, exceeding the recommended 64-character limit; (2) failed to identify the subject of the web page; (3) made no sense when read out of context; (4) included unnecessary repetitions; (5) included abbreviations without the expanded form, thus causing potential confusion and reading difficulties; and (6) included URL addresses.

These findings call for increased awareness of accessibility issues in website translation and localization. Generic accessibility guidelines and protocols do exist, but mechanisms are needed to effectively evaluate their proper implementation.

The COVID-19 pandemic exacerbated existing social and health inequalities around the world. Migrants, minorities, refugees, and disabled populations have been disproportionately affected by the ongoing spread of the disease. Timely, effective, and responsive communication with these communities, in this and other health emergences, has become increasingly important to all of us.

Translation technology can help. This book aims to offer updates and insights into its design, practical applications, and evaluation, whether for written, spoken, or signed varieties. Our hope is to help enable enhanced and more accessible healthcare communication with populations of diverse languages, cultures, and physical or mental abilities.

Meng Ji, Pierrette Bouillon, and Mark Seligman
September 2022

1

Speech and Translation Technologies
Explanations
MARK SELIGMAN

1.1 Introduction

The need for cross-language communication in healthcare is clear: Every day and everywhere, thousands of conversations take place between patients and caregivers – not only doctors and nurses, but administrators, volunteers, and others – whose native languages don't match. The circumstances vary widely, and the requirements for translation differ along with them. Some patients are literate, and some are not; some speak the caregivers' language sufficiently for effective communication concerning care, and some do not. Some patients are able to visit caregivers in person – or vice versa – while some must communicate remotely by phone, dedicated video, or internet audio and video.

Technology promising to assist this communication is developing explosively. The major linguistic technologies – machine translation (MT) of text, automatic speech recognition (ASR), text-to-speech (TTS) – have all improved dramatically in the era of neural networks, and so have the enabling elements of infrastructure – wireless communication, cloud computing, and mobile devices. By now, one would expect various forms of automatic translation and speech-enabled systems to have taken the healthcare world by storm, but adoption has in fact been sluggish. We'll examine the reasons for the speed bumps in Chapter 2, along with possible measures to surmount them.

One key factor in the lagging adoption, however, is the difficulty of understanding the relevant technologies, and thus the natural hesitation to trust them. Accordingly, this chapter aims to promote informed use by bridging the understanding gap for healthcare workers.

We begin with speech – its recognition (Section 1.2), its synthesis (Section 1.3), and related issues. Moving on to MT (Section 1.4), we'll first note the availability of systems covering only pretranslated phrases. We'll then go on to examine the major types of MT with broader coverage – "full MT," whether rule-based, statistical, or neural. As a bonus, we'll add extended discussion of transformer-based neural processing at the current state of the art. We'll conclude with some requisite cautions, and with a send-off to Chapter 2 shifting focus to practical applications of these technologies in the healthcare context.

1.2 Automatic Speech Recognition

1.2.1 Classical Automatic Speech Recognition

Automatic speech recognition has made dramatic progress in the last two decades. Throughout the 2000s, *speaker-dependent* ASR remained dominant: To achieve acceptable accuracy using commercially available ASR, each speaker had to provide speech samples, initially twenty minutes or more. In most systems, the speech signal to be converted into text was sliced into short segments, so that the system could estimate the probability of certain text sequences given a sequence of sound slices, generally using hidden Markov models (HMMs).[1] These estimates yielded possible words or word fragments and their probability rankings; and one could go on to estimate which *word* sequences were most likely, using compilations of word sequence probabilities called language models.[2] The search through the associated set of possibilities – the associated space of possible words and word sequences – was usually managed through some variant of Viterbi search techniques.[3]

By means of these techniques, and with sufficient speaker-specific and domain-specific recordings and accurate transcripts as training material, accuracies well above 90 percent became feasible in favorable environments. Necessary recording time dropped in a few years from twenty-plus minutes to less than a minute as processing power steadily increased according to Moore's law – the observation that computers' processing power doubles every two years or so[4] – and as usable recording databases became much larger. As a result, speaker-*independent* training had finally arrived by the early 2010s: That is, training time per new speaker had dropped to zero!

---

[1] "Hidden Markov Model." *Wikipedia*, Wikimedia Foundation, July 18, 2022, at 05: 21(UTC), https://en.wikipedia.org/wiki/Hidden_Markov_model.

[2] "Language Model." *Wikipedia*, Wikimedia Foundation, August 5, 2022, at 09: 29(UTC), https://en.wikipedia.org/wiki/Language_model.

[3] "Viterbi Algorithm." *Wikipedia*, Wikimedia Foundation, 12 March 2022, at 20: 26(UTC), https://en.wikipedia.org/wiki/Viterbi_algorithm.

[4] "Moore's law." *Wikipedia*, Wikimedia Foundation, July 30, 2022, at 18: 02(UTC), https://en.wikipedia.org/wiki/Moore%27s_law.

1.2.2 Neural Automatic Speech Recognition

Then neural speech recognition appeared on the scene: By the late 2010s, deep neural networks (DNNs) had essentially replaced HMM-based systems. Neural network models are fundamentally learners of input-to-output functions: When given certain patterns as input, they learn to yield certain patterns as output. (We'll look further into the details in Section 1.4.2.3.) And so, for ASR, when given suitably preprocessed speech signals, they can learn to deliver the most probable text transcripts. However, since speech recognition involves mediating between sequential patterns for both input (sequences of sounds) and output (sequences of graphemes – that is, letters or characters – and words), neural architectures specialized for sequences are essential. Until recently, recurrent and convolutional architectures were preferred – the first designed, when computing sound-to-text probabilities for the next step along a sequence in progress, to accumulate the output of all prior steps and include these as input, and the second designed to exploit a window moving across the sequence. These have now made room for transformer-based neural setups. These exploit a method called attention to focus upon the elements in a segment that will provide the most meaningful context to enable prediction of new sequences. (Transformers and attention are further discussed in Section 1.4.2.3.)

1.2.3 Automatic Speech Recognition Issues and Directions

1.2.3.1 Automatic Speech Recognition Issues

Numerous problems remain. Much speech, whether collected in real time or from recordings, is spontaneous rather than based upon written materials and consequently contains hesitations, stutters, repetitions, fragments, and other features unfriendly to recognition. Speech often occurs in noisy environments. It often involves multiparty conversations, with several voices that tend to overlap. The voices may be speaking different dialects and may even mix languages.

To address these and other issues, ASR development is continually in progress beyond neural network techniques themselves. Numerous possible architectural variations and component interactions can be tried according to the use case. For example, several varieties of noise reduction modules can deliver cleaner audio input (Li et al., 2014).

Integration of knowledge sources will also be a fruitful ongoing research direction. Presently, ASR still usually lacks any attempt to understand the objects and relationships in the speech situation.

1.2.3.2 Automatic Speech Recognition Directions

Considerations of understanding raise the question of future use cases for ASR. As one example, consider self-driving cars equipped with noise-resistant speech recognition: A car will "know" about its dynamic environment, having acquired from "experience" (multiple instances) visual "concepts" like CAR, TRUCK, and STREET, and their spatial and causative relations. And so, when recognizing user questions or commands concerning cars, trucks, streets, and so on, the car will be able to use knowledge about the referents – and not only the audio – to raise or lower probabilities of currently recognized text in context. And a car's concepts could include not only visual percepts but also sounds, vibrations, and lidar or radar data – a wide range of sensor data. In coming years, this incorporation of perceptually grounded knowledge is likely to transform all areas of artificial intelligence, speech recognition not least. The results will affect speech translation; transcription of all audio and video (real-time and otherwise); and, in fact, every use case demanding ASR – roughly, every use case involving speech.

To enable an informal impression of current speech recognition accuracy, we supply, in Appendix 1.1, healthcare-oriented ASR examples for English, using two current commercially available systems.

1.3 Speech Synthesis (Text-to-Speech)

Synthetic speech reached an acceptable quality level – understandable if colorless and unmistakably artificial – in the nineties. The problem was considered largely solved; and, partly for that reason, text-to-speech remained relatively static while speech recognition was rapidly and noticeably improving. We'll look at "classical" text-to-speech first, then move on to the current neural era.

1.3.1 Classical Text-to-Speech

1.3.1.1 Concatenative Text-to-Speech

The most widely used classical technology – still in use for some purposes – was concatenative: short, recorded audio segments associated with speech sounds (*phonemes* like /t/ or /o/ and their subparts or groupings) were stitched together (concatenated) to compose words and larger units.[5]

---

[5] "Speech Synthesis#Concatenation Synthesis." *Wikipedia*, Wikimedia Foundation, August 12, 2022, at 14: 44(UTC), https://en.wikipedia.org/wiki/Speech_synthesis#Concatenation_synthesis.

The segments in question were collected from large databases of recorded speech. Utterances were segmented into individual phones, syllables, words, and so on, usually employing a special-purpose speech recognition system yielding an alignment between sound elements and those linguistic units. An index of the units was compiled, based on the segmentation and on acoustic parameters (factors) including pitch, duration, and position among other units. And then, to build a target utterance given a text, the best chain of candidate units was selected, typically using a decision tree (sequence of program-based "questions") while extending the chain. Good results could be achieved, but maximum naturalness required large recording databases, up to dozens of hours. (Alternatives to such concatenative text-to-speech could synthesize utterances from scratch by artificially generating waveforms – the graphic representations of waves, describing them in terms of frequency and amplitude, which can be converted into actual sound. The resulting speech was less natural, but waveform methods had advantages, for example, in size, so that they lent themselves to implementations in small devices, even toys.)

1.3.1.2 General Text-to-Speech Issues

Concatenative or otherwise, any speech synthesis system confronts several issues.

Allophones and Coarticulation Phonemes are generally pronounced differently (as allophones, or phoneme variants) according to their place in words or phrases. For instance, in US English, phoneme /t/ may be pronounced with or without a puff of air (called *aspiration*, present in *top* but absent in *pot*). Moreover, even those variants – and all other speech sounds – will vary further in context according to the neighboring sounds (i.e., to coarticulation effects): For instance, the puffed /t/ sounds different before different vowels. (For this reason, diphones, or pairs of phonemes, are frequently used as speech sound groupings.) Coarticulation changes arising from some sound sequences can be dramatic in certain styles or registers, as when /t/+/y/ in *don't you* becomes the /ʧ/ of *doncha*. If classical TTS handled such cases – they usually didn't – it was through indicative spellings ("doncha") or through programs implementing handwritten combinatory rules.

Disambiguation Another problem is posed by text sequences that can be pronounced entirely differently according to their use in a sentence, like "record" in "For the *re*cord, ... " versus "We need to re*cord* this meeting."

Some analysis of sentences is needed to select the appropriate variant and resolve the ambiguity – that is, to perform *disambiguation*. In classical TTS, this need was often met by symbolic (handwritten) programs for sentence analysis.

Normalization Yet another challenge is presented by text elements whose pronunciation isn't specified in text at all but is instead left to the knowledge of the reader-out-loud. Numbers and dates are typical examples: 7/2/21 might be pronounced as "July second, twenty twenty-one" in the US – though variants are many, even leaving aside the matter of European writing conventions. Some ways must be found to convert such elements to pronounceable text – to normalize the input.

Pronunciation problems Foreign or unfamiliar words ("Just hang a U-ie on El Camino") present obvious difficulties for text-to-speech. They're normally addressed either through compilation of specialized or custom dictionaries or through use of a *guesser* – a program that uses rules (then) or machine learning (now) to guess the most likely pronunciation.

Prosody Some treatment is needed of *prosody* – movement of pitch (melody), duration (rhythm), and volume (loudness). In the classical era, the prosody of a sentence was superimposed on speech units via various digital signal processing techniques. For instance, via the Pitch Synchronous Overlap and Add (PSOLA) technique, the speech waveform is divided into small overlapping segments that can be moved further apart to decrease the pitch, or closer together to increase it. Segments could be repeated multiple times to increase the duration of a section or eliminated to decrease it. The final segments were combined by overlapping them and smoothing the overlap. The means of predicting the appropriate prosody were relatively simple – for example, by reference to punctuation – so the results were often repetitive and lacking in expression.

Extraprosodic speech features Extraprosodic speech features like breathiness, vocal tension, creakiness, and so on were only occasionally treated in research, for example, by simulating the physics of the voice tract. Using models of vocal frequency jitter and tremor and of airflow noise and laryngeal asymmetries, one system was engineered to mimic the timbre of vocally challenged speakers, giving controlled levels of roughness, breathiness, and strain (Englert et al., 2016).

1.3.2 Neural Text-to-Speech

As mentioned, neural technology learns input-to-output functions – usually from corpora of input-output examples. For neural speech synthesis, the synthesis job can be understood as two input-to-output problems or stages:

1. Given text (perhaps revised or augmented with markup), what should be the corresponding acoustic features (numbers indicating factors like segment pitch, duration, etc.)?

    ○ The acoustic features are represented as spectrograms, which show frequency changes over time: In an X/Y graph, the vertical (Y) axis shows frequency, and the horizontal (X) axis shows time. (These days, a modified frequency scale is often substituted for raw frequency: the mel frequency scale – mel for "melody" – which takes account of human perception.)

2. Given acoustic features, what actual sound should be generated? This is the function of a vocoder.[6]

However, the stages can be combined to yield an end-to-end neural text-to-speech solution.

The prerequisites for neural text-to-speech began as recently as 2016, when DeepMind demonstrated networks able to perform the second stage by generating speech from acoustic features.[7] In 2017, the technology was used by others (Sotelo et al., 2017) to produce an initial end-to-end solution – generating speech directly from text. At the same time, Google and Facebook offered Tacotron and VoiceLoop, which could perform the first stage – that is, generate acoustic features, as opposed to sound, from input text. Completing the R&D pathway, Google proposed Tacotron2 as a more mature end-to-end solution, combining a revised acoustic feature generator (the first stage) with the WaveNet vocoder (the second stage).[8]

Now that current end-to-end systems can generate speech whose color (timbre) and overall resemblance approaches that of humans, this methodology has been widely adopted (Tan et al., 2021). Good models for given speakers or languages can be created with little engineering. They're robust, since there are no components that can fail. And unlike classical concatenative models, they require no large databases at run time.

---

[6] "Vocoder." *Wikipedia, Wikimedia* Foundation, 7 August 2022, at 18: 38(UTC), https://en.wikipedia.org/wiki/Vocoder.

[7] "WaveNet." *Wikipedia, Wikimedia* Foundation, 18 July 2022, at 17: 07(UTC), https://en.wikipedia.org/wiki/WaveNet.

[8] "Deep Learning Speech Synthesis." *Wikipedia*, Wikimedia Foundation, June 6, 2022, at 17: 58 (UTC), https://en.wikipedia.org/wiki/Deep_learning_speech_synthesis.

1.3.2.1 Neural Text-to-Speech Issues

But, of course, challenges remain:

- Learning of models takes much time and computation. Resolution efforts have emphasized architectural variation: Transformer-based architecture (Section 1.4.2.3.1) can replace older methods, with several advantages, including efficiency.
- If training data is insufficient or low in quality, speech quality suffers. The quality problem is related to failures of alignment between text and speech sounds, so focus has been on improving alignment by leveraging the known relations between these elements.
- Control points are absent: What you hear is what you get. Research has stressed methods of learning representations of certain speech features as embeddings, or points in multidimensional (vector) space (Section 1.4.2.2). The points can represent emotions (like anger or sadness) as expressed through speech features like pitch or rhythm. Because that representation remains separate from, for example, the pronunciation, many combinations and blends are possible.
- Prosody and pronunciation tend to be flat, since they're averaged over large collections of training data. At or after synthesis time, users can interactively post-tune preliminary flat (emotionless, bland, boring) renderings via suitable user interfaces. In addition, TTS models can be made to generate speech with various speaker styles and characteristics by utilizing embeddings representing speakers and speaking styles.

1.3.2.2 Neural Vocoders

We mentioned that neural speech synthesis involves two stages, where the second is sound generation, as performed by a vocoder. That vocoder can exploit neural networks, as do the popular WaveNet ("WaveNet") and HiFi-GAN (Kong et al., 2021) vocoders.

1.4 Machine Translation

We now shift focus to MT. We'll glance at translation based on fixed phrases, postponing most discussion for Chapter 2, before shifting attention to various techniques for full (wide-ranging, relatively unrestricted) translation: rule-based, statistical, and neural. As an optional coda for AI-curious readers, we'll examine state-of-the-art neural translation techniques involving transformers – neural networks for sequence prediction that handle context in a powerful new way.

As we've seen, transformers can be applied advantageously to speech recognition and speech synthesis as well.

1.4.1 Machine Translation Based on Fixed Phrases

Several healthcare-oriented speech translation systems have been designed to handle pretranslated phrases only, rather than to attempt full MT of wide-ranging input. This design decision enhances reliability because it depends on (usually professional) translation in advance; and it aids customization per use case in that relevant phrases can be brought into the system as needed.

Speech translation systems of this type include a set of fixed and pretranslated phrases, each supplied with a prepared target-language translation. Within such a set, the task of speech recognition is to find the best match for the incoming source-language phrase so as to enable transmission of its prepared translation via text or text-to-speech. (Matches will often be inexact, so techniques for finding near misses will be required.) The translation may be augmented with, or even substituted by, audiovisual elements – images, videos, or audio clips. Chapter 2 offers further discussion of phrase-only speech translation systems, with description of sample systems.

1.4.2 Full Machine Translation: Beyond Fixed Phrases

We now survey development of MT from its beginnings in the 1950s to the current state of the art. Conveniently enough, progress in the field can be divided into three eras or paradigms:[9] those of rule-based, statistical, and neural MT. We'll devote a subsection to each paradigm. Each can be usefully viewed in terms of its treatment of meaning, or semantics: Rule-based methods have generally emphasized handmade semantic symbols; statistical methods have generally avoided semantic treatment or employed vector-based semantics, as will be explained; and neural methods have until now handled meaning as implicit within networks.

We aren't undertaking a full history of MT research and development. For that purpose, see instead for example Hutchins (2010). We postpone discussion of speech translation until Chapter 2.

---

[9] The word paradigm, when referring to a consensus among researchers about the legitimate concepts and procedures for a scientific enterprise, was introduced by (Kuhn, 1996). Here the progression of paradigms or eras tracks the shift from one way of handling machine translation to another.

1.4.2.1 Rule-Based Machine Translation

We begin our survey of MT with a review of rule-based approaches. These employ handwritten rules relating to grammar and word composition (morphology), side by side with handwritten programs, so that the style might instead have been termed handmade MT.

Handmade approaches are rare in current MT development, where neural approaches (Section 1.4.2.3) are now overwhelmingly favored. Still, legacy MT systems continue to employ them[10]; and examination of them is conceptually helpful in understanding neural approaches, which would otherwise appear as oracles – as "black boxes" whose inner workings are invisible and mysterious, into which one language enters and from which another language miraculously emerges.

Within the rule-based paradigm, then, three subapproaches can be distinguished: direct, transfer-based, and interlingua-based.

Throughout, we'll be referring to the source language (SL, the language we're translating *from*) and the target language (TL, the language we're translating *to*).

Intermediate Structures: Syntactic versus Semantic In comparing the three rule-based approaches, one important question is whether the approaches do or don't automatically derive steppingstones between the SL and TL. We'll call these *intermediate structures*.

Another significant consideration is the composition of any such go-between structures: Do they represent *syntactic* or *semantic* features of an utterance, or some mixture? Figure 1.1 illustrates this distinction.

Consider first the analysis of the Japanese phrase on the left. In their original order, the English glosses of the relevant Japanese words would be "car, (object marker), driving, do, person" – that is, "car-driving person," "person who drives/is driving a car." The analysis shows that we are dealing with a noun phrase; that it is composed of a verb phrase on the left and a noun on the right; that the verb phrase in turn contains a certain sort of phrase; and so on. This is strictly a part-to-whole analysis – a *syntactic* analysis, where syntax refers to the analysis of the parts of a speech segment (for example, a sentence) and their relation to the whole segment. It says nothing explicit about the *meaning* of the phrase.

By contrast, on the right, we do see an attempt to capture the meaning of this phrase. PERSON is this time shown as a semantic (meaning-related) object, presumably one which could be related within a graph relating classes,

---

[10] "Word Magic." URL: https://word-magic-translator-home-edition.software.informer.com/.

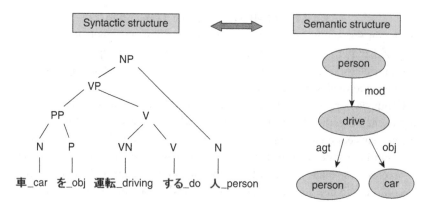

Figure 1.1 Contrasting syntactic and semantic intermediate structures

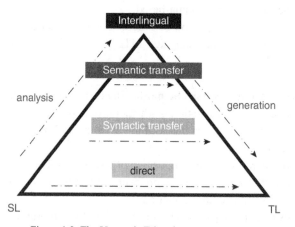

Figure 1.2 The Vauquois Triangle

subclasses, and instances – called an *ontology* – to other semantic objects such as ANIMALS, LIVING-THINGS, and so on. The PERSON in question is *modified* – a semantic rather than syntactic relationship – by the *action* DRIVE, and that modifying action has an *agent* (the same PERSON, though the identity is not shown) and an *object*, CAR.

In practice, such intermediate structures often mix syntactic (part-to-whole) and semantic (meaning-related) features, as we will see.

Vauquois Triangle We're ready now to contrast the three main approaches within the rule-based MT paradigm. For orientation, we refer to an often-used diagram of the relationships between direct, transfer-based, and interlingua-based methods (Figure tech.1.2), the *Vauquois Triangle* (Boitet, 2000).

The diagram depicts various paths for departing from the SL (at lower left) and arriving at the TL (at lower right).

Direct Translation We've drawn attention to this question for rule-based MT systems: are *intermediate structures* derived as go-betweens or steppingstones between SL and TL? The distinguishing feature of *direct* translation methods is precisely the absence of such midway points.

As a first step, *surface* elements of the SL – that is, the words and expressions in the input text – will undergo lookup to discover TL elements that can serve as their respective translations. (Several candidates might be found per element.) Programs will then be invoked to "massage" the target elements to compose a complete translation based upon them: to choose among translation candidates; to order the selected target elements properly; and to make necessary adjustments for TL morphology (word-building) and syntax (grouping and related modifications), for example, by handling agreement (making plural adjectives agree with plural nouns, for instance), adding function words or word parts (morphemes), and so on.

For such direct translation approaches, the diagram depicts a horizontal line between SL and TL which remains low in the triangle – low because, as mentioned, translation methods higher in the diagram use steppingstones (intermediate structures) on the way to a final translation, whereas direct methods do without them.

We've already seen examples of such steppingstones: the sample syntactic and semantic structures above. These intermediate structures are considered more *abstract* than the surface (text) elements; and height in the diagram is interpreted as degree of abstraction. (We'll say more about the interpretation of "abstraction" in a moment.) The intermediate structures include those derived through programs which perform *analysis* of the SL input (shown by the ascending line on the left): The structures produced by analysis should indicate the construction and meaning of the original SL input in ways not obvious from the surface language.

Transfer-Based Translation Above the horizontal line labeled "direct" is a line labeled "syntactic transfer." *Transfer-based* translation methods use *two* main intermediate structures. The first is the output of source-language analysis, as just described. The second intermediate structure should represent the construction and meaning of the input structure's translation into the TL. As such, it is intended to serve as the starting point for *generation* (construction) of the TL text (shown by the descending line on the right) and is derived from the analysis output through the *transfer process* for which transfer-based methods are named. Transfer processes are somewhat analogous to the processes of direct translation in that they, too, begin by selecting TL elements that will translate source elements, and then go on to "massage" by reordering, adding, or subtracting, and so on. However, instead of massaging surface language elements, they massage the associated analysis output structure, for example by replacing one substructure with another to account for structural differences between source and target. (For example, the English structure <x> LIKE<Y> might be replaced by <Y> PLEASE <X> in Spanish – in translating "Carlos likes books" to yield "A Carlos le gustan los libros," literally, "To Carlos, books please him.")

We said that intermediate structures are intended to be increasingly *abstract* in the following special sense: The more abstract an intermediate structure, the greater the number of SL utterances which may have given rise to it during analysis or the greater the number of target utterances which might result during generation.[11]

Interlingua-Based Translation If the tendency toward abstraction is taken to its extreme, analysis aims to produce a maximally meaning-oriented (semantic) result – one which could in principle result from any source utterance having an equivalent meaning, regardless of sentence or word structure. The result should then be an *interlingua representation*, one intended to represent the semantics for *both* SL and TL, and ideally for many, or even all, additional languages. Once this degree of abstraction has been reached, intermediate structures on the source and target side are no longer distinct, so there will be no need of a transfer process to mediate between them. For this reason, *interlingua-based* translation methods are shown at the apex of the Vauquois Triangle, where horizontal transfer lines will no longer fit.

Having outlined rule-based or handmade translation methods – direct, transfer-based, or interlingua-based – we can comment on their treatment of semantics.

Semantics in Rule-Based Machine Translation Of course, no translation could take place without at least implicit consideration of meaning. In purely direct rule-based MT, the meaning of an expression is shown implicitly only by

---

[11] In many linguistic discussions, "abstraction" is discussed in terms of "depth," as in "deep structure." This terminology can be confusing, and not only because elements *higher* in the Vauquois triangle would be described as "deeper." Several metaphors are in competition: "deeper" may mean "dominant in a phrase structure," as a verb phrase symbol may dominate a verb and its object; "superordinate in an ontology," as a class like AIRCRAFT may be superordinate to its subclasses like HELICOPTERS; "earlier in a derivation sequence," as analysis of a source utterance precedes TL generation; and so on.

its translations: One could say that the translations *are* the meanings. There are typically several possible translations for any given expression, and examination can reveal semantic relations like SL polysemy (an expression has multiple meanings: one or more SLs map to several groupings of synonymous TLs) and SL synonymy (several expressions mean the same: when several SLs map to one grouping of synonymous TLs).

However, for direct translation systems or any others, we can go on to examine the role, if any, of *explicit* semantic methods. And we can observe that, while direct MT methods do concentrate upon the surface (text) elements of SL and TL, explicit information concerning the *meanings* of words and phrases can still be useful, for example to aid in the selection of the correct word meaning, and thus the correct translation, for *ambiguous* expressions, or expressions (like English *bank*) with multiple meanings – that is, for *lexical disambiguation*. As is widely known, ambiguity has long plagued the MT enterprise. The difficulty of avoiding the meaning "writing instrument" when translating "The pig is in the pen" prompted an influential early misjudgment that automatic translation would prove a dead end.[12]

An example appeared in the direct MT system of Word Magic for English-to-and-from-Spanish, in which translation lexicons listed not only surface expressions but *word-senses*, for example, *bank1* ("financial institution"), *bank2* ("shore"), *bank3* ("row, e.g. of switches"), and so on, where each listed word-sense pointed to a set of synonymous Spanish translations, in which one member was the default translation. During analysis, the appropriate word-sense – that is, meaning – for the current translation segment was chosen according to handwritten rules taking account of the context. For maximum generality, the disambiguation rules referred to *semantic classes* (e.g., VEHICLES) rather than individual semantic instances (e.g., CAR.1); and those classes were collected and arranged in an ontology (categorization graph). Among direct rule-based approaches, this treatment is typical (Hutchins, 2005).

However, within the rule-based MT paradigm, while some direct systems have used semantic symbols to good advantage, such elements are most associated with transfer-based and interlingua-based methodologies.

The ASURA system for English, German, and Japanese, an early speech translation system, included a transfer-based MT component intended to operate at the semantic level, in order to better bridge the gap between the disparate languages involved. Consider Figure 1.3, a structure produced by the transfer process during translation of "Could you make the hotel arrangements?" into

[12] "History of Machine Translation#The 1960s, the ALPAC report and the seventies." *Wikipedia*, Wikimedia Foundation, July 9, 2022, at 18: 01(UTC), https://en.wikipedia.org/wiki/History_of_machine_translation#The_1960s,_theALPAC_report_and_the_seventies.

```
;;;=========== Transfer Result ============
 [[SEM [[RELN REQUEST]
        [AGEN !X3[[LABEL *SPEAKER*]]]
        [RECP !X1[[LABEL *HEARER*]]]
        [OBJE [[RELN MACHEN-V]
               [TENSE PRES]
               [AGEN !X1]
               [OBJE [[PARM !X2[]]
                      [RESTR [[RELN HOTELBUCHUNG-N]
                              [ENTITY !X2]]]
                      [INDEX [[DETERM DEFART]
                              [NUMBER SING]
                              [OWNER [[LABEL *UNKNOWN*]]]]]]]]]]
        [ATTD INTERROGATIVE]]]
 [PRAG [[RESTR [[IN [[FIRST [[RELN POLITE]]]
                     [REST [[FIRST [[RELN EMPATHY-DEGREE]
                                    [LESS !X1]
                                    [MORE !X3]]]
                            [REST [[FIRST [[RELN POLITE]]]
                                   [REST !X4[]]]]]]]]
               [OUT !X4]]]
        [HEARER !X1]
        [INTIMACY LOW]
        [POLITENESS [[DEGREE 3]]]
        [SPEAKER !X3]]]]
```

Figure 1.3 A hybrid intermediate structure from the ASURA system

German (Seligman, 1993). The structure contains the semantic symbols REQUEST and POLITE alongside syntactic symbols like MACHEN-V ("to make," a verb) and HOTELBUCHUNG-N ("hotel booking," a noun).

As might be expected, the most extensive use of explicit symbolic semantic tokens has been in interlingua-based MT. Here a mature example is the ATLAS system for English and Japanese, developed at Fujitsu under the direction of Hiroshi Uchida (1986). Uchida is also the founder of the most extensive multilingual and multipartner interlingua-based research effort, the Universal Networking Language (UNL) project.[13] Its foundation is a rich set of word senses, originally based upon that of a complete English dictionary. These can be combined, via special relational symbols like CAUSE, to enable construction of UNL representations for phrases, sentences, and so on. Figure 1.4, for instance, shows the combination representing the following sentence and its

---

[13] "UNL project." URL: www.undlfoundation.org/undlfoundation/.

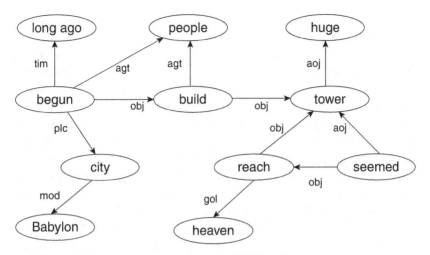

Figure 1.4 A sentence representation in the UNL interlingua

We have single, and twins and also Japanese rooms available on the eleventh.
a:give–information+availability+room (room–type=(single&twin&Japanese_style), time=md11)

I'd like a twin room, please.
c:accept+features+room(room–type=twin)

A twin room is fourteen thousand yen.
a:give–information+price+room(room–type=twin, price=(currency=yen, quantity=14000))

Figure 1.5 Sentence representations in the IF interlingua

many paraphrases and translations: "Long ago, in Babylon, the people began to build an enormous tower, which seemed to reach the sky."

Interlingua-based structures have been useful in speech translation research. See (Seligman and Waibel, 2018) and (Levin et al., 1998) regarding the Interchange Format (IF) structures used by the C-STAR consortium (Figure 1.5 shows three examples) and concerning a separate interlingua used in IBM's MASTOR project (Gao et al., 2006).

1.4.2.2 Statistical Machine Translation

A dramatic rise of *statistical machine translation* (SMT) (Koehn, 2009) erupted in the 1990s.

In initial implementations, statistical information was treated as a supplement or add-on to the existing rules and programs of rule-based MT (Brown et al., 1990, 1993). However, the new paradigm soon gravitated toward methods that in some respects recalled those of direct rule-based MT. Rather than manipulate abstract structures like those of transfer-based methods – structures representing some mixture of compositional and semantic common-alities among surface structures – statistical methods returned to operations upon the surface structures themselves. As in direct rule-based methods, the first step is to determine which TL surface segments might serve as translations for SL surface segments; and later steps relate to the ordering of target elements, possible additions or subtractions from them, possible grammatical adjustments, and so on. But while in rule-based methods these steps depend on rules and programs created by hand, in SMT they depend upon probabilities discovered in *parallel corpora* of human translations (for example, a large collection of English parliamentary transcripts in which each utterance is aligned with its French translation). The goal in SMT is to produce the most *probable* translation of a source segment given that training set (*corpus*), so actual production of a translation (*decoding*) becomes an *optimization* process – a search for the best solution among many candidates, often visualized as *hill climbing*: the probabilities of alternative translations are iteratively compared, and with each matchup, the better alternative is chosen as a step uphill. The goal is to arrive at the highest probability "peak" (and avoid getting stuck on a lower one).

In most SMT, the translations of words and phrases *are* their meanings (just as they are in "pure" or unadorned direct rule-based MT). SMT's translations are indicated in a system's *phrase table*, a listing of SL-to-TL correspondences (e.g., English *cool* to French *frais*), each with a probability determined during training (Figure 1.6). The rows in a table can be examined to discover semantic relations like polysemy (one expression, many meanings) and synonymy (many expressions sharing a meaning).

Vector-based semantics. Throughout its decade-long reign, mainstream SMT exploited explicit semantic symbols only rarely. In compensation, *vector-based* semantic treatments gradually became influential.

Source language expression	Target language expression	Probability
cool	frais	.34
cool	chouette	.21
nippy	frais	.88
man	homme	.68

Figure 1.6 Part of a phrase table for statistical machine translation

Vector-based semantic research aims to leverage the statistical relationships among text segments (words, phrases, etc.) to place the segments in an *abstract space*, within which closeness represents similarity of meaning (Turney and Pantel, 2010).

"Abstract space" sounds impressive but intimidating; however, everyday comparisons can reduce the fear factor. For example, any spreadsheet with several rows (representing, e.g., available flavors of an ice cream order) and several columns (available sizes of an order) exemplifies a "space" with two dimensions – up-down and right-left – in which the cell entry in row 2, column 3 ("strawberry, large") indicates a specific combination, seen as a "location" or "point" within that "space" (set of choices). We could stack such spreadsheets vertically to make room for a third dimension (perhaps available containers, as in cone vs. cup); and so on, in theory, to any number of dimensions or factors.

Vectors themselves, meanwhile, are just one-dimensional lists of numbers representing combinations of factors, with one number coding each factor: <strawberry, large, cone> might be coded as the vector <2, 1, 1>.

Closeness or similarity in such a "space" of choices can be represented as distance between "points" in the space (comparable to locations or cells in a spreadsheet): two ice cream orders that share several factors (flavor, size, or container) are closer (more similar) in the sheet than those with fewer commonalities.

This insight can enable comparison of words or expressions with respect to their meanings. Intuitively, words that occur in similar contexts and participate in similar relations with other words should turn out to be semantically similar. The intuition goes back to Firth's (1957) declaration that "You shall know a word by the company it keeps," and has been formalized as the *distributional hypothesis*. The clustering in this similar-neighbors space yields a hierarchy (ranking) of similarity relations, comparable to that of a handwritten ontology (symbol categorization graph). Figure 1.7 (Mikolov et al., 2013) shows two examples from English with corresponding examples from Spanish.

Representation of a given segment's meaning as a location in such a vector space can be viewed as an alternative to representation as a symbol located within a categorization graph. The vector-based approach is much more scalable (more extensible to large-scale use) in that there is no need to build graphs manually; but relations can be harder for humans to comprehend in the absence of appropriate visualization software tools.

Historically, the vector-based approach grew out of document classification techniques, whereby a document can be categorized according to the words in it and their frequency. The converse was then proposed: A word or other linguistic unit can be categorized according to the documents it appears in, or more

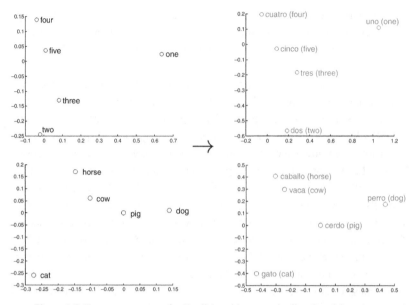

Figure 1.7 Two vector spaces for English, with corresponding Spanish spaces

generally, according to surrounding or nearby text segments of any size –
minimally, just the few words surrounding it.

Vector-based semantic approaches have been used experimentally to
improve statistical MT systems. Alkhouli et al. (2014) provide a clear example,
in which the elements located in vector space according to their respective
contexts are phrases (word groups) rather than only words. It then becomes
possible to measure distances between phrases, interpretable as similarity of
meaning; and this interpretation in turn enables enhancement of the translation
process via artificial enlargement of the relevant phrase tables – helpful because
the training set (corpus) rarely contains all the examples one would wish.

1.4.2.3 Neural Machine Translation

Neural machine translation (NMT) has proved to be a late bloomer. While early
neural experiments (Waibel, 1987; Waibel et al., 1987, 1991) garnered interest,
especially in view of potential insights into human language processing, the
computational infrastructure that would eventually make neural approaches
practical did not yet exist. Now that they do, the approach has experienced an
explosive renaissance: Google announced its first neural translation systems as
recently as 2016 (Johnson et al., 2016); Systran has since then gone fully neural

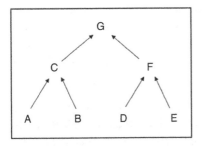

Figure 1.8 Connections among rules forming a network

(Senellart, 2018); and most other major MT vendors are converting at full speed.

A conceptual introduction to neural network operation may help to explain the methodology's application to translation. Think first of logical rules, for instance those of the predicate calculus:

If A and B, then C
If D and E, then F
If C and F, then G

If the premise-to-conclusion relations are depicted as lines, we obtain a tree-like diagram (Figure 1.8).

Imagine that the lines are electric wires, and that there is a bulb at each premise or conclusion which lights up if manually switched on, or if all incoming wires are active; and that, when a light is illuminated, the outgoing wire is activated. Switch on A, B, D, and E. Then C and F will be activated and will propagate activity to G. That is, since facts A, B, D, and E have been found to be true or in effect, fact G has been found to follow. *Et voilà*: a neural network! However, several refinements are needed to complete the picture.

- First, rather than being simply on or off, each line should have a *degree* of activation; and illumination of a conclusion bulb should require not full activation of all wires, but only summed activation passing a specified threshold.
- Second, some wires may inhibit rather than promote the conclusion – that is, their activation may subtract from the sum.
- Third, rather than only three "rules," there should be many thousands.
- And fourth, and perhaps most important, all of the network's parameters (numbers, factors) – the wires' activation levels, thresholds, and so on – should be learned from experience rather than set by hand. They may be

learned through a *supervised* process, whereby a trainer provides the expected conclusions given the switches thrown at the input, and appropriate programs work backwards to adjust the parameters; or through an *unsupervised* process, whereby adjustment depends on frequency of activation during training, perhaps assisted by hints and/or rewards or punishments.

Such networks can indeed be applied to translation, since they provide general-purpose computational mechanisms: With sufficient available wires, "rule" layers, and so on, they can in principle learn to compute any *function* – any mapping of input patterns to output patterns. Thus, they can learn to map input bulbs coding for SL segments into patterns analogous to the human-readable symbolic analysis results of an interlingua-based MT system – that is, to perform operations analogous to the analysis phase of such a system. (In NMT, the analysis phase is called *encoding*, and produces only human-opaque numbers.) Likewise, the networks can also learn to map those result patterns into the surface structures of the TL – that is, to perform operations (called *decoding*) analogous to a transfer-based system's generation phase. And they can learn the alignment between surface elements of the source segment with those of the target segment (that is, can learn which SL segments correspond to which TL segments), information helpful during TL generation (Figure 1.9). In Section 4.2.3.1, we'll see how it's done.

Neural networks were born to learn abstractions. The "hidden" layers in a neural network, those which mediate between the input and output layers, are designed to gradually form abstractions at multiple levels by determining which combinations of input elements, and which combinations of combinations,

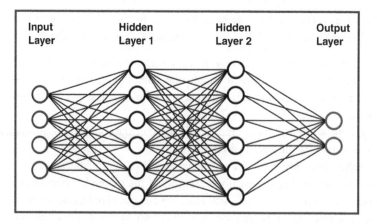

Figure 1.9 A neural network with input, output, and two hidden layers

are most significant in determining the appropriate output. (In our conceptual introduction above, each abstraction level was viewed as a stage in a chain of implied "rules." Rules close to the input layer of the network use surface elements specific to particular inputs as their "premises" or givens, while those further from the input use "premise" combinations taken from many inputs.) The more hidden layers, the more levels of abstraction become possible; and this is why *deep* neural networks are better at abstracting than shallow ones. This advantage has been evident in theory for some time; but deep networks only became practical when computational processing capacity became sufficient to handle multiple hidden layers.

Where MT is concerned, this hidden learning raises the possibility of training neural translators to develop internal meaning representations automatically and implicitly (Woszczyna et al., 1998). A new neural-network-based approach to meaning then suggests itself: Within a network, nodes or pathways shared by input elements having the same translation or translations can be seen as representing the shared meanings. Input elements sharing a translation can originate in a single SL (when in that language the source elements are synonyms in the current context) or in several SLs (when across the input languages in question the source elements are synonymous in their respective contexts). And, in fact, the shared translations, too, can be unilingual or multilingual.

Thus, if translation is trained over several languages, semantic representations may emerge that are abstracted away from – that become relatively independent of – the languages used in training. Taken together, they would compose a *neurally learned* interlingua, a language-neutral semantic representation comparable to the *handmade* symbolic interlingua discussed above in relation to rule-based systems. A successful neural interlingua could facilitate handling of languages for which data is sparse, thus opening a path to truly universal translation at manageable development costs. Several teams have begun work in this direction (Le et al., 2016; Kurzweil, 2016; Firat et al., 2016), and early results are already emerging: Google, for instance, has published on "zero-shot" NMT, so named because the approach allows translation between languages for which zero bilingual data was included in training corpora (Johnson et al., 2016); and SYSTRAN, in a similar spirit, has already announced combined translation systems for romance languages (Senellart, 2018). Not to be outdone, Meta (the company formerly known as Facebook) has recently announced a comparable push toward universal translation (Ramirez, 2022). Zero-shot NMT works because the encoding (analysis) phase of translation has been generalized across all currently trained SLs, while the decoding (generation) phrase has similarly been generalized across all currently trained TLs. Thus any current source can be paired with any current target. Expectations would be low, however, if completely untrained SLs or TLs were tried.

Transformers in Neural Machine Translation For many readers, the above account of NMT will suffice. Still, in the spirit of dispelling the mystery, we'll go on to provide an optional bonus: an intermediate-level account of the inner workings of neural translation at the state of the art, focusing on recent excitement over the *transformer* architecture (i.e., learning setup) and its advantages. We've repeatedly mentioned transformers as neural networks that can exploit a powerful technique called attention to predict sequences by analyzing their elements' contexts. Now we're ready to scrutinize the role of that technique in learning large language models (LLMs) like GPT-3 – subjects of intense research in the artificial intelligence community at the time of writing. While few healthcare workers may participate directly in this research, it will be helpful if those charged with selecting speech and translation components are conversant with it. Artificial intelligence is resurgent, and demystification should be healthy for most professionals.

Analyzing Sequences: The Role of Context As we've seen, all three of the major components that concern us here involve analysis of sequences, and more specifically, transformation of one sequence into another: For speech recognition, we transform a sequence of sound segments into a sequence of text elements; for speech synthesis we do the reverse, transforming a text sequence into a sequence of sound segments; and for MT, we normally transform a text sequence in the SL into a text sequence in the TL. ("Normally" because some research attempts to transform sound sequences directly into sound sequences, without passing through text on the way.) It will be convenient to focus our exposition of forefront research on MT. However, the techniques to be examined can serve to predict sequences quite generally – *single-strand sequences* (those with only one row of elements) as well as the aligned, *double-strand sequences* of most immediate interest (in which two interrelated rows are in question).

Our MT life would be sweet if we could simply replace each source word with its unique translation at its original place in the source sequence. However, as we've seen, there are several problems with this simplistic approach, all depending heavily on the source *context* – the surrounding source words. First, source words will in general be ambiguous: They may have several possible translations, possibly including *no* translation. Second, the order of target words may be different from that of the source words. Third, agreement may be required between certain elements of the target sequence. Finally, there will be pronouns and other referring words whose translation will depend on resolving the words they refer to.

How can we enable each word to be aware of its full context as we identify its translation counterpart? Until 2017, the standard answer was to step through the source word sequence one word at a time – for English, from left to right – while trying to "remember" earlier words and their translations. Information on all prior words and their translations was repeatedly fed to the process translating the current word. The setups that managed this recycling are called *recurrent neural networks* (RNNs), already mentioned in passing. They handled contextualization reasonably well for short sentences but less well when tackling longer ones, for several reasons.

- Memory of earlier elements tends to fade as the sequence progresses: The system forgets what happened early in the input as it progresses toward later elements. Consequently, only relatively recent context can have the desired, and crucial, influence.
- A related matter is the *vanishing gradient problem*. Neural networks learn by repeatedly measuring their errors from trial to trial so that they can adjust networks incrementally in the direction of the right outcome – up or down a metaphorical hill, or *gradient*; but if the differences between trials becomes too small and the hill flattens, such gradual adjustment becomes difficult, and learning grinds to a halt. This flattening is too frequent with recurrent techniques.
- Given the consecutive processing, elements *later* in the input can have no influence at all on the current word's analysis; and yet the entire sequence may have been accessible from the outset.
- The continuous recycling makes the entire progression resource-intensive and time-consuming.

Researchers attempting to alleviate these issues realized that *not all context is created equal*. For analysis of the current word, some neighbor words provide more significant context than others. So the relative context-worthiness of a word's neighbors should be estimated, and contextual influence on translation should be granted to them proportionately. But how can this be done?

"Attention" as Context-Worthiness We've already introduced the concept of vector-based semantics, in which words are categorized as semantically similar according to their respective contexts – their word neighbors. In neural MT, the vectors (embeddings) representing input words are just rows

of numbers, one number for each dimension (factor) in the abstract similarity "space." (These are supplied in advance, for instance by the BERT language model.[14]) Each word's vector represents its "location" in that "space": If there were only two dimensions, then a vector with two numbers referring to a standard X/Y axis would suffice, and we'd see the word's point somewhere in the plane thus defined; but the same principle applies for any number of dimensions. And here's the point: It turns out to be straightforward mathematically to measure the neighbor-based *similarity* of two words by calculating the distance between their vectors. Accordingly, we can let this sort of neighbor-based similarity be our measure for the context-worthiness, within the relevant segment, of each segment-mate word with respect to the current word. Context-worthiness, thus understood, is called *attention* in this technical sense; and it is in this sense that attention has captured the attention of the AI world.

Attention was initially used to augment the operation of RNNs; but in 2017, a seminal paper appeared: "Attention Is All You Need" (Vaswani et al., 2017). It showed that thoroughgoing use of attention could make unnecessary the massive recycling applied by RNNs: Instead, contextual influence could be calculated for each word separately. And this could be done by separate processors, and all at the same time – that is, in parallel! What's more, miraculous follow-on benefits were revealed: Context could become *much* larger and more complete, since it now became possible to consider the influence of segment-mate words at distances limited only by the length of the segment, rather than considering only the words recent enough to be clearly remembered. Then, too, similarity could be estimated not only for earlier words, but also for words *later* in a long segment. Parallel operation meant hugely faster operation than recurrent recycling; and hugely faster operation meant that huge amounts of data could be processed – essentially, *all* the text on the Internet! (And later, images and other types of data as well.) Meanwhile, the processing power that was saved could be spent on enlarging the neural networks themselves: They could be much wider and much deeper, with the number of connection strengths, and so on (i.e., of network *parameters*) to be learned during training reaching the billions. These fringe benefits jointly led to far greater abstraction and predictive power. What earlier was described as language models – we've encountered them earlier – had now become LLMs, *large* language models. First of these is Generative Pre-trained Transformer, version three – now famous in the field as GPT-3.

---

[14] "BERT language model." *Wikipedia*, Wikimedia Foundation, August 12, 2022, at 22: 00(UTC), https://en.wikipedia.org/wiki/BERT_(language_model).

Transformers can indeed be exploited for MT – we'll elaborate presently – but also, as we've seen, for speech recognition and speech synthesis.

Transformers as General-Purpose Predictors That's not all, however. They provide a general-purpose sequence prediction mechanism, so that any data that can be represented sequentially can be – and has been – fed to them and predicted by them. Images, video, audio, and action directives can all be chunked; and, given an initial sequence of chunks, GPT-3 and its successors (Wiggers, 2022) can predict the likely continuation (or several alternatives). Partial images can be completed or generated from scratch starting from a simple prompt. So can partial poems or novels, though quality is of course debatable. The system has in effect learned myriad schemas or templates, in which the fillers – the values of variables – are internally represented quite abstractly. Importantly, associations among different data types can also be learned – notably, between text and related images, so that perceptually grounded linguistic generalizations are formed: Certain abstract categories of images are associated with certain abstract categories of linguistic elements (Synced, 2021).

It turns out that, with sufficient input data and parameters, a single LLM can perform a wide range of tasks with varying degrees of measurable success.[15] In view of this progress, debate among AI researchers is ongoing: Is the general-purpose prediction ability gained by transformers the first step toward true general intelligence? What, if anything, is missing for true reasoning and understanding? Still, caution is warranted: Strikingly cogent predicted sequences are often accompanied by jarringly meaningless ones. And certainly, the appearance of understanding should not be mistaken for the real thing. On the other hand, I've suggested (Seligman, 2019) that a threshold would be crossed with the advent of *perceptually grounded* natural language processing, as opposed to processing based solely on text. That advent is now upon us. LLMs associating text and images are here, and those based on video with audio cannot be far off. These will bring the promise of true, if limited, *intentionality* – meaningful connection between linguistic elements and the perceived world.

Remember, too, that some of the best current systems in natural language processing – we're still focusing on translation – have not yet incorporated transformers at all, at least in system descriptions so far made public. For

[15] "Gato (Deep Mind)." *Wikipedia*, Wikimedia Foundation, June 25, 2022, at 21: 22(UTC), https:// en.wikipedia.org/wiki/Gato_(Deep Mind).

example, the DeepL automatic translator,[16] developed by DeepL SE of Cologne, Germany, has achieved the impressive results displayed in Appendix II with the convolutional neural network (CNN) architecture, a competitor to RNNs, in which context is learned by moving a window around in the sequence under analysis.

So attention is quite generally useful for tracking the relevance or inter-dependency of sequence elements. That relevance can be tracked *across* sequences, as when relating source sequences to target sequences to recognize potential translation relations among source and target words; or *within* a given sequence, for example, within the source or target sequence (in which case one speaks of *self*-attention). Relevance can also be assessed for various aspects of a task: for example, in analysis of the source sentence, with respect to syntactic dependencies (like the relation between subjects and predicates, or nouns and their associated adjectives), or to semantic co-reference (as when *my aunt's pen* and *it* refer to the same entity). Each sort of relevance can be handled by a dedicated transformer *head*, giving rise to *multi-headed transformers*.

Transformers in Neural Machine Translation Equipped with this general understanding of attention in transformers, we can return to the NMT process specifically. We pick up the story at the encoding phase, which aims for an abstracted analysis of the entire input, comparable to the result of handprogrammed analysis in the transfer-based MT style, and fit for passing to the decoding (TL generation) phase. Actually, several encoders are normally used, for reasons to be explained. Since they operate one after another, they can be pictured as a stack of *encoder layers*, in which (we'll say) the highest encoder layer is the earliest in the process, and later layers progress downward toward decoding and eventual translated output (Figure 1.10). (N.b., Encoder layers, and later decoder layers, shouldn't be confused with the neuron ("bulb") layers within a single neural network.)

In any one of these encoder layers, multi-headed self-attention is applied to augment each word with various sorts of contextualized information. One essential factor in a word's context is its actual location in the input sequence; so that information must be added to the word's enrichment by blending into the word's vector a *position vector* representing, via some mathematical magic, the word's numbered position in the sequential order. Also added for good measure is another vector representing the current word as it emerged from any

---

[16] "DeepL Translator." *Wikipedia*, Wikimedia Foundation, August 10, 2022, at 17: 37(UTC), https://en.wikipedia.org/wiki/DeepL_Translator)).

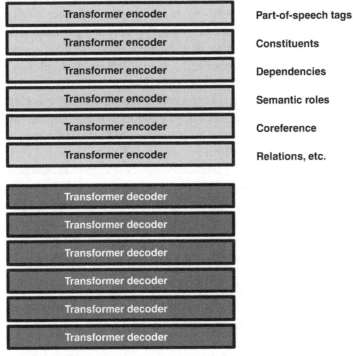

I am happy.

Transformer encoder	**Part-of-speech tags**
Transformer encoder	**Constituents**
Transformer encoder	**Dependencies**
Transformer encoder	**Semantic roles**
Transformer encoder	**Coreference**
Transformer encoder	**Relations, etc.**

Transformer decoder

Transformer decoder

Transformer decoder

Transformer decoder

Transformer decoder

Transformer decoder

私は幸せです。

Figure 1.10 Encoder and decoder layers in a transformer-based MT system

earlier encoder layers in the stack, in effect preserving some memory of past analysis.

Then, to complete an encoder layer's operation, the self-attention result for each word vector is run through a neural network to integrate the several information sources. This integration network is of the sort described above, where a row of "bulbs" representing "premises" is input and activation passes "forward" through neural network layers until "bulbs" representing "conclusions" are activated – a *feed-forward* neural network. These "conclusions" represent the encoder layer's integrated analysis of each word, performed for each word independently, so that the system's parallelism is never broken.

But again, there will typically be several encoder layers. Multiple *encoder* layers are employed for the same reason as multiple *neuron* ("bulb") layers are used within individual neural networks: abstraction. Earlier layers tend to learn concrete aspects of the relevant material, those close to the facts, while later ones tend to progressively generalize and address more global aspects. And, in fact, fascinating studies have confirmed this progression: Earliest encoder layers do seem most effective at recognizing part-of-speech tags (noun, verb, etc.), while subsequent layers – as we progress from earliest to latest – seem most efficient for identifying constituents (noun phrases, verb phrases); dependencies (e.g., between a verb and its direct or indirect objects); semantic roles (actor, location, etc.); coreference (pronouns referred to what?); and still more abstract roles. (The "probing" methods for making this determination are themselves of great interest, in view of the pervasive and frustrating opacity of neural networks (Tenney et al., 2019).)

The last layer in the *en*coder layer stack embodies the system's final and most abstracted analysis of the SL input. This can be passed to the earliest *de*coder layer – since decoder layers, like encoder layers, are normally stacked, again for reasons relating to abstraction. For decoders, however, the degree of abstraction progresses from more abstract to more concrete, culminating in the maximally specific decoder layer embodying the TL translation output.

Attention across Languages But how do SL words become TL words? Once again: through attention, in our technical sense. While attention in encoder layers entailed only *self*-attention – the learning of context-worthiness judgments among words *within* the source sequence – decoder layers also exploit such attention judgments *between* source and target word sequences. They indicate, for instance, that, when translating "rabbit" into German in "The rabbit ran because I scared it," we should attend to both "rabbit" and "it," because *source*-language self-attention has earlier found them to refer to the same entity. Both words then influence selection of "Hase" in the context of "Der Hase rannte, weil ich ihn erschreckt hatte."[17] This cross-sequence and cross-language attention is enabled by including a double-strand *encoder-decoder attention element* in each decoder layer, sandwiched between elements we've already encountered in *en*coder layers: a single-strand self-attention element (which analyzes the *TL* sequence on its own terms) and a feed-forward neural network (which integrates the various influences on each word vector) (Figure 1.11).

The decoder layers handle not only word translation – the alignment of source and target words, which will ultimately lead to target word selection – but also target word ordering and agreement (e.g., of nouns and their adjectives). Recall that each target word contains positional and dependency (e.g.,

---

[17] "The Transformer Neural Network Architecture Explained. 'Attention Is All You Need'." AI Coffee Break with Letitia. URL: www.youtube.com/watch?v=FWFA4DGuzSc&t=438s. July 5, 2020.

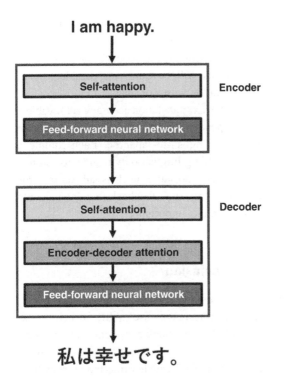

I am happy.

Self-attention — Encoder

Feed-forward neural network

Self-attention — Decoder

Encoder-decoder attention

Feed-forward neural network

私は幸せです。

Figure 1.11 Subelements of encoder and decoder layers in a transformer-based MT system

noun-to-adjective) information. In the full TL context, this information will suffice to influence ordering and selection of agreeing dependent words (e.g., forms of an adjective that agree with the associated noun in terms of singular vs. plural, male vs. female or neutral, etc.).

Delivery. The decoder stack's grand finale is the delivery of a TL word sequence. Each fully processed TL word vector, given its place in target-word similarity "space," yields a set of probabilities (a *probability distribution*), assigning each word in the target dictionary a probability score[18]. In our example above, "Hase" might receive a probability in the high nineties as the translation for "rabbit," while an unrelated word like "über" (German for English "over" or "above") would score very low. Once the most probable target word is selected from each set and all target words have found their positions in the sequence

[18] As arranged by a program with a puzzling name: *sofmax*. Its job is to ensure that a handful of probabilities, for example those for possible translations a given TL word, add up to 1.0. Here, if some translation probabilities are very high, others must be low.

according to their internal position indications, translation is complete. There you have it! *Et voilà! Bitte sehr! ¡Y ya está!* で、終わり*!*

(Again, the transformer-based neural sequence-to-sequence processing for speech recognition or speech synthesis will be quite comparable, though operating on sound segments rather than on words or images.)

To give an informal impression of the text translation accuracy achievable at the time of writing, we supply in Appendix II healthcare-oriented translation examples for English-to-Spanish and English-to-Japanese. Each sample is accompanied by a back-translation, enabling English-only readers to estimate the translation accuracy. Of course, back-translation itself is subject to error; but when the error rate is sufficiently small, such feedback remains valuable. Chapter 2 further discusses feedback and its importance.

1.5 Conclusion

As previewed, we've surveyed the methods and issues of several quickly developing technologies relevant to healthcare use cases: ASR, speech synthesis or TTS, and MT. With respect to MT, after a look at systems covering only pretranslated phrases, we went on to explain the major types of automatic translation with broader coverage – "full MT," whether rule-based, statistical, or neural. And finally, as an optional bonus for readers curious about recent developments in the artificial intelligence field, we focused attention (appropriately enough) on transformer-based neural processing.

Also as forecast, we've postponed for Chapter 2 discussion of practical applications for healthcare of speech and translation technologies, with special interest in their combined use for speech translation.

By dispelling the mysteries surrounding these truly epochal technologies, we hope to promote their wider use. However, utilization must also be responsible and cautious. Miscommunications concerning healthcare can be consequential, even deadly. Thus *reliability* – not only measurable accuracy but user confidence – will be essential. *Customization* per use case, too, will be vital, as Chapter 2 will emphasize.

References

Alkhouli, T., A. Guta, and H. Ney. 2014. "Vector Space Models for Phrase-Based Machine Translation." In *Proceedings of SSST-8, Eighth Workshop on Syntax, Semantics and Structure in Statistical Translation*. Doha, Qatar, October 25, pages 1–10.

Boitet, C. 2000. "Bernard Vauquois' Contribution to the Theory and Practice of Building MT Systems: A Historical Perspective." In *Early Years in Machine Translation: Memoirs and Biographies of Pioneers*, William John Hutchins (Ed.), Studies in the History of the Language Sciences 97, pages 331–349. Amsterdam: John Benjamins Publishing.

Brown, P. F., J. Cocke, S. A. Della Pietra, et al. 1990. "A Statistical Approach to Machine Translation." *Computational Linguistics*, 16 (2), June, pages 79–85.

Brown, P. F., S. A. Della Pietra, V. J. Della Pietra, and R. L. Mercer. 1993. "The Mathematics of Statistical Machine Translation: Parameter Estimation." *Computational Linguistics*, 19 (2), June, pages 263–311.

Englert, M., G. Madazio, I. Gielow, J. Lucero, and M. Behlau. 2016. "Perceptual Error Identification of Human and Synthesized Voices." *Journal of Voice*, 30 (5): 639.e17–639.e23. DOI: http://10.1016/j.jvoice.2015.07.017.

Firat, O., K. Cho, and Y. Bengio. 2016. "Multi-Way, Multilingual Neural Machine Translation with a Shared Attention Mechanism." In *Proceedings of the 2016 Conference of the North American Chapter of the Association for Computational Linguistics: Human Language Technologies*. San Diego, California, June, pages 866–875.

Firth, J. R. 1957. "A Synopsis of Linguistic Theory 1930–1955." In *Studies in Linguistic Analysis*. Oxford: Philological Society, pages 1–32. Reprinted in F. R. Palmer (Ed.), 1968, *Selected Papers of J.R. Firth 1952–1959*. London: Longman.

Gao, Y., Liang G., B. Zhou, et al. 2006. "IBM MASTOR SYSTEM: Multilingual Automatic Speech-to-Speech Translator." In *Proceedings of the First International Workshop on Medical Speech Translation, in Conjunction with NAACL/HLT*. New York, June 9.

Hutchins, W. J. 2005. "Towards a Definition of Example-Based Machine Translation." In *MT Summit X: Proceedings of Workshop on Example-Based Machine Translation*. Phuket, Thailand, pages 63–70.

Hutchins, W. J. 2010. "Machine Translation: A Concise History." *Journal of Translation Studies*, 13 (1–2), *Special Issue: The Teaching of Computer-Aided Translation*, Chan Sin Wai (Ed.), pages 29–70.

Johnson, M., M. Schuster, Q. V. Le, et al. 2016. "Google's Multilingual Neural Machine Translation System: Enabling Zero-Shot Translation." https://arxiv.org/abs/1611.04558.

Koehn, P. 2009. *Statistical Machine Translation*. Cambridge: Cambridge University Press.

Kong, J., J. Kim, and J. Bae. 2021. "HiFi-GAN: Generative Adversarial Networks for Efficient and High-Fidelity Speech Synthesis." arXiv:2010.05646v2. https://arxiv.org/abs/2010.05646.

Kuhn, T. S. 1996. *The Structure of Scientific Revolutions*. 3rd ed. Chicago, IL: University of Chicago Press.

Kurzweil, R. 2016. "Google's New Multilingual Neural Machine Translation System Can Translate between Language Pairs Even Though It Has Never Been Taught to Do So." www.kurzweilai.net/googles-new-multilingual-neural-machine-translation-system-can-translate-between-language-pairs-even-though-it-has-never-been-taught-to-do-so. November 25.

Le, T.-H., J. Niehues, and A. Waibel. 2016. "Toward Multilingual Neural Machine Translation with Universal Encoder and Decoder." In *Proceedings of the International Workshop on Spoken Language Translation (IWSLT) 2016*. Seattle, WA, December 8–9.

Levin, L., D. Gates, A. Lavie, and A. Waibel. 1998. "An Interlingua Based on Domain Actions for Machine Translation of Task-Oriented Dialogues." In *Proceedings of the Fifth International Conference on Spoken Language Processing, ICSLP-98*. Sydney, Australia, November 30–December 4.

Li, J., L. Deng, Y. Gong, and R. Haeb-Umbach. 2014. "An Overview of Noise-Robust Automatic Speech Recognition." *IEEE Transactions: Audio, Speech, and Language Processing*, 22 (4), pages 745–777.

Mikolov, T., Q. V. Le, and I. Sutskever. 2013. "Exploiting Similarities Among Languages for Machine Translation." arXiv preprint.

Ramirez, V. B. 2022. "Metaphor's Going After a Universal Translator. Its AI Now Works for 200 Languages." https://singularityhub.com/2022/07/07/metas-going-after-a-universal-translator-its-ai-now-works-for-200-languages. July 7.

Seligman, M. 1993. *A Japanese–German Transfer Component For ASURA*. ATR Technical Report TR-I-0368.

Seligman, M. 2019. "The Evolving Treatment of Semantics in Machine Translation." In *Advances in Empirical Translation Studies*, Christine (Meng) Ji, (Ed.), Cambridge: Cambridge University Press.

Seligman, M. and A. Waibel. 2018. "Advances in Speech-to-Speech Translation Technologies." In *Advances in Empirical Translation Studies*, Christine (Meng) Ji, (Ed.), Cambridge: Cambridge University Press.

Senellart, J. 2018. "Training Romance Multi-way Model." http://forum.opennmt.net/t/training-romance-multi-way-model/86.

Sotelo, J., S. Mehri, K. Kumar, et al. 2017. "Char2wav: End-to-End Speech Synthesis." International Conference on Learning Representations (ICLR). https://mila.quebec/wp-content/uploads/2017/02/end-end-speech.pdf.

Synced. 2021. "OpenAI Releases GLIDE: A Scaled-Down Text-to-Image Model That Rivals DALL-E Performance." https://syncedreview.com/2021/12/24/deepmind-podracer-tpu-based-rl-frameworks-deliver-exceptional-performance-at-low-cost-173/. December 24.

Tan, X., T. Qin, F. Soong, and T.-Y. Liu. 2021. "A Survey on Neural Speech Synthesis." arXiv: 2106.15561v3 [eess.AS] 23 July. Also in *Computer Science*, June 29, 2021. https://arxiv.org/pdf/2106.15561.pdf.

Tenney, I., D. Das, and E. Pavlick. 2019. "BERT Rediscovers the Classical NLP Pipeline." In *Proceedings of the 57th Annual Meeting of the Association for Computational Linguistics*, Florence, Italy, July, pages 4593–4601.

Turney, P. D. and P. Pantel. 2010. "From Frequency to Meaning: Vector Space Models of Semantics." *Journal of Artificial Intelligence Research* 37 (2010), pages 141–188.

Uchida, H. 1986. "Fujitsu Machine Translation System: ATLAS." In *Future Generation Computer Systems*, 2 (2), June, pages 95–100.

Vaswani, A., N. Shazeer, N. Parmar, et al. 2017. "Attention is All You Need." arXiv:1706.03762v5.

Waibel, A. 1987. "Phoneme Recognition Using Time-Delay Neural Networks." *Meeting of the Institute of Electrical, Information, and Communication Engineers (IEICE)*. Tokyo, Japan, December.

Waibel, A., T. Hanazawa, G. Hinton, and K. Shikano. 1987. "Phoneme Recognition Using Time-Delay Neural Networks." ATR Interpreting Telephony Research Laboratories, October 30.

Waibel, A., A. N. Jain, A. E. McNair, et al. 1991. "JANUS: A Speech-to-Speech Translation System Using Connectionist and Symbolic Processing Strategies." In *Proceedings of the International Conference on Acoustics, Speech and Signal Processing (ICASSP) 1991*. Toronto, Canada, May 14–17.

Wiggers, K. 2022. "*The emerging types of language models and why they matter.*" https://techcrunch.com/2022/04/28/the-emerging-types-of-language-models-and-why-they-matter/. 5:30 AM PDT, April 28.

Woszczyna, M., M. Broadhead, D. Gates, et al. 1998. "A Modular Approach to Spoken Language Translation for Large Domains." In *Proceedings of the Third Conference of the Association for Machine Translation in the Americas (AMTA)* 98. Langhorne, PA, October 28–31.

Appendix I Automatic Speech Recognition (ASR) Samples

We show two ASR results, for readers' inspection and informal evaluation:

1. iPhone X_R, Software Version 15.5, native (standard) speech recognition
2. Microsoft Windows 10, native (standard) speech recognition

Both results are based upon continuous dictation of the following healthcare-related text, copied without changes from www.cdph.ca.gov/Programs/CID/DCDC/Pages/COVID-19/PregnantandBreastfeedingWomenGuidance.aspx as originally published on May 18, 2021.

Summary
This document provides guidance for people who are pregnant and breastfeeding during the COVID-19 pandemic. The California Department of Public Health will update this guidance as new information becomes available.

Pregnancy: Based on what we know at this time, the Centers for Disease Control and Prevention (CDC) state "pregnant people are at an increased risk for severe illness from COVID-19 and death, compared to non-pregnant people. Additionally, pregnant people with COVID-19 might be at increased risk for other adverse outcomes, such as preterm birth (delivering the baby earlier than 37 weeks). It is especially important for pregnant people, and those who live with them, to protect themselves from getting COVID-19."

Breastfeeding: The Centers for Disease Control and Prevention (CDC) and the Academy of Pediatrics state that parents with COVID-19 can breastfeed. When breastfeeding, precautions should be taken to reduce the risk of passing COVID-19 to their baby.

For more information, visit Breastfeeding and Caring for Newborns.

iPhone Native ASR

Dictated to Google Keep note-taking app. Hand held 10 inches from mouth. Natural but clear pronunciation, with some white noise from refrigerator in neighboring room. Punctuation was dictated, for example as "period," "comma," or "colon," but not capitals or formatting, for example, for **bold** font.

Summary

This document provides guidance for people who are pregnant and breast-feeding during the COVID-19 pandemic. The California Department of Public health will update this guidance as new information becomes available.

Pregnancy: based on what we know this time, the centers for disease control and prevention (CDC) state "pregnant people are at an increased risk for severe illness from COVID-19 and death, compared to non-pregnant people. Additionally, pregnant people with COVID-19 might be at increased risk for other adverse outcomes, such as preterm birth (delivering the baby earlier than 37 weeks). It is especially important for pregnant people, and those who live with them, to protect themselves from getting COVID-19."

Breast-feeding: the centers for disease control and prevention (CDC) and the Academy of pediatrics state did parents with COVID-19 can breast-feed. When breast-feeding, precautions should be taken to reduce the risk of passing COVID-19 to their baby.

For more information visit breast-feeding and caring for newborns.

Microsoft Word on Windows 10

Dictation used standard Microsoft ASR on a Lenovo Yoga 730-13-inch laptop, with input via Microphone Array (Realtek High-Definition Audio (SST)) at 100 percent volume.

Note: Dictation was paused and restarted at two points: after "pregnant and breast-feeding" and "can breast feed." The initial words of the immediately following sentences were apparently missed as a result.

Summary

This document provides guidance for people who are pregnant and breastfeedingWith public health will update this guidance as new information becomes available.

Pregnancy: based on what we know at this time, the Centers for Disease control and prevention (CDC) state "pregnant people are at an increased risk for severe illness from COVID-19 and death, compared to non pregnant people. Additionally, pregnant people with COVID-19 might be at increased risk for other adverse outcomes, such as preterm birth (delivering the baby earlier than 37 weeks). It is especially important for pregnant people, and those who live with them,to protect themselves from getting COVID-19."

Breastfeeding: the Centers for Disease control and prevention (CDC) and the Academy of Pediatrics state that parents with COVID-19 can breast feed. The risk of passing COVID-19 to their baby.

For more information, visit breast feeding and caring for newborns.

Appendix II Translation Samples

Source Language Text to Be Translated

Our text sample for translation was the same as for the speech recognition sampling of Appendix I, copied without changes from https://www.cdph.ca.gov/Programs/CID/ DCDC/Pages/COVID-19/PregnantandBreastfeedingWomenGuidance.aspx as originally published on May 18, 2021.

We'll show the following translations and back-translations, all by DeepL (DeepL SE, Cologne, Germany), and all without editing or alterations:

1. Translation into Spanish
2. Back-translation from Spanish to English
3. Translation into Japanese
4. Back-translation from Japanese to English

1. Spanish Translation

Resumen

Este documento proporciona orientación para las personas que están embarazadas y amamantando durante la pandemia de COVID-19. El Departamento de Salud Pública de California actualizará esta guía a medida que se disponga de nueva información.

Embarazo: En base a lo que sabemos en este momento, los Centros para el Control y la Prevención de Enfermedades (CDC) afirman que "las personas embarazadas tienen un mayor riesgo de padecer enfermedades graves por COVID-19 y de morir, en comparación con las personas no embarazadas. Además, las personas embarazadas con COVID-19 podrían tener un mayor riesgo de sufrir otros resultados adversos, como el parto prematuro (dar a luz antes de las 37 semanas). Es especialmente importante que las personas embarazadas, y quienes conviven con ellas, se protejan de contraer COVID-19".

Lactancia: Los Centros para el Control y la Prevención de Enfermedades (CDC) y la Academia de Pediatría afirman que los padres con COVID-19 pueden dar el pecho. Al amamantar, se deben tomar precauciones para reducir el riesgo de transmitir COVID-19 a su bebé.

Para obtener más información, visite Lactancia y cuidado de los recién nacidos.

2. English Back-Translation from Spanish

Summary

This document provides guidance for persons who are pregnant and breastfeeding during the COVID-19 pandemic. The California Department of Public Health will update this guidance as new information becomes available.

Pregnancy: Based on what we know at this time, the Centers for Disease Control and Prevention (CDC) states that "pregnant persons are at increased risk of severe illness from COVID-19 and death compared to non-pregnant persons. In addition, pregnant persons with COVID-19 may be at increased risk for other adverse outcomes, such as preterm labor (giving birth before 37 weeks). It is especially important for pregnant women, and those living with them, to protect themselves from contracting COVID-19."

Breastfeeding: The Centers for Disease Control and Prevention (CDC) and the Academy of Pediatrics state that parents with COVID-19 can breastfeed. When breastfeeding, precautions should be taken to reduce the risk of transmitting COVID-19 to your baby.

For more information, visit Breastfeeding and Newborn Care.

3. **Japanese Translation**

概要
この文書は、COVID-19のパンデミック時に妊娠・授乳している人のためのガイダンスを提供するものです。カリフォルニア州公衆衛生局は、新しい情報が入手可能になり次第、このガイダンスを更新します。

妊娠中 現時点でわかっていることに基づいて、米国疾病対策予防センター (CDC) は、「妊娠中の人は、妊娠していない人に比べて、COVID-19による重症化や死亡のリスクが高くなる」と述べています。さらに、COVID-19に感染した妊娠中の人は、早産 (37週より早い出産) など、他の有害事象のリスクが高まる可能性があります。妊娠中の人と、その人と一緒に生活している人は、COVID-19に感染しないように身を守ることが特に重要です。"

母乳育児について 米国疾病対策予防センター (CDC) と小児科学会は、COVID-19を持つ親は母乳で育てることができるとしています。授乳の際には、COVID-19が赤ちゃんに感染するリスクを減らすための予防措置を取る必要があります。

詳細については、母乳育児と新生児の世話をご覧ください。

4. **English Back-Translation from Japanese**

Overview
This document provides guidance for pregnant and lactating women during a COVID-19 pandemic. The California Department of Public Health will update this guidance as new information becomes available.

　Pregnancy Based on what is known at this time, the Centers for Disease Control and Prevention (CDC) states that "pregnant individuals are at increased risk of severe illness or death from COVID-19 compared to non-pregnant individuals. In addition, pregnant women infected with COVID-19 may be at increased risk for other adverse events, such as premature delivery (birth earlier than 37 weeks). It is especially important for pregnant women and those living with them to protect themselves from becoming infected with COVID-19."

　Breastfeeding The Centers for Disease Control and Prevention (CDC) and the American Academy of Pediatrics state that parents with COVID-19 can breastfeed. When breastfeeding, precautions should be taken to reduce the risk of COVID-19 infecting the baby.

　For more information, see Breastfeeding and Caring for Your Newborn.

2

Speech and Translation Technologies
Healthcare Applications
MARK SELIGMAN

2.1 Introduction

Cross-language communication in healthcare is urgently needed. Daily and nightly throughout the world, thousands of conversations are required between caregivers – doctors, nurses, administrators, volunteers, and others – and patients or family members with differing native languages.

Chapter 1 describes and illustrates the exploding development of the relevant linguistic technologies – machine translation (MT) of text, automatic speech recognition (ASR), and text-to-speech (TTS). The related infrastructure – wireless communication, cloud computing, and mobile devices – has also been developing apace. This chapter will shift focus to the combination and application of these technologies in the healthcare context, with special interest in speech translation.

Given this impressive and accelerating progress, we'd expect various automatic translation and speech-enabled systems to be in widespread use by now; in fact, however, adoption remains slow. We'll examine the obstacles to adoption and directions for overcoming them in Section 2.2. In Section 2.3, we'll examine two major types of speech translation systems, concentrating on their respective approaches to the same obstacles. Section 2.4 will survey some healthcare-oriented communication systems, past and future. We'll conclude with an optimistic forecast for speech and translation applications in healthcare, tempered by due cautions.

2.2 Obstacles to Adoption and Potential Solutions

One key factor in the lagging adoption of linguistic technology in healthcare is the sheer difficulty of understanding the relevant technologies, and thus the natural hesitation to trust them. Accordingly, Chapter 1 aimed to bridge the understanding gap for healthcare workers by explaining speech recognition, speech synthesis, and MT.

However, even if potential users of speech and translation technologies in the healthcare field can gain sufficient understanding to realistically evaluate specific implementations, obstacles will remain. It will be helpful to group these under two major headings: reliability and customization per use case.

2.2.1 Reliability

In any field with demanding communication requirements, workers will hesitate to employ even exciting and progressing communication technology if they fear it may cause embarrassing, or even dangerous, errors. This tendency is compounded in the healthcare field, where communication errors can indeed have disastrous consequences. And it is further compounded for translation technology in particular, since users have until now usually been unable to judge the correctness of the results and have been unable to correct any errors even if recognized. Measurable *accuracy* is increasing in the three technologies of interest – most dramatically for translation, as informally demonstrated in Chapter 1; but this progress alone is unlikely to overcome high-tech hesitancy. Reliability must also be measured in terms of potential users' *confidence* – a psychological rather than technical matter. For our purposes, then, "reliability" implies accuracy *plus* trustworthiness. Trust can be fostered in several ways.

2.2.1.1 Offline Preparation of Output

Trust can be maximized through use of professionally prepared or confirmed output, as opposed to output generated on the spot. And, in fact, pre-vetted output of text translation is one important element of the approach to speech translation taken by fixed-phrase-based speech translators like BabelDr (Spechbach and Bouillon, 2019; Chapter 5). Because translations are prepared in advance by professionals, they can be assumed trustworthy – at least to the extent that one can trust the processes that select the appropriate prechecked translations by matching them against source-language inputs to be translated. (The matching processes are discussed in Chapter 1.)

Even in systems offering full translation, professionally prepared translations (or translations previously confirmed through other means to be discussed later) can be used in a preliminary step: If a sufficiently close match to the current input is found in the database of stored translations, the match's prepared translation will be used; if not, the input is passed to the subsystem designed for full translation. The repository of prepared translations thus serves as *translation memory*, an element of many MT systems, whether rule-based, statistical, or neural. This approach was employed, for instance, in the Converser for Healthcare prototype speech translation system (Seligman and Dillinger, 2006a, 2006b, 2008, 2011, 2012, 2013, 2014, 2015, 2016; Dillinger and Seligman, 2004; Zong and Seligman, 2005) under the proprietary name of Translation Shortcuts™. Section 2.3.3.7 will demonstrate its use in context.

Prepared translations can also be accessed more directly by literate users through text listings of the phrases to be translated, which can be browsed or automatically searched. To facilitate browsing or search, the listings can be categorized: For example, prepared translations can be categorized for pharmacy, nursing, or eye-care use; and translations for pharmacy can be subcategorized for consultation, prescription pickup, and so on (Section 2.3.2.7).

2.2.1.2 Feedback

Another approach to fostering trust is to provide effective feedback: Rather than blindly trusting speech recognition and translation outputs, users can see or hear recognition results and native-language retranslation, and perhaps correct any errors. For speech recognition, literate users can profit from textual feedback; and to enable eyes-free use or for illiterates, playback via TTS could additionally be offered. For MT, *back-translation* – that is, translation from the target language back to the original source language – can help to check whether a preliminary translation has conveyed the intended meaning. Various techniques can be applied to minimize back-translation errors (Seligman and Dillinger, 2014). Back-translation has usually been given only textually, but auditory feedback via TTS is also possible.

2.2.1.3 Correction

If users can be enabled to *recognize* errors, it may be feasible to enable error *correction* as well. For speech recognition, assuming results are made visible in text, literate users can correct any errors by first selecting the erroneous segment and then manually entering or pronouncing the correction.

With respect to translation errors, correction by monolingual users is more challenging, but still possible.

- A "Proceed with Caution Mode" can be offered, in which a preliminary back-translation, monitored by the staff member only, must be approved before transmission to the patient is authorized. If an error is seen, the users' paraphrase of the input, or of a selected part of it, may lead to a translation that can be approved.

- Users may note specific ambiguity errors in a back-translation – indicating translation of the wrong meaning for words or expressions with multiple meanings – such as translation of English *cool* as "chilly, nippy, somewhat cold ... " when "awesome, terrific, fantastic ... " was intended. They can then be enabled to select the erroneous segment and to choose among alternative meanings, which can be indicated in the native language via synonyms, definitions, examples, or pictures.

These correction possibilities are illustrated in context in Section 2.3.2.7.

Too Much Trouble? Monitoring of speech recognition and translation results inevitably takes attention and time, and any correction even more so. However, depending on the use case, the benefits in real-time accuracy and trust may sometimes justify the effort. Again, in healthcare, disastrous translations must be avoided at all costs.

And there is another justification for taking the trouble to correct, when and if enabled: Corrections can be captured and used in several ways. First, the corrections can become training material for machine learning that can substantially improve the systems in question. Corrections can be domain-specific, so that training of speech recognition and translation can be optimized for specific use cases. Second, corrected translations can be considered to have passed the trust test, and thus to have qualified as entries in translation memory.

Useful or not, correction mechanisms will likely be resented as intrusive unless interface facilities are provided for turning them on or off as appropriate. One system employed icons allowing switching between "Full Speed Ahead" mode, in which no verification stage would be used, and "Proceed with Caution" mode, in which a pause for verification would be imposed.

- Earring icons controlled handling of speech recognition: Selection of a green earring meant that ASR results would be sent to translation immediately, without pausing for pre-checking, while choice of a yellow icon did impose a pause. A red earring stopped all speech recognition, to block accidental use.
- A Traffic Light Icon controlled handling of translation: Green meant that translations would be immediately transmitted to users, while yellow meant that a verification dialogue would be presented first. A red light stopped all translation, to prevent accidental use.

These interface facilities, too, are illustrated in context in Section 2.3.2.7.

2.2.1.4 Record-Keeping

A final approach to building trust is regular recording of conversations. While audio recordings would be possible, transcripts may be enough for most purposes. These should include both the original inputs and the automatic translations. It may also be helpful to include any back-translations, so that monolingual staff or researchers can post-verify communication.

2.2.2 Customization per Use Case

One way to overcome obstacles to widespread use of speech and translation technologies within the healthcare field, we've suggested, is to ensure reliability – again, entailing not only increased measurable accuracy but increased user confidence. Another way is to ensure that the technologies can be used conveniently and practically in each use case – in other words, to ensure customization of the technologies per use case. Our motto here: "Magic is not enough!" While the relevant technologies have achieved levels of performance that would have seemed miraculous at the turn of the millennium, we've learned that awe alone cannot bring them across the proverbial chasm toward general acceptance. In every demanding field, but especially in health-care, responsible people are overloaded and properly conservative. The tools must be not only trustworthy but transparently easy to use and seamlessly convenient: They must fit the individual use cases like gloves. Fitting those gloves takes time and financial support, so implementing a solution becomes an organizational and business issue.

2.2.2.1 Platforms

The devices and software required for delivery of speech and translation services have evolved quickly. To dramatize the difference a decade makes, here's a look back at the equipment used in 2011 for a three-month pilot project involving full speech translation at a San Francisco hospital (Seligman and Dillinger, 2015).

At that time, most of the infrastructure we now take for granted was in the future:

- There were no modern flat tablets, so thick and heavy portable devices with built-in handles were used. An alternative setup aimed to accommodate staff members and patients facing each other across a desk. Staff could operate the full interface on a desktop computer serving as master, while patients could see, but not manipulate, a secondary computer showing the same view. For both arrangements, setup and maintenance were time-consuming and error prone.

- iPhones had appeared in 2007, but on-device memory capacity was limited, so processing was strained when running full speech translation. (Jibbigo (Eck et al., 2010) – a spinoff of Carnegie Mellon University research under Alex Waibel, later sold to Facebook – nevertheless released several on-device systems for individual language pairs, but their reliability was insufficient for demanding use cases.)
- Remote computing was thus a tempting alternative, but cloud computing was immature, and locally installed software remained the only practical option, with the attendant installation and maintenance headaches.
- Speech recognition software was still speaker-dependent, so each user needed to provide a voice sample during a short training session – doable for staff members, despite some scheduling annoyances, but impractical for patients, so translation was restricted to direction. (Soon after the pilot, zero-training ASR arrived, so that voice input from both sides would have been enabled.)
- Web conferencing with video was nascent and awkward to arrange, so extensive software integration work would have been required to enable remote conferencing with automatic translation.

Thankfully, ten years on, these handicaps have now been alleviated or resolved:

- A wide selection is now available of light and powerful computing devices – smartphones and tablets of various sizes.
- Cloud computing is now standard, making software installation a trivial matter of app download and registration.
- Speaker-independent speech recognition requiring no preparatory training is now taken for granted.
- Web conferencing has almost overnight become universal – with a boost from the pandemic era – and movement toward multilingual meeting capability is well underway. (Zoom has recently acquired relevant software (Marking, 2021).)

However, it is still proving difficult to engineer speech translation systems that offer an acceptable combination of reliability and use case customization. Ergonomic design is particularly challenging. An ideal system would be as unobtrusive as a skilled interpreter: It would offer highly reliable translation while allowing completely hands-free and eyes-free operation.

Unfortunately, two of the three major components of a speech translation system for demanding use cases like healthcare – speech recognition for spontaneous speech in noisy environments and automatic full translation – will still require some user monitoring until accuracy reaches an extremely high thresh-old, and may well continue to do so even beyond that point for user confidence ("reliability"). But that monitoring must be enabled without undue distraction from the work at hand.

Standard smartphones, tablets, and laptops are now available, but each format has its plusses and minuses. Smartphones, for instance, are easily portable, but their screens are small, so feedback may be hard to read at a distance; phones' onboard memory capacities are constrained; their speakers are limited in volume; their microphones may not work well if the device is far from a speaker; and, unless a holder is used, at least one hand will be occupied. Comparable pros and cons will apply to tablets and laptops.

In view of these issues, attempts have been made to build dedicated devices specialized for speech translation, and even for healthcare specifically. Fujitsu's Artificial Intelligence Laboratory, for instance, mounted a project to create two specialized microphone formats for this purpose. This effort is fully discussed in Section 2.3.2.9.

Several other companies have undertaken development of comparable dedi-cated devices for speech translation. Presently on sale are portable or wearable items marketed as ili, Pocketalk, Cheetah, and others. Voice translation is also available for Apple Watch, as powered by iTranslate, IHG Translator App, Speak & Translate, Microsoft Translator, Babbel, and TalkMondo. All these offerings address ergonomic – and therefore customization – issues to some degree, but none yet support reliability facilities.

In choosing between such dedicated devices and more standard ones like mobile phones and tablets, tradeoffs are unavoidable. Specialized equipment may be more narrowly directed at the given use case – desirable in principle, as we've stressed. But of course standard devices are everywhere: inexpen-sive, easy to obtain, familiar to use, and home to many apps developed at the makers' expense. In the end, the tradeoffs may fade as standard devices and software become ever more capable and versatile.

2.2.2.2 Peripherals

For any of the speech translation platforms just surveyed, auxiliary peripheral devices could provide ergonomic enhancements, some of which might prove decisive for usability per use case. For example, while auditory feedback for staff could boost reliability for both speech recognition and translation, it's likely to be confusing for patients. Earbuds – now connectable via Bluetooth to most devices – could ensure that only staff members heard appropriate confirmations.

More generally, Augmented Reality (AR) is quickly gaining popularity, and will likely experience an explosion with the imminent arrival of smart glasses. These will allow visual feedback to appear as "heads-up" displays visible through the lenses without head movement, and to be heard through embedded your-ears-only speakers. Translations, too, will be viewable and audible in the same way for both staff and patients.

Some AR devices will support not only visualization and sound for visual and auditory feedback, but also control capabilities for correction and guidance. They'll track hand movements in relation to virtual displays – if not immediately and affordably, then later. We can then expect AR to finally enable creation of maximally hands-free and eyes-free interfaces, and in this way to finally combine customization and reliability effectively.

2.2.2.3 Security

Translation and speech programs can be designed to run entirely in the "cloud" – that is, on servers which communicate with devices like smartphones or tablets; to run entirely on those devices; or to run in hybrid modes, with some elements (e.g., translation) online, and some (e.g., speech recognition and TTS) on the device. Related architecture decisions depend on the programs' processing requirements, on the necessary response time, and so on.

Most healthcare organizations worry about data security – certainly to protect their own operations, but often also to meet governmental requirements, such as those of the Health Insurance Portability and Accountability Act (HIPAA) in the US. Patient healthcare information is especially sensitive. Security requirements inevitably complicate adoption of technology for translation and speech. If associated software runs online (in the cloud), many organizations require that it be hosted on their own, usually local, servers. If the software runs on the device, it must often be integrated in approved official software *builds* (program sets).

2.3 Speech Translation Designs for Healthcare

Having discussed obstacles to adoption of speech translation systems, broadly grouped as relating to reliability and customization, and having considered a range of current and potential solutions, we now turn to examination of speech translation systems themselves.

Efforts to combine speech and translation technologies for healthcare have sorted themselves into two clear categories, largely based on systems' approaches to the tension between two major goals: On one hand, reliability is paramount in healthcare, as discussed, but wide applicability is also desirable. A tradeoff between these objectives is inevitable, since increased range will always give the opportunity for more errors. Several speech translation systems aiming for maximum reliability have opted for phrase-based design, while those aiming for greater range have risked full (that is, wide-ranging or relatively unrestricted) translation, while sometimes including phrase-based components.

Compromises between the phrase-based and full translation approaches are also possible, as already mentioned. A system enabling full translation can include a preliminary phrase-based stage, in which the input is matched against the set of remembered phrases, already supplied with prepared translations. We have introduced this approach as that of translation memory (Section 2.2.1.1). And again, a system can allow full translation when appropriate, while attempting to mitigate the associated risk of errors through facilities for verification and correction. Corrected translations can then enter the list of pretranslated inputs – that is, they can enter translation memory (Section 2.2.1.3.1). (Both of these strategies are illustrated in Section 2.3.2.7.)

We'll now look at phrase-based and full speech translation systems in turn.

2.3.1 Phrase-Based Speech Translation for Healthcare

Several healthcare-oriented systems have been designed to handle pretranslated phrases only, rather than attempting to provide full MT of wide-ranging input. This design decision addresses both of our desiderata: It enhances reliability because it depends on (usually professional) translation in advance, and it aids customization per use case in that relevant phrases can be brought into the system as needed. Here, we'll look at three strictly phrase-based systems.

2.3.1.1 S-MINDS and Phraselator

An early healthcare entry was the S-MINDS system by Sehda, Inc. (later Fluential) (Ehsani et al., 2008). At its center was an extensive set of fixed and pretranslated phrases, and the task of speech recognition was to match the appropriate one so as to enable pronunciation of its translation via TTS. A proprietary facility yielded the best available fuzzy match when no precise match was found. In this respect, the system represented further development of speech translation systems like the earlier Phraselator,[1] a ruggedized

---

[1] "Phraselator." *Wikipedia*, Wikimedia Foundation, 4 December 2021, at 20: 52(UTC), https://en .wikipedia.org/wiki/Phraselator.

handheld device likewise offering translation of fixed phrases only, provided in large quantities to the US military for use in the first Gulf War and later in various military, law enforcement, and humanitarian operations. To provide more flexible speech input, later versions of the Phraselator added technology licensed from Jibbigo (Eck et al., 2010), a commercial system for full speech translation produced by the research group of Alex Waibel.

2.3.1.2 BabelDr

The BabelDr system (Spechbach and Bouillon, 2019; Chapter 5), implemented by a team at the University of Geneva, is a recent example of phrase-only speech translation for healthcare. The system imposes two further constraints: (1) those phrases should generally be yes/no questions and (2) translation is unidirectional, in that patients are expected to respond only nonverbally to translated questions from healthcare staff. As compensation, however, these limitations enhance the overall practicality of the system by reducing the opportunities for error and the need for training. In addition, several interface refinements increase system reliability and facilitate customization for various use cases.

In terms of reliability, the system features transformation of each spoken or typed input phrase into a canonical text phrase, for which a translation has already been supplied and is ready for immediate transmission. In this respect, the system is comparable to the Phraselator and Sehda/Fluential speech-translation systems, as already described.

Importantly, however, the canonical phrases can also provide feedback to users concerning translation accuracy. This useful verification source has not previously been exploited. Experiments supplying confirmatory back-translations via neural networks appear promising as well (Mutal et al., 2019; DeepL commercial translation system[2]). For comparison, other feedback sources which have been used to date include semantically controlled back-translation (Seligman and Dillinger, 2016) and paraphrases generated via interlingua-based semantic representations (Gao et al., 2006).

Regarding customizability: In addition to using canonical phrases for verification of translations, users can access them more directly by browsing or by searching via keywords. The associated translations can then be transmitted without the need for further checking. Users can also focus on desired phrases by indicating the relevant topic through the GUI. These facilities enable quick

---

[2] "DeepL Translator." *Wikipedia*, Wikimedia Foundation, 10 August 2022, at 17: 37(UTC), https://en.wikipedia.org/wiki/DeepL_Translator.

customization of the system since new sets of canonical phrases and their translations can be created quickly.

While several central elements of BabelDr – robust matching of ASR results against a canonical set of pretranslated phrases, feedback to users concerning translation accuracy, enablement of searching and browsing among the phrase set – have been introduced by previous systems, this combination is new and promises to be especially practical, thanks to the imposed limitations and to the innovative handling of feedback.

Due in part to the same limitations, the reported evaluations demonstrate convincingly the usability of the system for successful diagnosis of simulated patients. Also reported are interesting results concerning the relative usability of speech as compared to text input.

2.3.2 Full Speech-to-Speech Translation for Healthcare

But now, on to full speech translation, in which vocabulary and grammar is relatively unrestricted – "relatively" because systems may still differ in the expected range of topics: Some may expect (and be trained on) only pharmaceutical matters, for instance, while others may invite conversations on roughly any topic.

Following decades of anticipation, automatic spoken-language translation (SLT) has finally entered widespread use. The Google Translate application, for instance, can bridge dozens of languages in face-to-face conversations, switching languages automatically. Microsoft speech-translation software now powers translated video chat among thirty languages, with sophisticated measures for cleaning up the stutters, errors, and repetitions of spontaneous speech.

Still emerging, however, are speech-translation systems directed at various demanding and socially significant use cases. Viewed from a high level, the main obstacle to widespread adoption has been that the essential components – speech-recognition and -translation technologies – are still error prone. While the error rates may be tolerable when the technologies are used separately, the errors combine and even compound when used together. The resulting translation output is often below the threshold of usability when accuracy is essential. Consequently, until now, use has been largely restricted to use cases – social networking, travel – in which no representation concerning accuracy is demanded or given.

Not that attempts to field systems for more demanding speech-translation applications have been missing. The Defense Advanced Research Programs Agency of the United States, for instance, has an extensive record of innovative work relating to law enforcement, disaster relief, and translation of broadcast news (Seligman and Waibel, 2019) – and healthcare, our main interest here.[3]

In examining healthcare-oriented SLT systems supporting full translation, we'll take as an example Converser for Healthcare, a prototype for communication between English-speaking healthcare staff and Spanish-speaking patients. The discussion is partly of historical interest since the system's pilot project took place in 2011 – an eon ago in computer years; however, most of the issues raised by that evaluation remain current. The system is also handy for present illustrative purposes, since it incorporated in a single application most of the reliability and customization features discussed: It applied interactive verification and correction techniques to the problem of reliability and offered Translation Shortcuts™, a form of translation memory, as its main aid to customization per use case.

Presently, we'll also touch on Fujitsu's healthcare-oriented system, emphasizing ergonomics as its customization approach (Section 2.3.2.2).

2.3.2.1 Converser for Healthcare

Converser was specialized for the healthcare market since the demand was most evident there. At the time of the pilot project, for example, San Francisco General Hospital received more than 3,500 requests for interpretation per month, or 42,000 per year, for 35 different languages. Requests for medical interpretation services are distributed among many wards and clinics (Paras et al., 2002). The resulting system was pilot tested in 2011 at the San Francisco Medical Center of Kaiser Permanente, the largest healthcare organization in the United States. An independent evaluation was carried out at the conclusion of the test.

The present section will

- describe Converser for Healthcare and its pilot project;
- summarize the resulting evaluation;
- provide an extended example of the revised system in use; and
- discuss the principal customization facility, Translation Shortcuts.

System Description We begin with a brief description of Converser's approach to interactive automatic interpretation, focusing upon the system's verification, correction, and customization features.

---

[3] For Project DIPLOMAT, see Frederking et. al. (2000); for BABYLON, see Waibel et al. (2003); for TRANSTAC, see Frandsen et al. (2008); and for GALE, see Cohen (2007) and Olive et al. (2011). Concerning Project BOLT, see "Broad Operational Language Translation (BOLT) (Archived)." Defense Advanced Research Projects Agency (DARPA). URL: www.darpa.mil /program/broad-operational-language-translation.

First, users could monitor and correct the speech-recognition system to ensure that the text which would be passed to the MT component was completely correct. Speech, typing, or handwriting could be used to repair speech-recognition errors.

Next, during the MT stage, users could monitor – and, if necessary, correct – one especially important aspect of the translation, lexical disambiguation.

The system's approach to lexical disambiguation was twofold: First, Converser supplied a back-translation, or retranslation of the translation from the target language back to the source. Using this paraphrase of the initial input, even a monolingual user could make an initial judgment concerning the quality of the preliminary MT output. Other systems, such as IBM's MASTOR (Gao et al., 2006), have also employed retranslation. Converser, however, exploited proprietary technologies to ensure that the lexical senses used during back-translation accurately reflected those used in forward translation.

In addition, if uncertainty remained about the correctness of a given word sense, the system supplied a proprietary set of Meaning Cues™ – synonyms, definitions, and so on – which had been drawn from various resources, collated in a database (called SELECT™), and aligned with the respective lexica of the relevant MT systems. With these cues as guides, the user could monitor the current, proposed meaning and, when necessary, select a different, preferred meaning from among those available. Automatic updates of translation and back-translation then followed.

The initial purpose of these techniques was to increase reliability during real-time speech-translation sessions. Equally significant, however, they could also enable even monolingual users to supply feedback for offline machine learning to improve the system. This feedback capability remains rare: Usually, only users with some knowledge of the output language can supply it, for example, in Google's Translate Community.

All translations were recorded in bilingual transcripts, including both the original source language and the target language translation. (In the latest system versions, transcripts also contained relevant back-translations.)

Converser adopted rather than created its speech and translation components, adding value through the interactive interface elements to be explained. Nuance, Inc., later acquired by Microsoft, supplied speech recognition; rule-based English and Spanish bi-directional MT were supplied by Word Magic of Costa Rica;[4] and TTS was again provided by Nuance.

Identical facilities were available for Spanish as for English speakers: When the Spanish flag was clicked, all interface elements – buttons and menus,

---

[4] "Word Magic." URL: https://word-magic-translator-home-edition.software.informer.com/.

onscreen messages, Translation Shortcuts (Section 2.3.2.8), handwriting recognition, and so on – changed to Spanish.

Multimodal Input In healthcare settings, speech input isn't appropriate for every situation. Current speech-recognition systems remain unfamiliar for many users. To maximize familiarity, Converser incorporated standard commercial-grade dictation systems for broad-coverage and ergonomic speech recognition, products with established user bases in the healthcare community. Even so, some orientation and practice were required. Also expected were problems of ambient noise (e.g., in emergency rooms or ambulances) and problems of microphone and computer arrangement (e.g., to accommodate not only desktops but counters or service windows, which may form barriers between staff and patient).

To deal with these and other usability issues, Converser provided a range of input modes: Also enabled, in addition to dictated speech, were the use of touchscreen keyboards for text input and the use of standard keyboards. All of these input modes had to be bilingual, and language switching needed to be arranged automatically when there was a change of active participant. Further, it was possible to change input modes seamlessly within a given utterance: For example, users could dictate the input if they wished but then have the option to make corrections using handwriting or one of the remaining two modes.

Of course, even this flexible range of input options hardly solved all problems. Illiterate patients pose special difficulties. The careful and relatively concise style of speech required for automatic recognition is often difficult to elicit, so that recognition accuracy remains low, and the ability to read and correct the results is obviously absent. Just as obviously, the remaining three text input modes would be equally ineffectual for illiterates. Converser's approach to low literacy was to supply Translation Shortcuts for the minimally literate. It was hoped that future versions would augment Shortcuts with TTS and iconic pictures.

Staff members are usually at least minimally literate, but they present their own usability issues. Their typing skills may be low or absent. Handling the computer and microphone may be awkward in many situations, for example, when examining a patient or taking notes. (Speech-translation systems are expected to function in a wide range of physical settings: in admissions or financial aid offices, at massage tables for physical therapy with patients lying face down, in personal living rooms for home therapy or interviews, and in many other locations.)

To help deal with the awkwardness issues, one version of the system provided voice commands, enabling hands-free operation. Both full interactive translation and the Translation Shortcuts facility could then be run hands free. To a limited degree, the system could be used eyes free as well: TTS could be used to pronounce the back-translation so that preliminary judgments of translation quality could be made without looking at the computer screen. These facilities, however, remained insufficiently tested in the pilot project to be discussed now.

Pilot Project In 2011, Converser for Healthcare 3.0 was pilot tested at the Medical Center of Kaiser Permanente in San Francisco. The project, supported by a grant from the company's Innovation Fund, ran for nine calendar months, with use in three departments during three of those months. At the conclusion, sixty-one interviews were conducted by an interpreter from an outside agency. A formal internal report gave the results. Reception was generally positive (Section 2.3.2.1.4); but departmental responsibility for next steps remained divided on project completion, and there has been no further use to date.

Converser was used and evaluated in four use cases in the Medical Center's Pharmacy, and one each in Inpatient Nursing and Eye Care. Each use case had its own workflow and equipment setup. In the Pharmacy, the master computer could be stationary (in the Consulting or Drop-off use case); handheld (in the Pickup use case); or on a cart (in the Greeter use case). In Inpatient Nursing, a handheld tablet personal computer was used throughout. In Eye Care, to facilitate typing, stationary use of the tablet was preferred. The hardware and software used in the project are described and assessed in Seligman and Dillinger (2011). The project's logistical issues are also discussed in detail.

Evaluation Evaluation of the Kaiser Permanente project relies on Kaiser's internal report, based as mentioned on a commissioned survey by an independent third party. The report itself is proprietary, but its findings are reproduced in essence in Seligman and Dillinger (2015; 2016). One significant finding: when asked whether the system met their needs, of the 79 percent of interviewed patients who answered the question, 94 percent responded either "completely" or "mostly." However, as would be expected in a system fielded a decade ago, qualifications and stumbling blocks were not lacking. The cited papers report on these, and on revisions subsequently undertaken to resolve them.

Revised System in Use Following is an extended example of the revised system in use, with emphasis on features addressing reliability and customization issues. For ease of exposition, we use the present tense, though the system isn't currently in use.

Again, depending on the platform, the system can offer up to four input modes: speech, typing, handwriting, and touchscreen. To illustrate the use of interactive correction for speech recognition as well as MT, we assume that the user has clicked on the round red Mic button to activate the microphone (Figure 2.1).

Still in Figure 2.1, notice the Traffic Light Icon™ and two Earring Icons™. These are used to switch between Precheck Mode and NoPrecheck Mode for translation and speech recognition, respectively. Both icons are currently green, indicating "Full speed ahead!" That is, verification has been temporarily switched off: The user has indicated that it is unnecessary to precheck either ASR or MT before transmitting the next utterance, preferring speed to accuracy.

Just prior to the figure's snapshot, the user said, "San Jose is a pleasant city." Since verification had been switched off for both ASR and MT, these functioned without interruption. The speech-recognition result appeared briefly (and in this case correctly) in the Input window. Immediately thereafter, the Spanish translation result (also correct in this case) appeared in the right-hand section of the Transcript window and was immediately pronounced via TTS. Meanwhile, the original English input was recorded in the left-hand section of that window.

Also on the English side of the Transcript window and just below the original English input is a specially prepared back-translation. The original input was translated into Spanish and then retranslated back into English. Proprietary

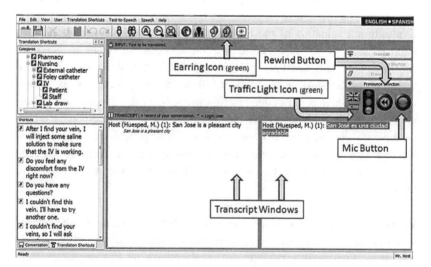

Figure 2.1 Earring and Traffic Light Icons are green: "Full speed ahead!"

techniques ensure that the Spanish-to-English back-translation means the same as the Spanish. Thus, even though pre-verification was bypassed for this utterance in the interest of speed, post-verification via the Transcript window was still enabled. (This window, containing inputs from both English and Spanish sides and the associated back-translations, can be saved for record-keeping. Participant identities can optionally be masked for confidentiality.)

Using this back-translation, the user might conclude that the translation just transmitted was inadequate. In that case, or if the user simply wants to rephrase this or some previous utterance, he or she can click the Rewind Button (round, with chevrons). A menu of previous inputs then appears (not shown). Once a previous input is selected, it will be brought back into the Input window, where it can be modified using any available input mode – voice, typing, or handwriting. In our example sentence, for instance, "pleasant" could be changed to "boring"; clicking the Translate button would then trigger transla-tion of the modified input, accompanied by a new back-translation.

In Figure 2.2, the user has selected the yellow Earring Icon, specifying that the speech recognition should "proceed with caution." As a result, spoken input remains in the Input window until the user explicitly orders translation. Thus, there's an opportunity to make any necessary or desired corrections of the ASR results. In this case, the user has said "This morning, I received an email from my colleague Igor Boguslavsky." The name, however, has been misrecognized as "Igor bogus Lovsky." Typed or handwritten correction can fix the mistake, and the Translate button can then be clicked to proceed.

Just prior to Figure 2.3, the Traffic Light Icon was also switched to yellow, indicating that translation (as opposed to speech recognition) should also "proceed with caution": It should be prechecked before transmission and pronunciation. This time the user said, "This is a cool program." Since the

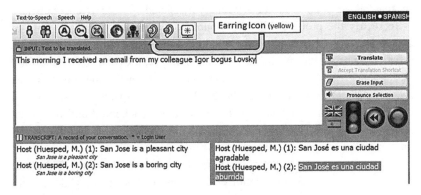

Figure 2.2 Earring Icon is yellow: "Proceed with caution!"

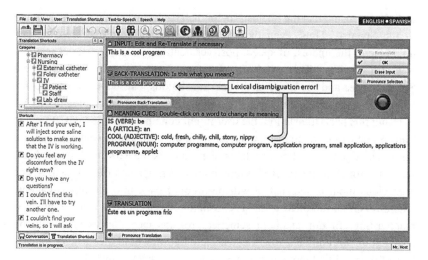

Figure 2.3 Verification Panel, with a lexical disambiguation error in "This is a cool program."

Earring Icon is still yellow, ASR results were prechecked and approved. Then the Verification Panel™ appeared, as shown in the figure. At the bottom, we see the preliminary Spanish translation, "Éste es un programa frío."

Unfortunately, despite the best efforts of the translation program to determine the intended meaning in context, "cool" has been mistranslated – as shown by the back-translation, "This is a cold program." Another indication of the error appears in the Meaning Cues window (third from the top), which indicates the meaning of each input word or expression as currently understood by the MT engine. Converser 4.0 employs synonyms as Meaning Cues; but pictures, definitions, and examples might also be used. In the present case, we see that the word "cool" has been wrongly translated as "cold, fresh, chilly ..."

To rectify the problem, the user double clicks on the offending word or expression. The Change Meaning Window™ then appears (Figure 2.4), with a list of all available meanings for the relevant expression. Here, the third meaning for "cool" is "great, fun, tremendous ..." When this meaning has been selected, the entire input is retranslated. This time the Spanish translation will be "Es un programa estupendo," and the translation back into English is "Is an awesome program." The user may accept this rendering, despite the minor grammatical error, or may decide to try again.

A side note concerning the Traffic Light Icon and Earring Icons: These help to balance a conversation's reliability with its speed. And again, while reliability is indispensable for serious applications like healthcare, some time is

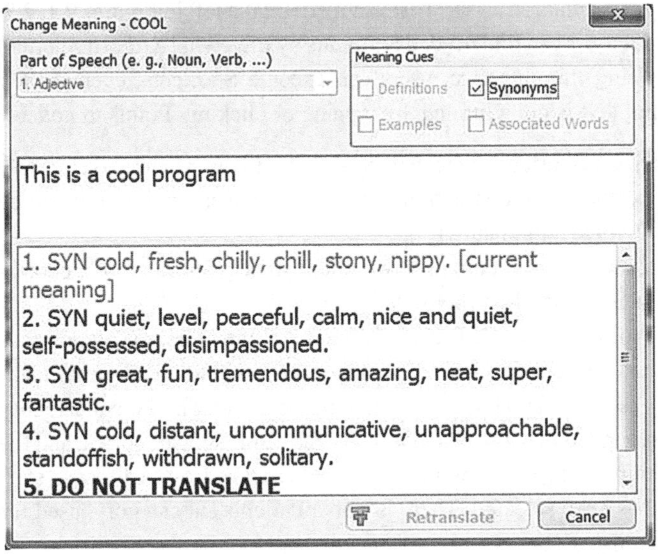

Figure 2.4 The Change Meaning Window, with four meanings of "cool"

required to interactively enhance it. The icons let users proceed carefully when accuracy is paramount, or a misunderstanding must be resolved. On the other hand, they can move ahead more quickly when throughput is judged more important. This flexibility, we anticipate, will be useful in future applications featuring automatic detection of start-of-speech: In NoPreCheck Mode, ASR and translation will proceed automatically without start or end signals, and thus without demanding the user's attention, but can be interrupted for interactive verification or correction as appropriate. (On the attention required for optional monitoring, compare Section 2.2.1.3.1.)

Translation Shortcuts We now shift focus from Converser's reliability features to its principal facility for customization and adaptation to multiple use cases: Translation Shortcuts – pre-packaged translations, providing a kind of translation memory. Shortcuts are designed to provide two main advantages.

First, translations have been professionally verified, so their reverification is unnecessary. They can be reliably transmitted as is. As such, they do double duty for reliability and customization.

Second, access to stored Shortcuts is very quick, with little or no need for text entry – a plus especially for busy use cases like healthcare. Several facilities contribute to meeting this design criterion.

- A Translation Shortcuts Browser™ is provided (on the left in Figures 2.1, 2.3, and 2.5) so that users can find needed Shortcuts by traversing a tree of Shortcut categories. Using this interface, users can execute Shortcuts, even if their ability to input text is quite limited, by tapping or clicking. Points to notice:

  o The Translation Shortcuts panel can be slid in and out of view to conserve screen space and avoid distraction. (In one Converser version, it could be operated by voice commands.)

  o The Shortcuts Browser contains two main areas, Shortcuts Categories (above) and Shortcuts List (below).

  o In the Categories section of Figures 2.1 and 2.3, the Nursing category has been selected. It contains several subcategories including External catheter, Foley catheter, IV (intravenous), and Lab draw. The IV subcategory has been expanded to show its Patient and Staff sub-subcategories, and the latter, containing expressions most likely to be used by healthcare staff members, has been selected. There is also a Patients subcategory, used for patient responses.

  o Below the Categories section is the Shortcuts List section, containing a scrollable list of alphabetized Shortcuts. (Various other sorting criteria could be enabled, for example, sorting by frequency of use, recency, etc.)

  o Double-clicking on any visible Shortcut in the list will execute it. (Clicking once will select and highlight a Shortcut, and typing Enter will execute any currently highlighted Shortcut.)

  o If a Shortcut from a Staff subcategory has been used, the associated Patient subcategory can be opened automatically to enable a response.

- A Shortcut Search™ facility can retrieve a set of relevant Shortcuts given only keywords or the first few characters or words of a string. The desired Shortcut can then be executed with a single gesture (mouse click or stylus tap) or voice command.

  o In Figure 2.5, the Mental Health category has been selected, and an icon (showing a magnifying glass containing a key) has been clicked to authorize Keyword Search.

  o The word "you" has been entered in the Input buffer – by voice, typing, or handwriting – and several Shortcuts containing this word have been found and gathered in a scrollable menu, ready for clicking.

  o Here, the results are sorted alphabetically. Various additional sorting possibilities might also be useful: by frequency of use, proportion of matched words, and so on.

  o Arrow keys or voice commands can be used to navigate the results.

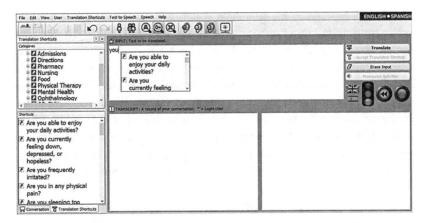

Figure 2.5 Automatic keyword search for Translation Shortcuts

o If the user enters the exact text of any Shortcut, a message will identify it as such, indicating that verification will not be necessary.

o However, final text not matching a Shortcut will be passed to the routines for full translation with verification. In this way, a seamless transition is provided between the Shortcuts facility and full, broad-coverage translation.

Again, because the Shortcuts Browser can be used without text entry, simply by pointing and clicking, it enables responses by minimally literate users. Use by completely illiterate users could be enabled through automatic pronunciation of Shortcuts and categories in the Shortcuts Browser via TTS, in effect reading the Shortcuts aloud while highlighting them. Shortcuts could also be augmented with pictures or symbols as clues to their meaning.

Having scrutinized Converser for Healthcare in terms of both reliability and customizability, we now turn to another healthcare-oriented SLT system supporting full translation. In this system, ergonomics – customization facilitating practical use in the specific settings – has been the central focus of research and development.

2.3.2.2 Fujitsu's Focus on Ergonomics

At Fujitsu Laboratories Ltd., the Artificial Intelligence Laboratory recently developed a system supporting full speech translation for healthcare under the direction of Senior Researcher Tomoki Nagase. The work was carried out in cooperation with Japan's Global Communication Plan Project associated with the planned-but-canceled Tokyo Olympics in 2020. This research and development, tightly focused on practical use in the healthcare setting, exemplifies purposeful customization for the assigned application.

Japan was expecting some 40 million visitors to the games, and the number of foreign residents in Japan had been increasing as well. The COVID-19 pandemic disrupted both expectations, but needs for healthcare translation can be expected to resurge. Prior to the disruption, in response to Fujitsu's questionnaires, about 70 percent of the healthcare institutional respondents anticipated language problems, so the need for communication aids appeared clear, particularly for minor languages and over holidays or at night. Human interpreters would have been preferred, but service might have been inefficient due to intermittent use, so interest was strong in technology-based solutions, with due recognition of their limits.

In preparation for clinical trials, Fujitsu organized cooperation with medical and research institutions, using interviews and translation logs to gather feedback concerning design. Principal partners were the International Medical Center of the University of Tokyo Hospital (which provided ethical review no. 10704) and the National Institute of Information and Communications Technology (NICT), which supplied crucial software and pursued performance improvements through analysis of speech-translation logs. Fujitsu's responsibility was to develop terminals and interfaces to be used at medical sites.

Preliminary simulation tests clarified several points. First, hands-free solutions would be needed, to leave both hands free for medical work and to help prevent infection. Second, a fallback would be needed in case of misunderstandings unresolved by repetition. To address the first requirement, two solutions were developed: (1) a fixed desktop terminal, with which staff and patient could interact face-to-face over a desk or counter, as in reception areas, medicine or cashier counters, blood sampling or inspection stations, and so on, and (2) a wearable terminal, usable by staff responding to foreign nationals in hospital wards, nursing stations, and so on. Tests confirmed stable operation in various noisy environments. To meet the fallback need, both terminals were equipped with a button for calling up a human interpreter.

Following these preparations, clinical trials were undertaken in 2016 and 2017, starting with six and progressing to twenty-one hospitals. English and Japanese were handled via the desktop terminal throughout, with Chinese>Japanese and wearable terminals added in the second year of trials. Use cases were selected freely by the institutions, without restrictions on conversations: Reception, hospital wards, and examinations were the most frequent users, along with medical interviews, intensive care units, inspections, medicine counters, emergency visits, cashiers, examination or treatment sessions, and others. Consent signatures were obtained from patients, and sessions were followed up with optional questionnaires for staff members and patients.

During the clinical trials, eighty-three English–Japanese sessions and seventy-six Chinese>Japanese sessions were recorded. Perhaps not surprisingly, speech was initiated by medical staff twice as often as by patients (67 percent compared to 33 percent). And, interestingly, there were more Chinese- than English-speaking users (53 percent and 47 percent). The optional questionnaire posed four questions to staff and patients: Was it useful during the conversation? Was what you spoke understood? Did you understand what the other person spoke? Was it easy to use? Five degrees of satisfaction could be registered, from "Highly rated" to "Lowly rated."

Combined scores for "Highly" or "Reasonably" ranged over these questions from about 60 percent to 70 percent for staff members and from about 70 percent to 75 percent for patients. The best result: About 60 percent of the English speakers responded that their understanding of Japanese was "Highly rated." By comparison, the "Highly rated" score for Chinese patients' comprehension of Japanese was about 35 percent.

With respect to the wearable terminal, in a briefing before clinical trials began, fifty staff members were interviewed. Forty-five, or 90 percent, said they were able to converse effectively. The terminal's size and weight were generally judged acceptable. Asked if they'd want to use the terminal at work, twenty-three said yes, as soon as possible; sixteen said they'd wait until the translation accuracy was improved; and the remainder would wait for an improved terminal or preferred not to use the system.

Actual trials followed improvements in the terminals, based on lessons learned. A number of positive staff reactions were claimed. Users said they were able to convey technical terms more easily with the device than with gestures; that they had more opportunities to converse with foreign patients and felt less hesitant to speak with them; and that they felt a sense of safety because the systems were available, even if there were few actual opportunities to use them.

Commercialization and deployment of the system remained for the future, but, until the disruption caused by the pandemic, plans were under way for expansion of language coverage, for example, to Korean, Vietnamese, and Brazilian Portuguese. Also anticipated were improvements in translation accuracy, especially for Chinese. Tools for training staff users, perhaps including instructional videos, were to be considered as well.

2.4 Past and Current Speech Translation Systems

We next point toward a range of further speech translation solutions available now or in the past, each supporting a subset of the reliability and customization features we've considered. Several useful studies and surveys will be cited.

2.4.1 Reliability of Machine Translation for Healthcare: A Study

As a component of speech-to-speech translation systems, translation technology development has been especially dynamic, with several changes of basic approach (Chapter 1). The consequent improvement in raw translation *accuracy* has brought improvement in speech translation *reliability* (accuracy plus user confidence), a critical factor in widespread adoption. But how much improvement?

Sample translations and back-translations were appended to Chapter 1 to give an informal impression of the state of the art in automatic text translation. We can now mention a pertinent formal study of the translation system sampled there: an evaluation of its Japanese-to-English translation in the medical domain (Takakusagi et al., 2021). Interestingly, back-translation into the original Japanese also figured prominently in this research.

The system in question is DeepL Translator, developed by DeepL GmbH, Cologne, Germany.[5] The test case was an already-published medical article in Japanese, automatically translated into English using DeepL Translator. The resulting English article was then back-translated into Japanese by three researchers. Three other researchers then compared the back-translated Japanese sentences with the original Japanese manuscript and calculated the percentage of sentences keeping the intended meaning. The match rate for the article as a whole was found to be 94.0 ± 2.9 percent. Different sections of the article fared differently, with significantly higher rate in the Results section, but lower rates in the Methods section. Helpfully, however, significant predictors for mismatched translations were found, with the most mismatches in compound sentences and sentences with unclear subjects and predicates. (Chapter 3 studies the usefulness of such predictors.) Overall, the translation was judged accurate.

While the system apparently delivered translation results in the 90 percent-plus range for *written* material – *and* on a famously challenging translation direction, *and* with a translation system not specifically trained on medical material – the added difficulties of translating recognized text from spontaneous speech must be considered (Chapter 1). Even so, from the translation viewpoint, the prospects for future speech translation systems do seem quite promising, especially since the usability of back-translation for verification and optional correction has already been demonstrated for at least this particular translation component. And so, with cautious optimism, we go on to refer readers to several surveys of speech translation systems.

---

[5] "DeepL Translator." *Wikipedia*, Wikimedia Foundation, 10 August 2022, at 17: 37(UTC), https://en.wikipedia.org/wiki/DeepL_Translator.

2.4.2 Surveys of Speech Translation Systems

"Enabling Medical Translation for Low-Resource Languages" (Musleh et al., 2016) briefly describes some speech translation systems available at the time of writing while developing text translation for Urdu, an under-resourced language closely related to Hindi and important for healthcare in Qatar. The paper provides useful historical context, even as several of the surveyed systems remain active.

2.4.2.1 Some Bi-directional Speech Translation Systems

The first group of systems cited by Musleh and colleagues are those for bi-directional doctor-patient communication, with special interest in systems requiring data collection for under-resourced languages. Most built until the time of writing (Bouillon et al., 2008; Dillinger and Seligman, 2006; Eck et al., 2010; Ehsani et al., 2006; Gao et al., 2006; Heinze et al., 2006) remained prototypes, with few fully deployed. Some did, however, work with under-resourced languages (Bouillon et al., 2008; Ehsani et al., 2006; Heinze et al., 2006; Gao et al., 2006). These relied on symbolic meaning representations rather than on statistical machine translation (while neural translation remained in in the future). Unfortunately, none of the systems addressed the top five languages of most interest to Qatar. In addition to Converser for Healthcare and S-MINDS, already discussed, the following systems are cited:

- MedSLT (Bouillon et al., 2008), an interlingua-based speech-to-speech translation system, covering a restricted set of domains for English, French, Japanese, Spanish, Catalan, and Arabic. The doctors' questions or statements to the patient could be translated, but not the patients' responses.
- Jibbigo (Eck et al., 2010), a travel and medical speech-to-speech MT system, deployed on iPhone mobile application (and requiring no Internet connection). Jibbigo covered English<>Spanish for medical translation.
- Accultran (Heinze et al., 2006), a prototype featuring back-translation to the doctor for confirmation and yes/no or multiple-choice questions to the patient. A cross-cultural adviser was included. Sensitive and hard-to-translate utterances were flagged. The SNOMED-CT or Clinical Document Architecture (CDA-2) standards were used as an interlingua.
- IBM MASTOR (Gao et al., 2006), a speech-to-speech MT system for English<>Mandarin and English<>Arabic dialects. Laptops and handhelds were accommodated.
- English-Portugese SLT (Santos Gomez Rodrigues, 2013), an English-Portuguese speech-to-speech system, usable as an online service or as a mobile app.

2.4.2.2 Some Phrase-Based Speech Translation Systems

The second group of systems discussed by Musleh et al. included several phrase-based mobile or web applications for doctor-to-patient translation only. The most popular were UniversalDoctor, MediBabble, Canopy, MedSpeak, MavroEmergency Medical Spanish, and DuoChart.[6] None enabled full (free, unseen, or spontaneous) translations, and none covered the language pairs of interest for Qatar. Some (e.g., UniversalDoctor) required paid subscriptions.

2.4.2.3 Fifteen Representative Apps: A Study

"Language Translation Apps in Health Care Settings: Expert Opinion" (Panayiotou et al., 2019) offers an assessment of fifteen apps. The concentration was on iPad-compatible language translation apps: Were they suitable for everyday conversations in healthcare settings? Apps found on the Apple iTunes Store and in the literature were considered if available free and able to translate at least one of the top ten languages spoken in Australia. These were reviewed in two stages: Stage 1 entailed a feature analysis by two independent researchers, with evaluation for offline use, input and output methods, and available languages; in Stage 2, two independent professionals with expertise in translation and cross-cultural communication analyzed app suitability for everyday communication in healthcare. Importantly, however, apps were considered unsuitable if they aimed at aspects of care for which professional interpreters were normally responsible. These included assessment, treatment and discharge planning, and elicitation of consent for medical treatments.

Eight of the fifteen evaluated apps contained voice-to-voice and voice-to-text translation options. Six were phrase-only systems, and one supplied a combination of free input and preset phrases. Five apps were excluded before Stage 2. Of the ten remaining apps, six were specifically designed for healthcare translation purposes. Of these, two were rated as suitable for everyday communication in the healthcare setting: Assist and Talk to Me. Both were found to be culturally and linguistically diverse and to contain simple and appropriate preset health phrases. Neither attempted conversations normally handled by professional interpreters.

The study concluded cautiously: All iPad-compatible translation apps require caution and consideration in healthcare settings, and none should

---

[6] "Universal Doctor." URL: www.universaldoctor.com; "Medibabble." URL: http://medibabble
.com; "Canopy." URL: www.canopyapps.com; "Medspeak." URL: https://apptopia.com/ios/
app/313250795/about; "MavroEmergency Medical Spanish." URL: http://mavroinc.com/med
ical.html; "DuoChart." URL: http://duochart.com.

replace professional interpreters. However, a few apps were found suitable for everyday conversations, especially phrase-based systems treating subjects not requiring a professional interpreter.

2.4.2.4 Some Additional Links

Finally, several additional healthcare-related studies have been kindly suggested by Meng Ji, co-author of this volume: Van de Velde et al. (2015); Thonon et al. (2021); Chen et al. (2017); and Turner et al. (2019).

2.5 Conclusions

This chapter's introduction promised an optimistic conclusion concerning the future of speech translation systems for healthcare. Optimism is certainly warranted – firstly, in view of recent technological progress, not only in the speech and translation components but in the related ecosystem of platforms, peripherals, and security; and secondly, considering the prospects for continued improvements in the associated reliability and customizability.

However, as (almost) goes without saying, technological optimism must be tempered by prudent and informed caution – especially in healthcare, where errors can be deadly. While we do advocate progressive adoption of speech translation technologies in many healthcare-related use cases, we do so with these caveats:

- Staff responsible for tech selection require basic grounding in the relevant tech: How does it work, and what are its limitations per use case? We hope that this volume can help to supply that foundation. While the technology is challenging and quickly developing, it should not be treated as oracular. While systems unavoidably remain black boxes to some extent in current stages of the neural network era, blind or awestruck acceptance is unhealthy – in healthcare, quite literally.
- Further, while responsible staff should strive for at least high-level understanding, they shouldn't fly solo. Professionals in the prospective technologies must also be consulted, with reference to specific intended use cases.
- All responsible parties – staff, consultants, and patients – must be helped to fully understand that speech recognition and translation errors are inevitable in automatic systems of whatever quality, since even human interpreters make mistakes. An aforementioned tradeoff must be acknowledged: the broader the coverage of the system, the less its expected accuracy. And so, if the use case is inherently narrow (as, e.g., for patient intake) and demands

reliability with little staff interaction or monitoring, phrase-based rather than full translation systems may be sensible choices. As continued improvement in accuracy raises the reliability of full translation systems, or as increased staff interaction becomes possible or desirable, systems providing broader translation can be reconsidered.

Arthur C. Clarke said, "Any sufficiently advanced technology is indistinguishable from magic" – and he was not far wrong. But as we've seen, for healthcare and many other challenging use cases, "Magic is not enough" – not without determined attention to reliability and customization. Still, we find ourselves in the unaccountably fortunate position of not only witnessing but – to some degree, anyway – actually understanding developments that would have seemed purely magical even in recent decades. So while blind or awestruck adoption of speech translation services is not recommended, awed appreciation, with eyes wide open, definitely is. We sorcerers' apprentices would be ungrateful not to exploit this sorcery to improve well-being and save lives. But with care.

References

Bouillon, Pierrette, Glenn Flores, Maria Georgescul, et al. 2008. "Many-to-Many Multilingual Medical Speech Translation on a PDA." In *Proceedings of the Eighth Conference of the Association for Machine Translation in the Americas*, AMTA'08, pages 314–323, Waikiki, Hawaii, USA.

Chen X, S. Acosta, and A. Barry. 2017, "Machine or Human? Evaluating the Quality of a Language Translation Mobile App for Diabetes Education Material." *Journal of Medical Internet Research*, 2(1): e13. URL: https://diabetes.jmir.org/2017/1/e13. DOI: 0.2196/diabetes.7446.

Cohen, J. 2007. "The GALE Project: A Description and an Update." In *Proceedings of the IEEE Workshop on Automatic Speech Recognition and Understanding* (ASRU), Kyoto, Japan.

Dillinger, M., and M. Seligman. 2004. "System Description: A Highly Interactive Speech-to-Speech Translation System." In *Proceedings of the Association for Machine Translation in the Americas* (AMTA-04). Washington, DC.

Dillinger, M., and M. Seligman. 2006. "Converser: Highly Interactive Speech-to-Speech Translation for Healthcare." In *Proceedings of the COLING-ACL 2006 Workshop on Medical Speech Translation*, pages 36–39, Sydney, Australia.

Eck, M., I. Lane, Y. Zhang, and A. Waibel. 2010. "Jibbigo: Speech-to-Speech Translation on Mobile Devices." In *Proceedings of IEEE Spoken Language Technology Workshop*, SLT2010, pages 165–166, Berkeley, California, USA.

Ehsani, F., J. Kimzey, D. Master, et al. 2006. "Speech to Speech Translation for Medical Triage in Korean." In *Proceedings of the COLING-ACL 2006 Workshop on Medical Speech Translation*, pages 13–19, New York, NY, USA.

Ehsani, F., J. Kimzey, E. Zuber, D. Master, and K. Sudre. 2008. "Speech to Speech Translation for Nurse Patient Interaction." In *Coling 2008: Proceedings of the Workshop on Speech Processing for Safety Critical Translation and Pervasive Applications*, pages 54–59, Manchester, England: COLING 2008 Organizing Committee.

Frandsen, M. W., S. Z. Riehemann, and K. Precoda. 2008. "IraqComm and FlexTrans: A Speech Translation System and Flexible Framework." In *Innovations and Advances in Computer Sciences and Engineering*, pages 527–532, Singapore: Springer.

Frederking, R., A. Rudnicky, C. Hogan, and K. Lenzo. 2000. "Interactive Speech Translation in the DIPLOMAT Project." *Machine Translation*, 15, pages 27–42.

Gao, Y., Liang G., B. Zhou, et al. 2006. "IBM MASTOR System: Multilingual Automatic Speech-to-Speech Translator." In *Proceedings of the COLING-ACL 2006 Workshop on Medical Speech Translation*, pages 53–56, Sydney, Australia.

Heinze, D. T., A. Turchin, and V. Jagannathan. 2006. "Automated Interpretation of Clinical Encounters with Cultural Cues and Electronic Health Record Generation." In *Proceedings of the COLING-ACL 2006 Workshop on Medical Speech Translation*, pages 20–27, Sydney, Australia.

Marking, M. 2021. "Zoom Bolts on Speech Translation in What Is Only Its Second-Ever Acquisition." *URL*: https://slator.com/zoom-bolts-on-speech-translation-in-what-is-only-its-second-ever-acquisition/. June 30, 2021.

Musleh, A., N. Durrani, I. Temnikova, S. Vogel, and O. Alsaad. "Enabling Medical Translation for Low-Resource Languages." 2016. In *Proceedings of 17th International Conference on Intelligent Text Processing and Computational Linguistics*, Konya, Turkey.

Mutal, J., P. Bouillon, J. Gmerlach, P. Estrella, and H. Spechbach. 2019. "Monolingual Backtranslation in a Medical Speech Translation System for Diagnostic Interviews – A NMT Approach." In *Proceedings of the MT Summit XVII: The 17th Machine Translation Summit*, Dublin, Ireland.

Olive, J., C. Christianson, and J. McCary (eds.). 2011. *Handbook of Natural Language Processing and Machine Translation: DARPA Global Autonomous Language Exploitation*. New York, NY: Springer Science and Business Media.

Panayiotou, A., A. Gardner, S. Williams, et al. 2019. "Language Translation Apps in Health Care Settings: Expert Opinion." *JMIR Mhealth Uhealth*, 7(4), April 9, 2019. e11316. DOI: 10.2196/11316. PMID: 30964446; PMCID: PMC6477569.

Paras, M., O. Leyva, T. Berthold, and R. Otake. 2002. "*Videoconferencing Medical Interpretation: The Results of Clinical Trials.*" Oakland, CA: Health Access Foundation.

Santos Gomes Rodrigues, J. A. 2013. *Speech-to-Speech Translation to Support Medical Interviews*. PhD thesis, Universidade de Lisboa, Portugal.

Seligman, M. 2020. "Socially Significant Applications of Speech-Translation Technology." In *The Oxford Handbook of Translation and Social Practices*. M. Ji and S. Laviosa, eds. Oxford University Press (Oxford Handbooks). New York. December 15, 2020. Chapter 27, pages 561–586.

Seligman, M., and M. Dillinger. 2006a. "Usability Issues in an Interactive Speech-To-Speech Translation System for Healthcare." In *HLT/NAACL-06: Proceedings of the Workshop on Medical Speech Translation*, pages 1–4, Stroudsburg, PA: Association for Computational Linguistics.

Seligman, M., and M. Dillinger. 2006b. "Converser: Highly Interactive Speech-to-Speech Translation for Healthcare." In *HLT/NAACL-06: Proceedings of The Workshop on Medical Speech Translation*, pages 36–39, Stroudsburg, PA: Association for Computational Linguistics.

Seligman, M., and M. Dillinger. 2008. "Rapid Portability Among Domains in an Interactive Spoken Language Translation System." In *Coling 2008: Proceedings of the Workshop on Speech Processing for Safety Critical Translation and Pervasive Applications*, pages 40–47, Manchester, England: Coling 2008 Organizing Committee.

Seligman, M., and M. Dillinger. 2011. "Real-time Multi-Media Translation for Healthcare: A Usability Study." In *Proceedings of the 13th Machine Translation Summit*, Xiamen, China.

Seligman, M., and M. Dillinger. 2012. "Spoken Language Translation: Three Business Opportunities." In *Proceedings of the Association for Machine Translation in the Americas* (AMTA-12), San Diego, CA.

Seligman, M., and M. Dillinger. 2013. "Automatic Speech Translation for Healthcare: Some Internet and Interface Aspects." In *Proceedings of the 10th International Conference on Terminology and Artificial Intelligence* (TIA-13), Paris, France.

Seligman, M., and M. Dillinger. 2014. "Behind the Scenes in an Interactive Speech Translation System." In *Proceedings of the Association for Machine Translation in the Americas* (AMTA-14), Vancouver, BC, Canada.

Seligman, M., and M. Dillinger. 2015. "Evaluation and Revision of a Speech Translation System for Healthcare." In *Proceedings of the 12th International Workshop on Spoken Language Translation*, Da Nang, Vietnam.

Seligman, M., and M. Dillinger. 2016. "Automatic Interpretation for Healthcare." *MultiLingual Computing*, pages 38–42.

Seligman, M., and A. Waibel. 2019. "Advances in Speech-To-Speech Translation Technologies." In *Advances in Empirical Translation Studies*, M. Ji, ed., pages 217–251, Cambridge, England: Cambridge University Press.

Spechbach, H., and P. Bouillon. 2019. "BabelDr – An Innovative and Reliable Translation Tool." In *Proceedings of the 18th European Congress of Internal Medicine*, Lisbon, Portugal.

Takakusagi, Y., T. Oike, K. Shirai, et al. 2021. "Validation of the Reliability of Machine Translation for a Medical Article from Japanese to English Using DeepL Translator." *Cureus*, September 6; 13 (9): e17778. DOI: 10.7759/cureus.17778. PMCID: PMC8494522.

Thonon F, S. Perrot, A. Yergolkar, et al. 2021. "Electronic Tools to Bridge the Language Gap in Health Care for People Who Have Migrated." *Systematic Review, Journal of Medical Internet Research*, 23 (5): e25131 URL: www.jmir.org/2021/5/e25131. DOI: 10.2196/25131.

Turner A, Y. Choi, K. Dew, et al. 2019. "Evaluating the Usefulness of Translation Technologies for Emergency Response Communication: A Scenario-Based Study." *Journal of Medical Internet Research, Public Health Survey*, 5 (1): e11171. URL: https://publichealth.jmir.org/2019/1/e11171. DOI: 10.2196/11171.

Van de Velde, S., L. Macken, K. Vanneste, et al. 2015 "Technology for Large-Scale Translation of Clinical Practice Guidelines: A Pilot Study of the Performance of a Hybrid Human and Computer-Assisted Approach." *JMIR Medical Informatics*, 3(4), e33. URL: https://medinform.jmir.org/2015/4/e33. DOI: 10.2196/medinform.4450.

Waibel, A., A. Badran, A. W. Black, et al. 2003. "Speechalator: Two-way Speech-To-Speech Translation on a Consumer PDA." In *EUROSPEECH-2003, the Eighth European Conference on Speech Communication and Technology*, pages 369–372, Baixas, France: International Speech Communication Association.

Zong, C., and M. Seligman. 2005. "Toward Practical Spoken Language Translation." *Machine Translation*, 19(2), pages 113–137.

3

Predicting Errors in Google Translations of Online Health Information

MENG JI

3.1 Introduction

The use of machine translation in cross-lingual health communication and clinical settings is growing (Ragni and Viera, 2021; Manchanda and Grunin, 2020; Dew et al., 2018). Patients, medical professionals, and even common people with different language and cultural backgrounds have found these low-cost online translation systems very convenient. The technology can be especially useful for those with special needs, such as those with speech and hearing impairments. Overall, the use of online machine translations is on the rise across the world, but research shows that there are risks and uncertainties associated with these emerging technologies (Santy et al., 2019; Almagro et al., 2019; Mathur et al., 2013b; Kumar and Bansal, 2017). There is thus a pressing need to learn about the types and levels of mistakes and errors that machine translation systems make when deployed in health and medical domains. Policies and regulations are needed to reduce the risks and safety issues associated with the use of automated translation systems and mobile apps by clinicians and patients; and systematic empirical analyses of human and machine translation discrepancies of health and medical resources can inform their development.

Many online machine translation systems, such as Google Translate (GT), are constantly improving the quality of automated translation outputs by adapting technologies such as neural machine translation (NMT). Compared to traditional rule-based or statistical machine translation, NMT offers greater coherence, naturalness, and logical accuracy (Popel et al., 2020; Đerić, 2020; Jia et al., 2019), and is therefore more likely to gain trust from users who lack sufficient knowledge of the language pair being translated and consequently cannot judge the relevance and safety of translation outputs related to medical or health information. Research shows that several issues can in fact lead to serious errors in machine-translated health and medical resources.

To be specific, the following features of English source texts were linked to clinically significant or life-threatening mistakes in machine translation outputs: (1) low readability of English long sentences (Flesch-Kincaid scores greater than Grade 8); (2) the use of atypical words, medical terminology, or abbreviations not explained in the source texts; (3) spelling and grammar anomalies; and (4) colloquial English (Khoong et al., 2019).

Nevertheless, despite its importance for reducing inequalities in healthcare services for vulnerable populations, improvement of translation technologies in medical and healthcare settings remains an understudied field of research.

In medicine and healthcare research, machine learning is becoming increasingly important. The detection and prediction of diseases, or of populations at risk of developing diseases, is an important application of machine learning, as early targeted interventions can improve the cost-effectiveness and efficiency of existing medical treatments significantly. The use of complex machine learning models can reduce investment in advanced medical experiments and clinical equipment but can also improve diagnostic precision by exploiting characteristics of the study subjects that are relatively easy to obtain. In general, classifiers that use machine learning tend to outperform the standard parameters and measurements of medical research in predicting health risks and diseases. It is true that the use of machine learning in health research has sometimes been criticized as overfitting learning algorithms due to small samples. However, some machine learning models, including sparse Bayesian classifiers such as relevance vector machines (RVMs), have proven to be highly effective in controlling algorithmic overfitting and thus improving the generality and applicability of findings (Madhukar et al., 2019; Langarizadeh and Moghbeli, 2016; Tipping 2001; Zhang and Ling, 2018; Silva and Ribeiro, 2006; Tipping and Faul, 2002).

This study examined whether it would be possible to improve diagnostic performance using Bayesian machine learning to combine easy-to-obtain English source health material features (both structural and semantic). It is anticipated that the results may lead to the automated combination and analysis of natural language features of English medical and health resources to improve detection of fundamental conceptual errors in translations into various languages. Success in detecting source text features associated with higher probabilities of conceptual errors in machine translation will support the use of machine learning techniques for the purpose of this study: the assessment and prediction of risk profiles of specific machine translations (Daems et al., 2017; Voita et al., 2019; Ashengo et al., 2021; Banerjee and Lavie, 2005).

For machine translations predicted to have high probabilities (>50 percent) of containing conceptual errors, a human evaluation and expert scrutiny would be required to reduce potential risks and clinically significant errors for both users and communities. Translation error detection and prediction based on machine learning would improve awareness – among medical and health professionals and throughout the public at large – about how to safely use online translation software. In addition, this study examined the social implications of setting probability thresholds for Bayesian machine learning classifiers of machine translation error detection. Probability thresholds associated with higher classifier sensitivities and lower specificities imply higher predicted error rates in machine translation outputs; and these will result in increased investments in human review and greater burden on the healthcare systems of multicultural societies.

3.2 Methods

3.2.1 Research Hypothesis

As with human translation errors, conceptual errors in machine translation outputs can be predicted based on the likelihood of occurrence; and machine learning models can facilitate the prediction. For the purpose of this study, Bayesian machine learning classifiers were developed to predict the probability of critical conceptual mistakes (clinically misleading instructions) in outputs of state-of-the-art machine translation systems (Google). To develop the classifiers, the structural and semantic features of the original English source texts were used to estimate their risk profiles when submitted to machine translation tools online. The probabilistic output of sparse Bayesian machine learning classifiers is more intuitive for clinical use than machine learning output converted to nonlinear scales by postprocessing, and for this reason is more informative and preferable for the purpose of this study.

3.2.2 Screening Criteria for Text

MSD Manuals offer comprehensive medical resources developed by global health experts. Most of the original English sources have been translated into twelve world languages by professional translators and reviewed by domain experts since 2014. In China, these manuals are an important source of health education for the public and medical students (Liao et al., 2017). On the website of MSD Manuals' Consumer Edition, translated health resources are categorized by various common topics to facilitate search and retrieval of health information. Taking advantage of this resource for this study, 200 original

English texts were collected and, after removing texts not long enough for structural analysis, kept 185 articles of comparable lengths.

3.2.3 Topics of Infectious Diseases

With the aim of developing machine learning algorithms that are generalizable or topic-independent in predicting critical conceptual errors in Chinese machine translation, a cross-section of health resources on infectious diseases were selected. The collected texts related to the following diseases, among others: dengue, Ebola, Marburg virus, Hantavirus, hemorrhagic fevers, Lassa fever, lymphocytic choriomeningitis, Zika, bacteremia, botulism, clostridioides difficile infection, gas gangrene, tetanus, gram-negative bacteria such as brucellosis, campylobacter infections, cat-scratch disease, cholera, Escherichia Coli infections, haemophilus influenzae infections, klebsiella, Enterobacter, Serratia infections, legionella infections, pertussis, plague, Yersinia infections, pseudomonas infections, salmonella infections, shigellosis, tularaemia, typhoid fever, gram-positive bacteria such as anthrax, diphtheria, enterococcal infections, erysipelothricosis, listeriosis, nocardiosis, pneumococcal infections, staphylococcus aureus infections, streptococcal infections, toxic shock syndrome, and clostridioides difficile infection. Professional translators matched the original English texts with their Chinese translations, verified them in consultation with domain experts and published them on the Chinese edition of the MSD Manuals website.

3.2.4 Labeling of Machine Translations

Machine translations were generated using GT, using the original English source texts (May 2021). Chinese translations were labeled as human and machine translations respectively before being thoroughly analyzed by two native Chinese speakers trained as university researchers. They were asked to assess the severity of any discrepancy between paired Chinese translations (human versus machine). Language variability was allowed without causing clinically significant misunderstanding of original English source texts. A third trained observer adjudicated any discrepancies between the assessors. Machine translations exhibited two types of errors: terminological inconsistencies and conceptual errors. Conceptual errors were the focus of this study, in view of their higher severity and of the potential harm if machine-translated medical materials remained undetected by users lacking adequate medical training or the ability to appraise the materials.

3.2.5 Conceptual Mistakes in Machine Translations

In machine translation, conceptual mistakes are errors that can cause life-threatening actions or misinterpretations of original English materials. In this study on machine translation of public-oriented medical materials, these can include erroneous interpretation of medical advice, or clinical instructions on the detection, prevention, and treatment of infectious diseases and viruses. As an example, in an English text on preventing Ebola and Marburg virus infections, the original instruction was, "Do not handle items that may have come in contact with an infected person's blood or body fluids." Upon back-translation into English, the human translation closely matched the original meaning of the phrase, "Do not touch any objects that may have been contaminated with the blood or body fluids of the infected." However, the machine translation was "Do not dispose of objects which may have been touched by the blood or body fluids of the infected people." This discrepancy between human and machine translations was marked as a conceptual error since it was suspected that naive users of the machine translation output, lacking enough medical knowledge of the disease, might be unaware of the high risk of infection if they misunderstood the straightforward intent of the original medical instruction: not to clean or reuse Ebola patients' personal items.

In the same text, another critical, life-threatening conceptual mistake was found in the translation of the original English text "Avoiding contact with bats and primates (such as apes and monkeys) and not eating raw or inadequately cooked meat prepared from these animals." The human translation again matched the original meaning well: "Avoid touching bats and primates (like apes and monkeys) and not to eat the raw or not properly cooked meats of these animals." Machine translation by GT contained critical conceptual mistakes, as it read, "Avoid touching bats and primates (like apes and monkeys) and do not eat the raw and cooked meats of these animals." In another text on the prevention of Zika virus infection, the original text was, "Currently, men who may have been exposed to the Zika virus are not tested to determine whether they are infected and thus at risk of transmitting the virus through sexual intercourse. Instead measures to prevent transmission are recommended whenever people who may have been exposed to the Zika virus have sexual intercourse."

The human translation was close to the original meaning:

> Currently, men who may have been exposed to the Zika virus are not tested to confirm whether they are infected, as a result, the risk of getting infected through sexual intercourse exists. It is recommended that when having sex with men who may have been exposed to the virus, protective measures are taken to prevent infection.

When back-translated into English, Google's translation into Chinese meant, "Currently, men who may have been exposed to Zika virus are not tested to confirm whether they are infected, therefore there are risks of getting infected via sextual intercourse. By contrast, when having sex with men who probably have already been infected with the virus, protective measures are recommended to stop infection." The discrepancy in the Chinese translation of "whenever people who may have been exposed to the Zika virus" was marked as a critical conceptual mistake by machine translation, as the risk of virus infection via sexual transmission was clearly misinterpreted and downplayed. An ordinary Chinese user of machine translation might well be misled into believing that, as long as the individual has not been clinically diagnosed with Zika virus, it is safe to have sexual relations with that individual.

3.2.6 Prevalence of Conceptual Mistakes in Machine Translations

An extensive comparison of human and machine translations of the same English source text revealed similar conceptual mistakes in 89 texts (48 percent) of the total 185 texts collected for this study. In some cases, a machine-translated text contained as many as four or five conceptual errors. While the translation pair studied (English to Chinese) has been relatively well studied by machine translation researchers (including Google's), the high rate of persisting conceptual mistakes in machine translation of medical materials was alarming. Machine translation into and from less-researched languages is likely to generate higher rates of conceptual errors, especially for high-risk communities and populations speaking those languages.

3.2.7 Annotation of Features of English Source Texts

The English source texts were annotated with structural features using Readability Studio (Oleander Software). These features serve to quantify the morphological, syntactic, and logical complexity of original health materials in English. The following features are annotated: average paragraph length in sentences, number of difficult sentences (of more than twenty-two words), number of longest sentences, average sentence length in words, number of unique words, number of syllables, average number of characters per word, average number of syllables per word, number of proper nouns, number of monosyllabic words, number of unique monosyllabic words, number of complex (more than three syllable) words, number of unique multi-syllable (more than three) words, number of long (more than six characters) words, number of unique long words, misspellings, overused words, wordy expressions, passive voice, and sentences beginning with conjunctions. In addition, to determine which words in English source texts are likely to cause conceptual errors when machine-translated into Chinese, the words of the original texts were annotated with their semantic categories, using the comprehensive automatic semantic tagging system developed by the University of Lancaster, USAS.

USAS contains twenty-one large semantic categories which are further divided into more than 100 sub-categories covering general and abstract words (A1–A15), the body and the individual (B1–B5), arts and crafts (C1), emotions (E1–E6), food and farming (F1–F4), government and the public (G1–G3), architecture, housing and home (H1–H5), money, commerce and industry (I1–I4), entertainment, sports and games (K1–K6), life and living things (L1–L3), movement, location, travel and transport (M1–M8), numbers and measurement (N1–N6), substances, materials, objects and equipment (O1–O4), education (P1), language and communication (Q1–Q4), social actions, states and processes (S1–S9), time (T1–T4), world and environment (W1–W5), psychological actions, states, process (X1–X9), science and technology (Y1–Y2), names, and grammars (Z1–Z99). These two sets of features are widely used in the development of machine learning models based on natural language processing techniques because they can be automatically annotated and interpreted relatively easily from the perspective of applied linguistics. In sum, in the final feature set, there were 20 structural features and 115 semantic features – composing a feature set sufficiently rich to enable exhaustive analysis and modeling of English source text features that may help to predict the occurrence of conceptual mistakes in the English-to-Chinese machine translation output.

3.2.8 Bayesian Machine Learning Classifier Relevance Vector Machine

The RVM is a variation of Support Vector Machines (SVM) (Cortes and Vapnik, 2005) which uses Bayesian inference and has the same functional form as SVMs (Tipping, 2001, 2004). As a Bayesian-based method, it offers probabilistic predictions and enables intuitive interpretations of uncertainty (Bishop and Tipping, 2003). The RVM model is also quite practical, in that it does not require large amounts of training data and generalizes well (Tipping, 2001; Bowd et al, 2008; Caesarendra et al., 2010). With these characteristics and advantages, it provides an ideal method for medical research and disease prediction. In these use cases, it is often necessary to determine the probability of a disease based on observed symptoms, even though the relevant data is usually sparse and hard to collect (Bowd et al, 2008; Langarizadeh and Moghbeli, 2016). In this paper, an RVM model, enhanced by structural and semantic features, is applied to estimate the probability that machine translation of specific health education material s concerning infectious diseases will contain critical conceptual errors.

3.2.9 Training and Testing of Relevance Vector Machines with Three Different Full Feature Sets

In order to train and test machine learning classifiers, 70 percent of the data was used for training an RVM with three full feature sets, while 30 percent of the data was withheld for testing the three RVM models. The training data (129 texts in total) included 63 English source texts accompanied by machine translations containing conceptual errors, and 66 English source texts accompanied by machine translations without conceptual errors. There were 26 English source texts whose Chinese translations by GT contained conceptual mistakes, and 30 English source texts whose machine translations were correct. RVMs were trained using three feature sets to enable comparison of feature types: the full structural feature set (20); the full semantic feature set (115); and the combined feature set (135). To minimize bias in the classifier training process, five-fold cross-validation was applied to the training data (129). In particular, English source texts (the training data, 70 percent of the total data) linked or not with detected machine translation errors, were randomly divided into five approximately equal, exhaustive, and mutually exclusive subsets. Afterward, RVM classifiers were trained on four subsets combined and then tested on the fifth subset. The process was repeated five times, with each subset serving as the test data once. In this way, each tested English source text was never part of the training data and was only tested once. During cross-validation, a mean AUC (area under the curve receiver operating characteristic) and its standard deviation were calculated for the RVM trained on each full feature set. The remaining 30 percent of the testing data was used to evaluate the performance of the trained classifiers and to generate their sensitivity, specificity, accuracy, AUC, and F1.

3.2.10 Classifier Optimization

It was found that, in the current study, the large dimensionality (number of features: 135) and small sample size (185) of the data sets adversely affected the performance of the Bayesian RVM classifier in locating the separating surface for classification. This classification uncertainty was reduced by using automated feature optimization to identify the best sets of structural and semantic features of the original English health texts, using backward feature elimination and 5-fold cross-validation to reduce bias in the optimized RVM classifier.

3.2.11 Backward Feature Elimination: RFE-SVM Method

Due to RVM's lack of "nuisance" parameters and its ability to automatically set regularization parameters to avoid overfitting, no hyper-parameter tuning was necessary to optimize the model (Tipping, 2001). To improve the performance of RVM, Recursive Feature Elimination (RFE) with SVM was applied as the base estimator (denoted as RFE-SVM) (Guyon et al., 2002) to reduce the feature dimension and automatically select the most important features that could improve RVM. For the RFE-SVM model, the parameter "min_features_to_select" (the minimum number of features to be selected) was set as "1" and set the "step" parameter (the number of features to be removed at each iteration) as "1." Z-score normalization was performed of the optimized features to improve the performance of the RVM classifier. As a result, the normalized data had zero mean and one unit deviation. The total set of health materials on infectious diseases was randomly split into training data (129) and test data (56) at a split rate of 0.7. The training data were used for feature optimization by 5-fold cross-validation and the performance of RVM with four different feature sets were evaluated on the remaining 30 percent test data. The cross-validation process of RVM classifier optimization was similar to the process used to train and test the full-dimension RVM classifier on the three feature sets (structural, semantic, and combined). First, the training data were divided into five subsets of approximately equal size. Four of the five subsets were used to determine the optimized feature set based on the maximum cross-validation score, using 5-fold cross- validation. The optimized feature set trained on the initial four subsets was then tested on the 5th subset to allow evaluation of the trained classifier with optimized features.

3.2.12 Separate and Joint Feature Optimization

The first step was to repeat the same process for the structural and semantic features separately, resulting in two separate optimized feature sets: the optimized structural feature set (OFT) and the optimized semantic feature (OSF) set. Features retained in the OFT set were as follows: average number of sentences per paragraph, average number of characters per word, average number of syllables per word, passive voice, and sentences that begin with conjunctions. Features retained in the OSF set were these: expressions indicating probability (A7), possession (A9), food (F1), general substances and materials (O1), physical attributes (O4), speech acts (Q2), obligation and necessity (S6), power relationships (S7), time (general) (T1), time (beginning/ending) (T2), time (early/late) (T4), mental actions and processes (X2), sensory (X3), intention (X7), science and technology in general (Y1), and geographical names (Z2). Next, the two sets of separately optimized structural and semantic features were combined and labeled as "Combined Features via Separate Optimization" (CFSO) comprised of 21 features (5 optimized structural features and 16 optimized semantic features).

Lastly, the same feature optimization was repeated on the combined full feature set (135), using 5-fold cross- validation, yielding the "Combined Features through Joint Optimization" (CFJO: 48), a distinct optimized feature set with 11 structural and 37 semantic features. Structure and semantic features selected in separate optimization processes were quite different from those selected in the machine learning process, suggesting that the importance of individual features in machine learning depends largely on other optimized features. (Compare the situation in standard statistical analysis, where p values indicate whether variables are statistically significant.) The 11 structural features in CFJO were as follows: average number of sentences per paragraph, longest sentence, average number of characters, number of monosyllabic words, number of complex words of more than three syllables, number of unique multi-syllable words (more than three syllables), number of unique long words, misspellings, overused words, wordy items, and passive voice. The 37 semantic features in the CFJO set were: verbs/nouns indicating modify/change (A2), classification (A4), evaluation (A5), comparison (A6), probabilities (A7), possession (A9), degrees (A13), Anatomy and physiology (B1), health and diseases (B2), bravery and fear (E5), food (F1), furniture and household fittings (H5), life and living things (L1), numbers (N1), measurements (N3), quantities (N5), general substances/materials (O1), general objects (O2), linguistic actions, states, processes (Q1), speech acts (Q2), social actions, states, processes (S1); people (S2); obligation and necessity (S6); power relationship (S7); helping/hindering (S8); time: general (T1); time: beginning /ending (T2); time: old/new (T3); time: early/late (T4); sensory (X3); intention (X7); ability (X9); science/technology in general (Y1); geographical names (Z2); discourse connectors (Z4); grammatical expressions (Z5); and conditional expressions (Z7).

3.3 Results

The performance of RVM classifiers were compared using different optimized feature sets on the test data (Table 3.1, Figure 3.1): optimized structural features (OTF) (5), OSF (16), jointly optimized structural and semantic features (CFJO) (48), and separately optimized structural and semantic features (CFSO) (21). Table 3.1 shows that while the performance of optimized RVMs did not always improve over non-optimized RVMs on the *training* data (5-fold cross-validation), optimized RVMs were consistently much better than non-optimized RVMs on the *test* data. For example, AUCs of RVMs increased from 0.451 using original structural features to 0.587 using optimized structural features (OTF); AUCs of RVMs increased from 0.628 using original semantic features to 0.679 using OSF; AUCs of RVMs increased from 0.679 using original combined features to 0.689 using combined structural and semantic

Table 3.1 *Performance of RVMs with different feature sets on test dataset*

Feature Sets	Training Data (5-fold CV) AUC Mean (SD)	Test data				
		AUC	Accuracy	Macro F1	Sensitivity	Specificity
Original Combined Features (135)	0.6166 (0.179)	0.679	0.625	0.60	0.42	0.80
Original Structural Feature (20)	0.6319 (0.144)	0.451	0.4821	0.48	0.54	0.53
Original Semantic Features (115)	0.6299 (0.166)	0.628	0.6607	0.66	0.62	0.70
Optimized structural features: OTF (5)	0.6245 (0.078)	0.587	0.5536	0.55	0.58	0.53
Optimized semantic features: OSF (16)	0.6837 (0.120)	0.679	0.625	0.62	0.58	0.67
Combined features through joint optimization: CFJO (48)	0.6159 (0.105)	0.689	0.6429	0.64	0.54	0.73
Combined features through separate optimization: CFSO (21)	**0.6840 (0.111)**	**0.684**	**0.6786**	**0.68**	**0.73**	**0.63**

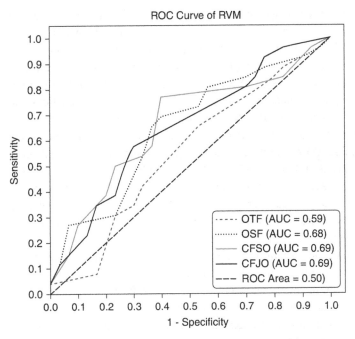

Figure 3.1 ROC curves of RVMs with different optimized feature sets

optimized features (CFJO). AUCs of RVMs did not improve using CFSO (0.684) over CFJO (0.689), but the total number of features was reduced by more than half from 48 (CFJO) to 21 (CFSO), and sensitivity of the RVM increased significantly from 0.54 using the CFJO features to 0.73 using the CFSO features. Specificity of RMV classifiers decreased from 0.73 using the CFJO features to 0.63 using the CFSO features. Since the goal of this study was to develop Bayesian machine learning classifiers that would detect and predict critical conceptual errors in machine translation outputs based on the observed features of the English source materials, higher sensitivity classifiers were deemed more useful for detecting mistakes in machine-translated Chinese health resources.

3.4 Comparison of Optimized RVMs with Binary Classifiers Using Readability Formula

This best-performing Bayesian RVM identified twenty-one features by separately optimizing structural and semantic features. The five optimized structural features were: average number of sentences per paragraph, average number of characters per word, average number of syllables per word, passive voice, and sentences that begin with conjunctions. The sixteen optimized semantic feature were: expressions indicating probability (A7), possession (A9), food (F1), general substances and materials (O1), physical attributes (O4), speech acts (Q2), obligation and necessity (S6), power relationships (S7), time (general) (T1), time (beginning/ending) (T2), time (early/late) (T4), mental actions and processes (X2), sensory (X3), intention (X7), science and technology in general (Y1), and geographical names (Z2). The structural features included in the best-performing RMV resembled those incorporated in widely used readability formulas (Table 3.2). For example, the Flesch Reading Ease Score was based on average sentence length and average number of syllables per word; the Gunning Fog Index used average sentence length and percentage of hard words; and the SMOG Index used polysyllabic words (more than three syllables per word).

It was found the structural complexity of original English materials to have a significant impact on the quality of machine translation. In studying this relationship, the performance of the optimized RVM and binary classifiers was evaluated using some popular readability formulas (Flesch Reading Ease, Gunning Fog Index, SMOG Index) in terms of AUC, sensitivity, specificity, and whether the predictions of the optimized RMV and readability-formula-derived binary classifiers achieved statistically significant improvements over the reference line (AUC=0.5) (Table 3.3, Figure 3.2). The threshold of Flesch Reading Ease was 60, as texts with scores below 60 are considered fairly difficult to read, and texts with scores over 60 are easily understood by students ages 13 to 15. The threshold of SMOG Index and Gunning Fog Index was set at 12 to indicate a relatively easy reading level of medical texts in English, since scores above 12 tend to create reading difficulties and may increase the likelihood of conceptual errors in the machine translation output.

Table 3.2 *Readability formulas*

Readability tools	Formulas
Flesch Reading Ease Score	Score=206.835-(1.015*ASL[a]) – (84.6*ASW[b])
Gunning Fog Index	Score =0.4*(ASL[a]+PHW[c])
SMOG Index	Score = 3 + Square Root of Polysyllable Count

a ASL: average sentence length.
b ASW: average number of syllables per word.
c PHW: percentage of hard words.

Table 3.3 *Performance of the best-performing RVM with binary classifiers using readability formula*

Test Result Variable and Thresholds	Area under the Curve	Std. Error[a]	Asymptotic Sig.[b]	Asymptotic 95% Confidence Interval	
				Lower Bound	Upper Bound
RVM (CFSO)	**0.685**	**0.074**	**0.012 ****	**0.540**	**0.829**
SMOG (12)	0.538	0.083	0.642	0.376	0.701
Gunning Fog (12)	0.533	0.080	0.677	0.376	0.690
Flesch Reading Ease (60)	0.492	0.082	0.925	0.333	0.652

a. Under the nonparametric assumption b. Null hypothesis: true area = 0.5

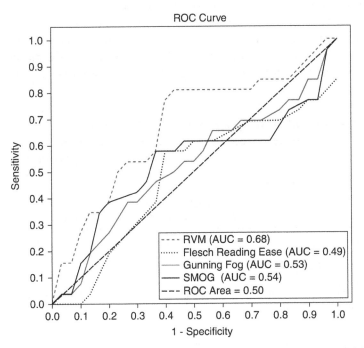

Figure 3.2 ROC curves of Flesch Reading Ease, Gunning Fog, and SMOG

Table 3.3 shows that AUC of the optimized RVM (using CFSO features) achieved statistically significant improvement of the reference (AUC= 0. 685, p=0.012, 95 percent confidence interval: 0.540, 0.829).

The three readability- formula derived binary classifiers did not improve over the reference (AUC=0.5): the AUCs of the SMOG Index and the Gunning Fox Index based classifiers were only slightly better than the threshold – respectively, 0.538 (p=0.642, 95 percent CI: 0.376, 0.701) and 0.533 (p=0.677, 95 percent CI: 0.376, 0.690); and the binary classifier using Flesch Reading Ease Scores was even less than effective than a random guess (AUC=0.492, p=0.925, 95 percent CI: 0.333, 0.652). Notably, according to this finding, the complexity of original English health materials, as measured by standard (currently available) readability parameters, cannot predict the presence of conceptual errors in machine-translated health and medical resources on infectious diseases. By contrast, however, a Bayesian machine learning classifier optimized based on the structural and semantic features of English input texts to the machine translation system did achieve statistically significant improvements in the prediction of conceptual mistakes in machine translation.

Table 3.4 shows the result of a pairwise resampled t test of the four classifiers: the optimized RVM and the three readability-formula based binary classifiers. It shows that although RVM achieved statistically significant improvement over the reference AUC (p=0.012), the improvement in AUC

Table 3.4 *Paired-sample area difference under the ROC curves*

Test Result Pair(s)	Asymptotic		AUC Difference	Std. Error Difference[b]	Asymptotic 95% Confidence Interval	
	z	Sig. (2-tail)[a]			Lower Bound	Upper Bound
RVM vs. Flesch Reading Ease	1.634	0.102	0.192	0.396	−0.038	0.423
RVM vs. Gunning Fog	1.512	0.131	0.151	0.390	−0.045	0.347
RVM vs. SMOG	1.466	0.143	0.146	0.393	−0.049	0.342
Flesch Reading Ease vs. Gunning Fog	−0.268	0.789	−0.041	0.415	−0.341	0.259
Flesch Reading Ease vs. SMOG	−0.302	0.763	−0.046	0.417	−0.346	0.254
Gunning Fog vs. SMOG	−0.131	0.895	−0.005	0.389	−0.082	0.071

a. Null hypothesis: true area difference = 0 b. Under the nonparametric assumption

was not statistically significant when compared with the three binary classifiers: the largest increase in AUC was between RVM and Flesch Reading Ease (0.192, p=0.102), followed by the AUC difference between RVM and Gunning Fog Index (0.151, p=0.131) and the AUC difference between RVM and SMOG Index (0.146, p=0.143). The AUC of the SMOG Index based classifier improved by 0.046 over the AUC of Flesch Reading Ease based classifier (p=0.763) and improved by

0.005 over the AUC of Gunning Fog Index based classifier (p=0.895).

3.4.1 Discussion

RVM produces probabilistic outputs through Bayesian inference, as opposed to SVMs. Bayesian probabilistic prediction enables relatively intuitive interpretation of classification results, and accordingly is relatively informative and helpful for clinical use and decision-making. According to this study, the best RVM classifier (AUC=0.685), based on two sets of separately optimized structural and semantic features, was able to usefully predict the probability that each specific original English text would belong to the group of texts associated with critical conceptual errors in machine-translated outputs. The RVM classified the original English text as a 'safe' text if its predicted probability was less than 50 percent, and as a 'dirty' text if its predicted probability was more than 50 percent. The RVM's probabilistic output gave an average mean probability of 0.388 (SD: 0.326, 95 percent CI: 0.266, 0.509) for 'safe' or error-proof English source texts and 0.606 (SD: 0.336, 95 percent CI: 0.472, 0.740) for 'risky' or error-prone English source texts.

Figure 3.3 is a histogram showing the percentage of English source texts in each 10 percent probability bin of the RVM probabilistic output for which conceptual errors in machine translations were detected (based on a comparison with human translations). 73 percent of the English source texts whose translations by Google contained critical conceptual errors were assigned a probability of "error-prone English text (EPET)" >= 50 percent (sensitivity: 0.73 percent); and 63 percent of English texts not linked with conceptual errors were assigned a probability of "non-error-prone English text (non- EPET)" > 50 percent (specificity: 63 percent).

The RVM results showed that most of the test English source texts associated with conceptual errors in machine translation belonged to the EPET group. (The distribution was negatively skewed, Figure 3.3.) For English source texts without conceptual mistakes in machine translation, the distribution of probabilities was less skewed. This result may be explained by the wide range of structural and semantic features of English source texts that are *not* related to

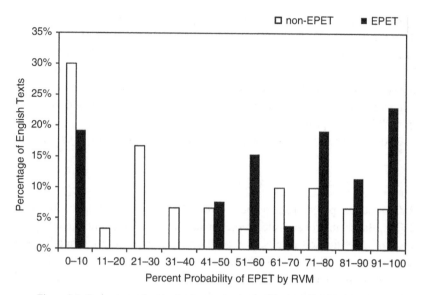

Figure 3.3 Percentage of non-mistake or mistake texts assigned by RVM classifier to 10 percent probability bins

conceptual errors in machine translation. 18 percent of the English source texts linked with machine translation errors were assigned to the 0–10 percent probability bin. This assignment indicated that there was still some uncertainty in the RVM probabilistic prediction, as some error-prone source texts were misclassified as "safe" source texts for machine translation systems.

Table 3.5 presents the various probability thresholds and associated sensitivity-specificity pairs of the best- performing RVM classifier, using a combination of structural and semantic features undergoing separate optimization. In real life, a meaningful probability threshold depends on the desired sensitivity-specificity pair. Classifiers of higher sensitivities are more suitable for screening purposes. Using the RVM, increasing numbers of English source texts were identified that would cause critical conceptual errors if translated using current machine translation tools, such as GT. However, increasing sensitivity can reduce specificity. And when specificities are lower, false-positive rates are higher (1-specificity), which means that more "safe" English source texts will be classified as error-prone or risky, even when the current translation technology can actually avoid life-threatening conceptual mistakes. And so, for health educational resource development and translation, lower screening classifier sensitivities imply heavier budgetary investments in human expert evaluation and assessment;

Table 3.5 *Under different probability thresholds, Sensitivity, Specificity and Positive Likelihood Ratios of the best-performing RVM with CFSO optimized features*

SE-SP Pairs	Probability Cut-Offs	Sensitivity (SE)	Specificity (SP)	Positive Likelihood Ratio (LR+)
1	0.075	0.846	0.300	1.209
2	0.415	0.808	0.600	2.019
3	0.494	0.769	0.633	2.098
4	0.496	0.769	0.633	2.098
5	0.586	0.577	0.633	1.573
6	0.625	0.577	0.667	1.731
7	0.703	0.5	0.767	2.143
8	0.757	0.385	0.800	1.923
9	0.799	0.346	0.833	2.077
10	0.876	0.269	0.900	2.692

and this issue in turn can result in further gaps in the provision of quality healthcare services and in support to populations and communities that rely on translated health resources and information for self-health management and disease prevention.

Another important indicator of the diagnostic utility of machine learning classifiers is the *positive likelihood ratio* (LR+), which is the ratio between sensitivity and false-positive (1-specificity) rates. Diagnostic utility increases with the positive likelihood ratio. In Table 3.5, sensitivity-specificity pairs (2, 3, and 4) showed high sensitivities (0.769–0.808) and moderate specificities (0.6–0.633), while positive likelihood ratios (2.019–2.098) showed small effects on post-test probabilities of English source texts causing critical conceptual errors in machine translations. The probability thresholds for these desirable sensitivity-specificity pairs (2, 3, and 4) were between 40 percent and 50 percent. As probability cut-offs increased over 50 percent, sensitivity decreased sharply, and specificity increased steadily. SE-SP pairs (5 and 6) produced the lowest positive likelihood ratios (1.573–1.731) and their probability thresholds were in the 50 percent-60 percent range. Finally, the pairs (7, 8, 9, and 10) were all impractical, as their sensitivities and specificities were very low, despite a positive likelihood ratio of 1.923–2.692. Since these models' sensitivities were low, they couldn't identify most English source texts that would likely result in critical conceptual errors if machine-translated using current systems. True, these high specificities did indicate that they were unlikely to over-predict the risk level of English source materials, thus requiring less expert evaluation and intervention, reducing healthcare budgets; however, in consequence, more clinically significant errors would be likely, because the screening classifiers would make professionals less aware of the high risks of using machine translation technologies clinically.

3.5 Conclusion

In cross-lingual health communication and clinical settings, machine translation is becoming increasingly common. It is true that these developing language technologies are associated with numerous risks and uncertainties, as research has shown. Still, in order to help reduce the risks of using such systems in clinical or patient settings, perhaps policies and regulations can be formulated based on evidence derived from systematic empirical analyses of discrepancies between human and machine translations of health and medical resources. With this goal in mind, the present study has sought to determine the probabilistic distribution of mistakes in neural machine translations of public-oriented online health resources on infectious diseases and viruses, using as predictors various linguistic and textual features that characterize English health-oriented educational materials. Two-hundred English-language source texts on infectious diseases and their human translations into Chinese were obtained from HON.Net-certified websites on health education. Native Chinese speakers compared human translations with machine translations (GT) to identify critical conceptual errors.

To overcome overfitting problems in machine learning for small, high-dimensional data sets while aiming to identify possible source text features associated with clinically significant translation errors, Bayesian classifiers (RVM) were trained on language-specific source texts classified as yielding, or not yielding, machine translation outputs containing critical conceptual grammatical errors. Among the best-performing models, the RVM trained on the CFSO (16 percent of the original combined features) performed best. RVM (CFSO) outperformed binary classifiers (BCs) using standard English readability tests. The accuracy, sensitivity, specificity of the three BCs were as follows: FRE (accuracy 0.457; sensitivity 0.903, specificity 0.011); GFI (accuracy 0.5735; sensitivity 0.685, specificity 0.462); and SMOG (accuracy 0.568; sensitivity 0.674, specificity 0.462).

In this study, Bayesian machine learning classifiers with combined optimized features did in fact identify certain features of English health materials features as associated with (and possibly causing) critical conceptual errors in state-of-the-art machine translation systems. It was found that machine-generated Chinese medical translation errors were most associated with certain

English structures (e.g., passive voice or sentences beginning with conjunctions) and semantic polysemy (different meanings of the same word when used in different contexts), since these features tend to lead to critical conceptual errors in NMT systems (English to Chinese) of health education information on infectious diseases. This finding challenges the hypothesis that complex medical terminology and low linguistic readability are the main causes of critical translation errors, since none of the predictor features appeared to be related to these factors.

Overall, this study underlines the need for clinical and health education settings to be cautious and informed when using the latest translational technology. It also points toward provision of helpful aids in exercising that caution. Classifiers can be trained using machine learning models like ours to identify texts containing features likely to yield clinically significant translation errors. Tools found to cause more such errors for the same texts could be avoided. At the same time, recommendations could be made for preemptively revising the original source texts to minimize likely errors. Additionally, machine learning might be applied to *automatically* revise source texts. Finally, the findings and procedures might be used to augment existing confidence scores for real-time translations, so that users could be warned that a current translation was suspect, and that paraphrase might be advisable.

Reference

Almagro, M., Martínez, R., Montalvo, S., & Fresno, V. (2019). A cross-lingual approach to automatic ICD-10 coding of death certificates by exploring machine translation. Journal of Biomedical Informatics, 94, 103207. https://doi.org/10.1016/j.jbi.2019.103207.

Ashengo, Y. A., R. T. Aga, and S. L. Abebe. 2021. "Context Based Machine Translation with Recurrent Neural Network for English–Amharic Translation," *Machine Translation*, 35 (1), pages 19–36. https://doi.org/10.1007/s10590-021-09262-4.

Banerjee, S., and Lavie, A. 2005. "METEOR: an automatic metric for MT evaluation with improved correlation with human judgments," in Proceedings of the Workshop on Intrinsic and Extrinsic Evaluation Measures for MT and/or Summarization at the 43th Annual Meeting of the Association of Computational Linguistics, Ann Arbor, MI.

Bishop, C. M., & Tipping, M. E. 2003. "Bayesian regression and classification," *NATO Science Series sub Series III Computer And Systems Sciences*, 190, pages 267–288.

Bowd, C., J. Hao, I. M. Tavares, et al. 2008. "Bayesian Machine Learning Classifiers for Combining Structural and Functional Measurements to Classify Healthy and Glaucomatous Eyes," *Investigative Ophthalmology and Visual Science*, 49 (3), 945–953.

Caesarendra, W., Widodo, A., and Yang, B. S. 2010. "Application of Relevance Vector Machine and Logistic Regression for Machine Degradation Assessment," *Mechanical Systems and Signal Processing*, 24 (4), pages 1161–1171.

Cortes, C., & Vapnik, V. 1995. "Support vector machine," *Machine Learning*, 20 (3), pages 273–297.

Daems, J., Vandepitte, S., Hartsuiker, R. J., and Macken, L. 2017. "Identifying the Machine Translation Error Types with the Greatest Impact on Post-editing Effort," *Frontiers in Psychology*, 8. https://doi.org/10.3389/fpsyg.2017.01282.

Đerić, I. 2020. Google Translate Accuracy Evaluation, in Sinteza https://doi.org/10.15308/Sinteza-2020-80-85. http://portal.sinteza.singidunum.ac.rs/paper/745.

Dew, K. N., A. M. Turner, Y. K. Choi, A. Bosold, and K. Kirchhoff. 2018. "Development of Machine Translation Technology for Assisting Health Communication: A Systematic Review," *Journal of Biomedical Informatics*, 85, pages 56–67, https://doi.org/10.1016/j.jbi.2018.07.018.

Guyon, I., Weston, J., Barnhill, S., and Vapnik, V. 2002. "Gene Selection for Cancer Classification Using Support Vector Machines," Machine Learning, 46 (1) pages 389–422.

Jia, Y., Carl, M., and Wang, X. 2019. "Post-editing Neural Machine Translation versus Phrase-Based Machine Translation for English–Chinese." *Machine Translation*, 33 (1), pages 9–29.

Khoong, E. C., Steinbrook, E., Brown, C., and Fernandez, A. 2019. "Assessing the Use of Google Translate for Spanish and Chinese Translations of Emergency Department Discharge Instructions." *JAMA Internal Medicine*, 179 (4), pages 580–582.

Kumar, A., and Bansal, N. 2017. Machine translation survey for Punjabi and Urdu languages. In 2017 3rd International Conference on Advances in Computing, Communication & Automation (ICACCA)(Fall) (pages 1–11). IEEE.

Langarizadeh, M., and Moghbeli, F. 2016. "Applying Naive Bayesian Networks to Disease Prediction: a Systematic Review." *Acta Informatica Medica*, 24 (5), 364. https://doi.org/10.5455/aim.2016.24.364-369.

Liao XP, Chipenda-Dansokho S, Lewin A, Abdelouahab N, Wei SQ. 2017. "Advanced Neonatal Medicine in China: A National Baseline Database," *PLOS ONE*, 12(1): e0169970. https://doi.org/10.1371/journal.pone.0169970

Madhukar, N. S., Khade, P. K., Huang, L., et al. 2019. "A Bayesian Machine Learning Approach for Drug Target Identification Using Diverse Data Types." *Nature Communications*, 10 (1), pages 1–14.

Manchanda, S., and G. Grunin. 2020. Domain Informed Neural Machine Translation: Developing Translation Services for Healthcare Enterprise, In Proceedings of the 22nd Annual Conference of the European Association for Machine Translation, Lisbon, Portugal, European Association for Machine Translation. www.aclweb.org/anthology/2020.eamt-1.27.

Mathur, P., Ruiz, N., and Federico, M. 2013b. "Recommending Machine Translation Output to Translators by Estimating Translation Effort: A Case Study." *Polibits*, 47, pages 47–53. https://doi.org/10.17562/pb-47-5.

Popel, M., Tomkova, M., Tomek, J., Kaiser, Ł., Uszkoreit, J., Bojar, O., and Žabokrtský, Z. 2020. "Transforming Machine Translation: A Deep Learning System Reaches News Translation Quality Comparable to Human Professionals." *Nature Communications*, 11 (1), pages 1–15.

Ragni, V. and L. N. Vieira. 2021 "What has changed with neural machine translation? A critical review of human factors." *Perspectives*, 30, (1), pages 1–22.

Santy, S., S. Dandapat, M. Choudhury, and K. Bali. 2019. Interactive Neural Machine Translation Prediction, in Proceedings of the 2019 Conference on Empirical Methods in Natural Language Processing and the 9th International Joint Conference on Natural Language Processing (EMNLP-IJCNLP): System Demonstrations, Hong Kong, Association for Computational Linguistics.

Silva, C. and B. Ribeiro. 2006. "Scaling Text Classification with Relevance Vector Machines," *Systems Man and Cybernetics. SMC'06*, 5, pages 4186–4191.

Tipping, M. E. 2000. "The Relevance Vector Machine." In *Advances in neural information processing systems*, pages 652–658.

Tipping, M. E. 2001. "Sparse Bayesian Learning and the Relevance Vector Machine," *Journal of Machine Learning Research*, 1 (Jun), 211–244.

Tipping, A. and A. Faul. 2002. "Analysis of Sparse Bayesian Learning," *Advances in Neural Information Processing Systems*, 14, pages 383–389.

Voita, E., R. Sennrich, and I. Titov. 2019. When a Good Translation is Wrong in Context: Context-Aware Machine Translation Improves on Deixis, Ellipsis, and Lexical Cohesion, In arXiv:1905.05979v2

Zhang, Y., and C. Ling. 2018. "A Strategy to Apply Machine Learning to Small Datasets in Materials Science," *NPJ Computational Materials*, 4 (1). https://doi.org/10.1038/s41524-018-0081-z

4

Cultural and Linguistic Bias of Neural Machine Translation Technology

MENG JI

4.1 Introduction

Neural translations are not neutral. On the contrary, as a new dilemma for neural machine translation as neural machine translation systems have learned to recognize patterns in lexical and semantic units in human languages (Johnson et al., 2017; Pope et al., 2020; Grechishnikova, 2021) to translate more fluently, increasing cultural bias in the target language has emerged. Given that language use is heavily influenced by the culture of the host country and carries with it deeply ingrained perceptions, beliefs, and attitudes (Downes, 1998; Fishman, 2019; Thomas and Wareing, 1999; Montgomery, 1995), increasingly fluent translations can increasingly convey those cultural aspects, and sometimes bring cultural biases along with them. In this respect, machine biases induced by translation are inevitable consequences of algorithms designed to achieve near-native level linguistic naturalness and communicative fluency in automatic translation outputs (Weng et al., 2020; Feng et al., 2020; Martindale et al., 2019; Koehn, 2020; Wu et al., 2016). And in fact, University of Cambridge researchers have indeed discovered gender bias in machine translations of English into German, Spanish, and Hebrew, chosen for their distinct linguistic and cultural properties (Saunders and Byrne, 2020). Their studies revealed that, in MT output, gender bias in particular was an inevitable consequence of language use in training datasets that included genres such as news reports and speeches. Similarly, several studies of machine translation quality assessment revealed widespread racial, as well as gender, bias (Tomalin et al., 2021; Font and Costa-jussà, 2019; Salles et al., 2018; Best, 2017). In the machine translations of job titles in the U.S. Bureau of Labor Statistics, Prates et al. (2019) showed a strong tendency toward male defaults in as many as twelve languages

(Hungarian, Chinese, Japanese, Basque, Yoruba, Turkish, Malay, Armenian, Swahili, Estonian, Bengali, Finnish)[1].

While commendable progress has been made in developing scalable approaches to reducing such bias in machine translations, the problem persists. Significant human effort is still required to revise MT training data, and the resulting MT datasets still do not address all forms of social discrimination inherited from target-language datasets. In our current study, we will speak of this issue as inevitably arising from the social and cultural constraints of artificial intelligence. Since human thoughts and behaviors do have social and cultural contexts, sexist, racial, class, and other types of bias are inevitable in MT output; and artificial intelligence, as our brainchild, will inevitably amplify these tendencies. Nevertheless, they are predictable and preventable. We argue that MT quality assessment should incorporate social, ethical, and cultural sensitivity, rather than focusing solely on linguistic accuracy and fluency. And specifically, for materials generated by neural translation, it is necessary to develop mechanisms to support decision-making concerning the trade-offs involving linguistic fluency and cultural biases. Special attention is needed in specialized domains. One such, multicultural mental healthcare, provides the focus of our study.

Globally, anxiety disorders are the largest burden on mental health (3.76 percent in 2017). Countries with the highest prevalence of anxiety disorders (5 percent–6 percent) are some of the most advanced economies in their regions (Argentina, Brazil, Chile, Uruguay) and worldwide (U.S., Canada, UK, Germany, Australia, Sweden, Spain, France, Italy, Norway, New Zealand, Denmark, Ireland), as well as a few countries in the Middle East and Africa (Algeria, Iran). In Asia, only a few countries ranked within this range (5–6 percent), even though anxiety disorders are traditionally prevalent in countries like Japan, South Korea, and, more recently, India and China. Developing Latin American countries, too, have a tradition of anxiety. However, we can ask whether mental disorders are openly treated in different countries, and whether differences in openness might affect these statistics. The use of medical and mental healthcare can be subject to discrimination and stigma. And in fact, we do find that, in some rapidly developing countries, mental health issues are underrepresented, even though their populations are exposed to environmental, social, and economic stressors. This underrepresentation might be a result of traditional cultural beliefs stigmatizing people with mental illnesses, and perhaps from a related lack of access to mental healthcare support.

---

[1] Some of the language choices have been criticized, however. Chinese and Japanese are not gender neural languages, for example.

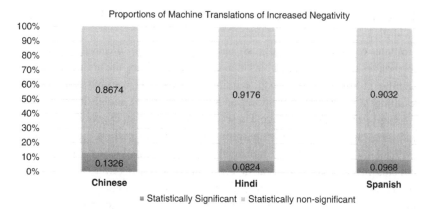

Figure 4.1 Ratios of machine translations of statistically increased negative emotions

We would expect such negative social sentiments or attitudes. Thus, to test our hypothesis, we gathered and generated translations into Chinese, Hindi, and Spanish of public health materials on anxiety disorders developed by health-promotion organizations in English-speaking countries. The back-translations from these three languages were paired with their original English health materials, and the distribution of negative emotion words in each pair was statistically analyzed (Figure 4.1).

4.2 Data Collection

We developed a set of quality control criteria based on five considerations for searching English public health materials on anxiety disorders. In gathering our training data, we screened online mental health information on this topic according to these criteria. Our intent has been to ensure the usefulness of the machine learning classifiers we have developed for health organizations and their wide applicability in research and clinical settings for effective, positive cross-lingual health communication concerning mental health disorders among multicultural populations.

- **Topic Relevance**: Our study focuses on anxiety disorders, due to their high prevalence
- **Information accessibility**: The materials we selected were written in an accessible, familiar style. Materials of this type are more likely to be translated by Google into language that the general public, as opposed to health

professionals, can understand. As the linguistic difficulty of English material increases, training data will be restricted to professional-oriented health resources. These will be less suitable for learning about the common language in a given country and the social attitudes toward mental disorders conveyed in its language.

- **Information credibility**: The English health materials selected were developed by national or charitable health-promotion organizations to ensure credibility (see Appendix 4).
- **Understandability**: Online health information materials may be intended for professionals or for patients. We chose English materials intended for the public, since their translations can be better understood by machine translation users from diverse cultural and linguistic backgrounds and thus can impact their opinions on mental health conditions. This criterion was significant because an important objective of our research was to develop machine learning classifiers that would improve translation quality – that is, that would help to produce less biased machine translations that could contribute to more positive understanding of anxiety disorders. With this goal in mind, we developed classifiers to process English health materials in an accessible and understandable manner.
- **User relevance:** While understudied, relevance to specific users is another key indicator of mental health resource quality. The causes, symptoms, and treatment of mental disorders vary considerably among people of varying demographic characteristics – people of different ages, genders, socioeconomic classes, and so on. We assume that health information can be significantly improved by tailoring it to specific user groups, and accordingly collected online English materials concerning anxiety disorders developed for children, teens, young adults, the elderly, men, women, and transgender people.

As part of the quality control process, we identified websites of national, charitable health-promotion organizations and selected original English health materials that met the above criteria. There were 557 original English health materials. There are three sets of natural language features annotated on the original English and back-translation health materials: multiple semantic categories using the university of Lancaster Semantic Annotation System (USAS); word frequency bands (WFB); and lexical dispersion rates (LDR), with the last two based on the British National Corpus. The total number of annotation classes was 153 including semantic classes (115), WFB (18), and LDR (20) (see Appendix 2).

4.3 Development of Machine Learning Classifiers

We collected 557 original English health materials regarding anxiety disorders that met all our search criteria. We generated their machine translations into Chinese, Hindi, and Spanish using the Google Translate API. We then compared the original English with their matching back-translations from the three languages and used the Linguistic Inquiry and Word Count System (LIWC) (University of Texas at Austin) to find the distribution of words expressing negative emotions in both sets of English materials, original and back-translation. A Wilkson signed-rank test found back-translations from the target languages showed a statistically significant increase ($p*0.05$) in expressions of negative emotions when compared to their original English texts.

The original English texts were chosen since they yielded back-translations showing statistically increased sentiment negativity concerning anxiety disorders. Since our goal was to develop neural programs that could distinguish texts relatively likely to produce biased translations, we then manually developed training corpora as follows. We classified the original English texts into risky (1) versus safe (0) classes: risky English texts were associated with back-translations of increased negativity in at least one language of Chinese, Hindi, or Spanish; and safe texts were associated with back-translations in which negativity increase was statistically insignificant ($p>=0.05$) in all three test languages. Of the 557 texts collected to train and test machine learning classifiers, 428 texts were classified as safe (class 0) and 129 texts as risky (class 1).

Again, our goal was to distinguish texts that were safe, or unlikely to contain biased language, from those that were risky, or like to contain such language. We faced some analytical problems, however, in that (1) the languages we studied differed in their respective degrees of negativity and (2) our corpus contained many more safe than risky texts. The most negative translations were found in Chinese (13.26 percent), followed by Hindi (8.24 percent) and Spanish (9.68 percent); and within the three target languages, the ratio of English materials associated with increased negativity in machine translations and those without any negative machine translations was 3:10.

In other words, in statistical terms, our data was imbalanced – as would be the case, for example, if we attempted to distinguish legitimate credit card transactions from fraudulent ones, since the former will greatly outnumber the latter in any corpus. Fortunately, various techniques have been developed for handling such data imbalance. Synthetic Minority Oversampling Technique (SMOTE) (Chawla et al., 2002) in Python was applied to improve the balance between the two classes of machine translation output in terms of negative emotion words. We divided the whole dataset, after oversampling, into training (70 percent) and testing datasets, and performed five-fold cross-validation on the training dataset (see Table 4.1).

Table 4.1 *Training and testing datasets*

Training/Testing Classifiers		Class 0	Class 1
Before Oversampling	Before total	428	129
After oversampling	Training (70%)	303	296
	Testing (30%)	125	132
	Total	428	428

4.4 Feature Optimization

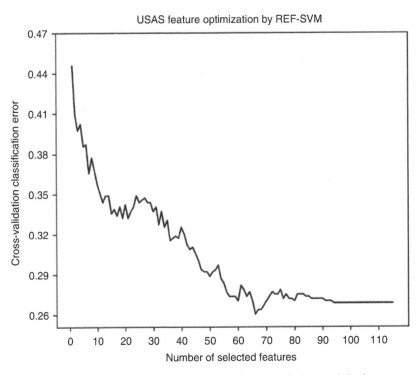

Figure 4.2 Recursive Feature Elimination with Automatic Feature Selection as the Base Estimator

Cross-validation classification error (CVCE)

(a) automatic optimization of English lexical dispersion features (from 20 to 9 feature, CVCE= 0.333)

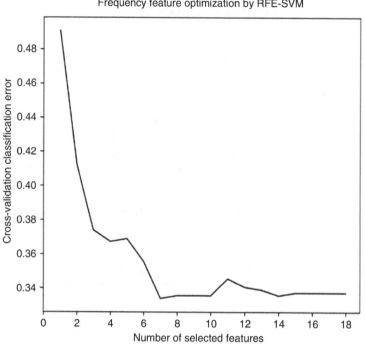

(b) automatic optimization of English lexical frequency range features (from 18 to 7 features, CVCE= 0.333)

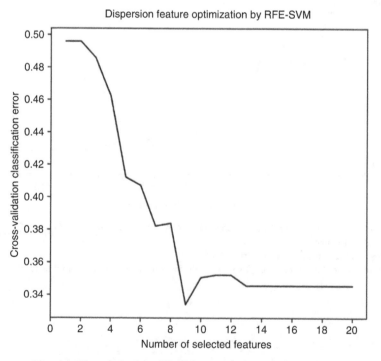

(c) automatic optimization of English semantic features (from 115 to 66 features, CVCE= 0.260)

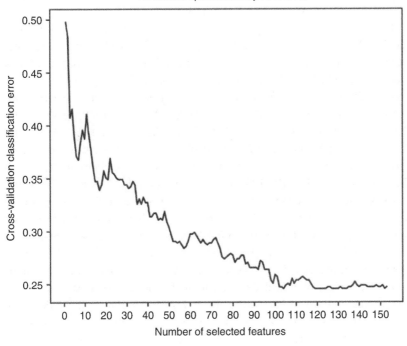

(d) automatic optimization of all features (a, b, c) (from 153 to 119 features, CVCE=0.245)

4.5 Separate and Combined Feature Optimization

The dataset has 153 features, including 115 semantic classes, 18 WFB, and 20 LDR. By reducing high-dimensional feature sets, machine learning classifiers can be made more efficient and interpretable. Accordingly, support vector machine (SVM) methodology was used as the base estimator (RVM_SVM) in recursive feature elimination.

Figure 4.2 (a) shows the automatic optimization of English lexical dispersion rate features. After reduction of the LDR from 20 to 9, the cross-validation classification error reached its minimum (0.333). English lexis dispersion rates range from 0 to 1, with higher dispersion rates indicating wider distribution of the words across different textual genres, and thus indicating whether the relevant language is general or specialized. Both spoken and written dispersion rates were optimized: for very specialized words in spoken English (DiSp1:0.0–0.1, DiSp3:0.2–0.3); for general words in spoken English (DiSp6:0.5–0.6, DiSp9:0.8–0.9, DiSp10:0.9–1.0); and for medium-to-very-general words in written English (DiWr4:0.3–0.4, DiWr6:0.5–0.6, DiWr8:0.7–0.9, DiWr10:0.9).

In a comparable way, Figure 4.4 (b) shows the automatic optimization of English lexical frequency band features. When the number of features was reduced from 18 to 7, the minimal cross-validation classification error was obtained (0.333). In the British National Corpus (BNC), frequency bands refer to the ordinal ranges of word occurrence frequencies. For written materials, we listed nine frequency bands: FrWr1:0–500, FrWr2:500–1000, FrWr3:1000–1500, FrWr4:1500–2000, FrWr5:2000–2500, FrWr6:2500–3000, FrWr7:3000–3500, FrWr8:3500–4000, and FrWr9:4000–64420. The words that appear most frequently in the BNC corpus are those in the higher bands. For example, only 30 English words in the FrWr9 band occur more than 4,000 times in the entire database. Generally, the smaller the frequency bands, the less frequent or familiar the words are to the public. We also provided nine frequency bands for spoken materials: FrSp1:0–500, FrSp2:500–1000, FrSp3:1000–1500, FrSp4:1500–2000, FrSp5:2000–2500, FrSp6:2500–3000, FrSp7:3000–3500, FrSp8:3500–4000, and FrSp9:4000–57010. Again, higher frequencies indicate greater familiarity with words. We note that optimization of frequency band features reduced the original number of bands from 18 to 7: FrSp1:0–500, FrSp5:2000–2500, FrSp9:4000–57010, FrWr4:1500–2000, FrWr7:3000–3500, FrWr8:3500–4000, and FrWr9:4000–64420.

Finally, the automatic optimization of English semantic features is shown in Figure 4.4 (c). There were in total 115 semantic features covering as many as 21 semantic categories: general and abstract terms (A1-A15, 15 features); the body and the individual (B1-B5, 5 features); arts and crafts (C1); emotion (E1-E6, 6 features); food and farming (F1-F4, 4 features); government and public (G1-G3, 3 features); architecture, housing and the home (H1-H5, 5 features); money and commerce in industry (I1-I4, 4 features); entertainment, sports and games (K1-K6, 6 features); life and living things (L1-L3, 3 features); movement, location, travel and transport (M1-M8, 8 features); measurements (N1-N6, 6 features); substances, materials, objects and equipment (O1-O4, 4 features); education (P1), language communication (Q1-Q4, 4 features); social actions, states, processes (S1-S9, 9 features); time (T1-T4, 4 features); environment (W1-W5, 5 features); psychological actions, states and processes (X1-X9, 9 features); science and technology (Y1-Y2, 2 features); and names and grammar (Z0-Z9, Z99, 11 features).

The minimal classification error (0.260) was reached when the original semantic feature sets was reduced by almost half from 115 to 66: A12 (easy/ difficult); A13 (degree, extent); A15 (safety/danger); A7 (probability); B1 (anatomy, physiology); B2 (health and disease); B3 (medicines, medical treatment); E2 (liking); E3 (calm/violent/angry); E4 (happiness, contentment); E5 (bravery, fear); E6 (worry, confidence); G2 (crime, law); I1 (money); I3 (employment); O4 (physical attributes); Q1 (linguistic actions, states, processes); S1 (social actions, states, processes); S2 (people); S8 (helping/hindering); S9 (religion); W1 (environment); W3 (geographical terms); X1 (psychological actions, states, processes); X3 (sensory); X4 (mental object); X5 (attention); X6 (Deciding); X7 (wanting, planning); X8 (trying); X9 (Ability); Z6 (negative); Z8 (pronouns); and so on. Figure 4.4 (d) shows the automatic optimization of the three sets of natural language features combined. The minimal classification error (0.245) was reached when the full feature set (153 features) was reduced to 119.

4.6 Classifier Training and Development

Relevance vector machine (RVM) methodology was used to develop Bayesian machine learning classifiers in Table 4.2. Different RVM models were compared using paired optimized and unoptimized feature sets, as well as their normalized versions, using three different techniques for feature normalization: min-maximal normalization (MMN), L2 normalization (L2 N), and Z-score normalization (ZSN). On the testing data, optimized feature sets of English LDR (Disp_9) achieved a higher area under the receiver operator characteristic (area under curve (AUC)=0.7023) than its matching unoptimized feature set (Disp_20) (AUC=0.7013). Feature normalization increased AUC of optimized and non-optimized feature sets to varying degrees. Optimization did not improve the performance of the feature set of WFB, since the AUC of Freq_7 on the testing data set (0.6626) was lower than Freq_18 (0.6784). By contrast, optimization did enhance the performance of RVMs using semantic features, as USAS_66 (0.7894) had a higher AUC than USAS_115 (0.773). With min-max normalization as the best technique, the AUC of the optimized model USAS_66 also increased.

The results of the separate optimizations of the English feature sets are shown in Table 4.2. Table 4.3 shows the results of combining the three feature sets. Although the optimized full feature set (F119) (AUC=0.778) did not achieve a higher AUC than the unoptimized full feature set (F153) (AUC=0.830), feature normalization significantly increased the AUC of classifier F119. The most effective normalization technique was min-max normalization, which increased the AUC of classifier F119 from 0.778 to 0.896, very similar to that of classifier F153 after the same normalization process (0.897).

Table 4.2 *Comparison of RVMs with full vs. separately optimized features sets*

RVM	Training data Mean AUC (STD)	Testing data AUC	Accuracy	Sensitivity	Specificity	Macro-F1
Full Feature Set (English LDR: Disp)						
Disp_20	0.6738 (0.0389)	0.7013	0.6381	0.6818	0.592	0.6367
Disp_20 (Min-Max normalization: MMN)	0.7943 (0.0329)	0.8147	0.7315	0.7121	0.752	0.7315
Disp_20 (L_2 normalization: L_2 N)	0.6632 (0.038)	0.7049	0.6304	0.7652	0.488	0.6212
Disp_20 (Z-score normalization: ZSN)	0.7899 (0.0275)	0.859	0.7899	0.7803	0.8	0.7899
Automatically Optimized Feature Set (English LDR: Disp)						
Disp_9	0.6709 (0.0409)	0.7024	0.6148	0.6742	0.552	0.6124
Disp_9 (MMN)	0.792 (0.0294)	0.8014	0.7588	0.7576	0.76	0.7587
Disp_9 (L_2 N)	0.6666 (0.0417)	0.7062	0.6459	0.7424	0.544	0.641
Disp_9 (ZSN)	0.8134 (0.0082)	0.8254	0.7626	0.7348	0.792	0.7626
Full Feature Set (English Lexical Frequency Bands: Freq)						
Freq_18	0.6906 (0.0429)	0.6784	0.6615	0.7652	0.552	0.6561
Freq_18 (MMN)	0.7911 (0.046)	0.8334	0.7626	0.8106	0.712	0.7615
Freq_18 (L_2 N)	0.6673 (0.0503)	0.652	0.6381	0.75	0.52	0.6317
Freq_18 (ZSN)	0.8052 (0.0326)	0.8343	0.786	0.8788	0.688	0.783
Automatically Optimized Feature Set (English Lexical Frequency Bands: Freq)						
Freq_7	0.6808 (0.0185)	0.6626	0.6381	0.7424	0.528	0.6324
Freq_7 (MMN)	0.6905 (0.0334)	0.6908	0.6148	0.6288	0.6	0.6144
Freq_7 (L_2 N)	0.6668 (0.0246)	0.6378	0.6226	0.7197	0.52	0.6174
Freq_7 (ZSN)	0.7163 (0.0277)	0.7905	0.7198	0.7348	0.704	0.7195

Table 4.2 *(cont.)*

	Training data	Testing data				
RVM	Mean AUC (STD)	AUC	Accuracy	Sensitivity	Specificity	Macro-F1
Full Feature Set (English Semantic Classes: USAS)						
USAS_115	0.7893 (0.0202)	0.773	0.7043	0.7045	0.704	0.7042
USAS_115 (MMN)	0.8623 (0.0302)	0.9219	0.856	0.8485	0.864	0.856
USAS_115 (L_2 N)	0.7767 (0.0413)	0.8092	0.751	0.7803	0.72	0.7503
USAS_115 (ZSN)	0.8652 (0.0302)	0.9092	0.856	0.8258	0.888	0.856
Automatically Optimized Feature Set (English Semantic Classes: USAS)						
USAS_66	0.8464 (0.0221)	0.7894	0.751	0.8106	0.688	0.7493
USAS_66 (MMN)	0.8814 (0.0347)	0.9053	0.8366	0.8182	0.856	0.8366
USAS_66 (L_2 N)	0.842 (0.0286)	0.8539	0.786	0.8485	0.72	0.7844
USAS_66 (ZSN)	0.8728 (0.0325)	0.8885	0.8249	0.8182	0.832	0.8249

Table 4.3 *Comparison of RVMs with full vs. jointly optimized features sets*

	Training data	Testing data			
Relevance Vector Machine (RVM)	Mean AUC (STD)	AUC	Accuracy	Sensitivity	Specificity
Full Feature Set (including Disp, Freq and USAS)					
Disp_20 + Freq_18 + USAS_115 = F153	0.780 (0.021)	0.830	0.755	0.765	0.744
F153 (MMN)	0.833 (0.045)	0.897	0.825	0.849	0.800
F153 (L_2 N)	0.774 (0.033)	0.780	0.697	0.735	0.656
F153 (ZSN)	0.863 (0.053)	0.878	0.809	0.788	0.832
Automatically Optimized Full Feature Set (including Disp, Freq and USAS)					
F119	0.776 (0.033)	0.778	0.689	0.674	0.704
F119 (MMN)	0.844 (0.058)	0.896	0.844	0.864	0.824
F119 (L_2 N)	0.788 (0.018)	0.803	0.735	0.765	0.704
F119 (ZSN)	0.846 (0.045)	0.893	0.817	0.803	0.832
Combinations of separately optimized feature Sets					
Freq_7 + Disp_9 + USAS_66 = F82	0.792 (0.013)	0.794	0.724	0.750	0.696
F82 (MMN)	0.853 (0.025)	0.906	0.837	0.841	0.832
F82 (L_2 N)	0.790 (0.025)	0.774	0.700	0.742	0.656
F82 (ZSN)	0.879 (0.023)	0.891	0.813	0.788	0.840

Table 4.3 *(cont.)*

Relevance Vector Machine (RVM)	Training data Mean AUC (STD)	Testing data			
		AUC	Accuracy	Sensitivity	Specificity
Freq_ 7 + USAS_ 66 = F73	0.815 (0.022)	0.803	0.763	0.826	0.696
F73 (MMN)	0.856 (0.031)	0.903	0.825	0.856	0.792
F73 (L_2 N)	0.832 (0.032)	0.834	0.770	0.796	0.744
F73 (ZSN)	0.874 (0.014)	0.880	0.809	0.841	0.776
Disp_ 9 + USAS_ 66 = F75	0.811 (0.016)	0.805	0.739	0.765	0.712
F75 (MMN)	0.877 (0.039)	0.919	0.848	0.803	0.896
F75 (L_2 N)	0.803 (0.034)	0.783	0.732	0.780	0.680
F75 (ZSN)	0.878 (0.031)	0.890	0.837	0.833	0.840
Freq_ 7 + Disp_ 9 = F16	0.676 (0.03)	0.707	0.646	0.712	0.576
F16 (MMN)	0.768 (0.035)	0.793	0.728	0.735	0.720
F16 (L_2 N)	0.677 (0.029)	0.689	0.634	0.720	0.544
F16 (ZSN)	0.765 (0.030)	0.822	0.732	0.735	0.728

Pairwise comparisons were conducted of any two optimized feature sets to determine the best combination of features. The results show that the combination of optimized dispersion rates (Disp_9) and optimized semantic features (USAS_66) yielded the highest AUC on the testing data: F75 (AUC=0.919, sensitivity=0.803, specificity=0.896, accuracy=0.848), followed by the combination of all three optimized feature sets: F82 (AUC=0.906, sensitivity=0.841, specificity=0.832, accuracy=0.837). F75 thus emerged as the best model.

4.7 Statistical Refinement of the Optimized Classifier

In order to further improve the performance of the optimized classifier F75, we performed statistical analyses of the dispersion rate features and semantic features in the two sets of English mental health materials: labeled as 0, indicating no back-translation associated with statistically increased negative emotions, and labeled as 1, indicating back-translations with strong negative connotations in one or more of the three languages – Chinese, Hindi, and Spanish (Table 4.4). Appendix 3 shows the results of the Mann Whitney U test between the two sets of original English texts. As compared to "safe" original English materials, five features yielded statistically different distributions with respect to their respective probabilities of being translated into Chinese, Hindi, or Spanish with strong negativity: DiSp9:0.8–0.9 (p<0.001), DiSp10:0.9–1.0 (p<0.001), DiWr6:0.5–0.6

Table 4.4 *Comparison of RVMs with full vs. combined, separately optimized features sets*

Relevance Vector Machine (RVM)	Training data	Testing data			
	Mean AUC (STD)	AUC	Accuracy	Sensitivity	Specificity
Statistically Refined Feature Set based on the Automatic Optimization					
Disp_ 5 + USAS_66 = F71	0.817 (0.012)	0.807	0.755	0.796	0.712
F71 (L₂ N)	0.798 (0.029)	0.783	0.732	0.78	0.68
F71 (MMN)	0.884 (0.036)	0.865	0.829	0.849	0.808
F71 (ZSN)	0.867 (0.028)	0.886	0.856	0.856	0.856
Disp_ 9 + USAS_59 = F68	0.818 (0.018)	0.805	0.774	0.841	0.704
F68 (L₂ N)	0.805 (0.030)	0.766	0.728	0.803	0.648
F68 (MMN)	0.863 (0.034)	0.911	0.833	0.841	0.824
F68 (ZSN)	0.863 (0.035)	0.883	0.825	0.856	0.792
Disp_ 6 + USAS_59 = F65	0.815 (0.013)	0.806	0.751	0.788	0.712
F65 (L₂ N)	0.801 (0.028)	0.77	0.712	0.788	0.632
F65 (MMN)	0.866 (0.030)	0.881	0.848	0.856	0.84
F65 (ZSN)	0.867 (0.023)	0.885	0.833	0.841	0.824
Disp_5 + USAS_59 = F64	0.816 (0.017)	0.806	0.759	0.818	0.696
F64 (L₂ N)	0.804 (0.031)	0.767	0.716	0.796	0.632
F64 (MMN)	0.867 (0.039)	0.883	0.841	0.841	0.84
F64 (ZSM)	0.865 (0.021)	0.885	0.829	0.841	0.816
Disp 4 + USAS_59 = F63	0.822 (0.023)	0.799	0.743	0.773	0.712
F63 (L₂ N)	0.802 (0.036)	0.77	0.712	0.788	0.632
F63 (MMN)	0.866 (0.038)	0.885	0.825	0.826	0.824
F63 (ZSN)	0.868 (0.021)	0.887	0.829	0.841	0.816
Disp best 5 + USAS_59 = F best 64	0.817 (0.015)	0.805	0.77	0.826	0.712
F_ best 64 (L₂ N)	0.792 (0.045)	0.77	0.712	0.773	0.648
F_ best 64 (MMN)	0.870 (0.025)	0.886	0.848	0.849	0.848
F_ best 64 (ZSN)	0.865 (0.023)	0.893	0.852	0.864	0.84

(p=0.045), DiWr8:0.7–0.9 (p<0.001), and DiWr10:0.9–1.0 (p<0.001). The automatically selected features of LDR were reduced from 9 to 5. Similarly, the number of semantic features was reduced from 66 in the automatic feature selection (RVM_SVM) to 59. The classifier was subsequently fine-tuned by comparing four combinations of optimized LDR with optimized semantic features (USAS_59). (For details on the different dispersion rates used, see Appendix 2.) With ZSN, F (best 64) emerged as the best-performing classifier (AUC=0.893, accuracy=0.852, sensitivity=0.864, specificity=0.84).

RVM classifiers with different feature sets are compared in Tables 4.5 and 4.6. The comparison was to determine whether the sensitivity and specificity of the best-performing model were significantly higher than those of other classifiers.

Table 4.5 *Paired sample t test of the difference in sensitivity between the best model with other models*

No.	Pairs of RVMs	Mean Difference	S.D.	Lower	Upper	P value	Rank	(i/m)Q	Sig.
				95% Confidence Interval of Difference					
1	F best 64 (ZSN) vs. F75 (MMN)	0.0606	0.0093	0.0375	0.0837	0.0078	1	0.0056	**
2	F best 64 (ZSN) vs. F63 (ZSN)	0.0227	0.0039	0.0131	0.0323	0.0095	2	0.0111	**
3	F best 64 (ZSN) vs. F64 (MMN)	0.0227	0.0039	0.0131	0.0323	0.0095	3	0.0167	**
4	F best 64 (ZSN) vs. F68 (MMN)	0.0227	0.0039	0.0131	0.0323	0.0095	4	0.0222	**
5	F best 64 (ZSN) vs. F82 (MMN)	0.0227	0.0039	0.0131	0.0323	0.0095	5	0.0278	**
6	F best 64 (ZSN) vs. F153 (MMN)	0.0151	0.0026	0.0086	0.0216	0.0098	6	0.0333	**
7	F best 64 (ZSN) vs. F65 (MMN)	0.0075	0.0013	0.0042	0.0109	0.0103	7	0.0389	**
8	F best 64 (ZSN) vs. F71 (ZSM)	0.0075	0.0013	0.0042	0.0109	0.0103	8	0.0444	**
9	F best 64 (ZSN) vs. F119 (MMN)	0	0	0	0	1	9	0.0500	

To control for any false discovery rate, we applied the Benjamini–Hochberg correction procedure.

With respect to sensitivity, the results show that F (best 64) yielded statistically higher sensitivity than the other seven high-performing classifiers selected from the 72 classifiers we developed. There was no statistically significant difference between F (best 64) and F119 (jointly optimized features and normalized using min- max optimization). However, F (best 64) was much less complex with only 64 features.

With respect to specificity, F (best 64) gave statistically greater specificity than five high-performing classifiers (F63, F153, F68, F119, and F82), while F (best 64) gave statistically similar specificity to classifiers F64 and F65. The specificity of F (best 64) was statistically lower than that of F75 (MMN) and F71 (ZSM), but the sensitivity of F (best 64) was statistically higher than F75 (MMN) and F71 (ZSM).

As the primary aim of our study is to detect English texts that are more likely to be translated with strong negative connotations in the target languages, model sensitivity is more important than specificity. Therefore, F (best 64) was chosen as the best-performing classifier.

Table 4.6 *Paired sample t test of the difference in specificity between the best model with other models*

No	Pairs of RVMs	Mean Difference	S.D.	95% Confidence Interval of Difference		P value	Rank	(i/m)Q	Sig.
				Lower	Upper				
1	F best 64 (ZSN) vs. F63 (ZSN)	0.0240	0.0037	0.0149	0.0331	0.0077	1	0.006	**
2	F best 64 (ZSN) vs. F153 (MMN)	0.0400	0.0059	0.0255	0.0545	0.0071	2	0.011	**
3	F best 64 (ZSN) vs. F68 (MMN)	0.0160	0.0025	0.0098	0.0222	0.0080	3	0.017	**
4	F best 64 (ZSN) vs. F119 (MMN)	0.0160	0.0025	0.0098	0.0222	0.0080	4	0.022	**
5	F best 64 (ZSN) vs. F82 (MMN)	0.0080	0.0013	0.0048	0.0112	0.0083	5	0.028	**
6	F best 64 (ZSN) vs. F71 (ZSM)	−0.0160	0.0027	−0.0228	−0.0092	0.0095	6	0.033	**
7	F best 64 (ZSN) vs. F75 (MMN)	−0.0560	0.0108	−0.0827	−0.0293	0.0121	7	0.039	**
8	F best 64 (ZSN) vs. F64 (MMN)	0.0000	0.0000	0.0000	0.0000	1.0000	8	0.044	
9	F best 64 (ZSN) vs. F65 (MMN)	0.0000	0.0000	0.0000	0.0000	1.0000	9	0.050	

4.8 Model Stability

On the testing data set, Figure 4.3 shows how AUC varies when the size of the training data was adjusted from 150 to 550 on 100 intervals. The RVMs show themselves unlikely to have overfitting issues, unlike other classifiers such as extreme gradient boosting trees, random forests, and neural networks that require hyperparameter tuning. The RVM classifiers all demonstrated stability and scalability, as their performance (AUC) increased gradually as we increased the training dataset size. F (best 64) outperformed other classifiers when the size of training data exceeded that of testing data. Figure 4.4 shows the mean AUC of RVM classifiers on test data and Table 4.7 shows the paired sample t test of the AUC of these classifiers. Even though F (best 64) employed the smallest number of features, its mean AUC was comparable to that of other high-dimensional classifiers.

To review, then, we have succeeded in developing a high-performing relevance vector machine (RVM) classifier to predict the likelihood of a certain English health text being translated by Google as having statistically increased negative connotations when compared to the original English text.

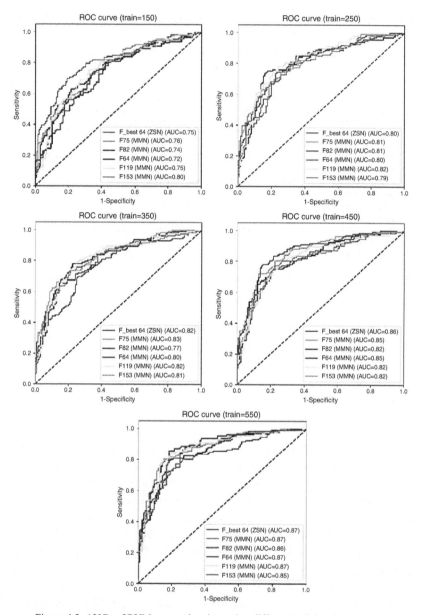

Figure 4.3 AUCs of RVMs on testing data using different training dataset sizes (150, 250, 350, 450, 550).

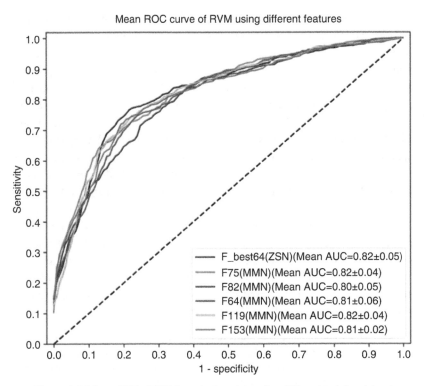

Figure 4.4 Mean AUC of RVMs on testing data using different training dataset size (150, 250, 350, 450, 550).

Table 4.7 *Paired sample t test of AUC of the best-performing classifier with other high-performing classifiers*

| | | Paired Mean Differences | Std. Error Mean | 95% Confidence Interval of the Difference | | Sig. (2-tailed) |
				Lower	Upper	
Pair 1	Fbest 64 – F75	−0.0021	0.0053	−0.0167	0.0124	0.7039
Pair 2	Fbest 64 – F82	0.0201	0.0110	−0.0103	0.0506	0.1404
Pair 3	Fbest 64 – F64	0.0093	0.0047	−0.0037	0.0223	0.1176
Pair 4	Fbest 64 – F119	0.0043	0.0099	−0.0231	0.0318	0.6848
Pair 5	Fbest 64 – F153	0.0076	0.0156	−0.0357	0.0508	0.6526

Among the three languages we studied, the negative emotions and attitudes toward mental health – specifically, toward anxiety disorders – introduced by automatic translation were widespread. To understand the reasons, we carefully read the original English health texts in our database and their corresponding back-translations from the target languages. We found some illuminating examples, collected in Appendix 1. In some cases, mental health disorders have been translated by Google into Chinese as mental health diseases; people with anxiety disorders are describe in translation as mental illness patients; in Spanish, mental health conditions are translated as mental illnesses; in Hindi, shyness is translated as general shame, and panic is translated as nervousness. In Chinese, there is a subtle difference in word connotation: neural verbs such as "have a mental disorder" are replaced by "suffer from a mental disease." As discussed above, neural machine translation emphasizes naturalness and fluency of translations, as compared with the more literal translations characteristic of statistical machine translation. The overall translation does improve significantly in terms of readability, fluency, and grammar; however, the accuracy of local translations may be compromised at the lexical and lexico-grammatical levels.

As Way noted in the following text:

> [Neural] MT output can be deceptively fluent; sometimes perfect target-language sentences are output, and less thorough translators and proofreaders may be seduced into accepting such translations, despite the fact that such translations may not be an actual translation of the source sentence at hand at all!

As we have seen, a direct result of the target-language-oriented approach to neural MT in mental health translation has been unintentional increased negativity and discrimination in the translation output, even though such connotations were absent in the original English mental health materials. And as discussed, we have developed machine learning classifiers mitigate this undesirable effect by detecting English mental health information that might lead to biased translation in the three languages.

Our RVM classifier reached its statistically highest sensitivity (mean=0.864, 95 percent C.I.: 0.805, 0.922) and specificity (mean=0.832, 95 percent C.I.: 0.766, 0.898) when the probability threshold was set at 0.5. However, the default threshold of 0.5 can be adjusted further to fine-tune the classifier. When the threshold of the classifier was increased, sensitivity decreased, while specificity increased; conversely, when the threshold was decreased, sensitivity increased, and specificity decreased. Thus, one can select the best sensitivity and specificity pairing according to the practical circumstances.

For example, high-sensitivity classifiers can be useful for screening purposes – to identify mental health materials in English which cannot be adequately translated by full, unverified automatic machine translation, due to their heightened likelihood of biased or discriminatory translations. By contrast, a low-sensitivity classifier is relatively unlikely to identify potentially problematic original English mental health information – that is, to screen out any materials that are not safe and suitable for neural machine translation. Thus, any social biases or discrimination against mental disorders still present in the target language would unfortunately be reinforced in machine-translated mental health resources, even if indirectly or unintentionally – clearly not the intent of global mental health promotion.

As for classifiers with high specificity, they are more suitable for identifying original English mental health texts which are suitable for neural machine translation, at least for the three languages we studied, Chinese, Hindi, and Spanish. On the other hand, when a classifier with a low specificity is used, there is a raised likelihood of false positive predictions: that is, even safe and suitable original English mental health information may be erroneously considered unsuitable for neural MT. While subsequent human post-evaluation could correct such inaccurate predictions, logistical burdens and staff costs would increase. This extra effort might well be impractical or prohibitive in low-resource healthcare service scenarios, often subject to tight budget constraints or lacking bilingual workers with sufficient knowledge of the relevant languages.

4.9 Conclusion

In comparison with earlier statistical machine learning models, current neural machine translation technologies exhibit greater linguistic fluency. However, as noted, while improving linguistic fluency, neural machine translation also learns, inevitably if unconsciously, to reflect the sentiments, attitudes, and biases of the target cultures, societies, and communities. Since the design favors the most natural sequence of translated words and phrases in the target language – its natural lexical and syntactic patterns – its results inevitably convey the social and cultural connotations of the cultures from which the languages sprang.

In many countries and cultures, mental disorders are still stigmatized and subject to discrimination. In associated languages, this deeply rooted sentiment comes to be reflected in conventional lexical and semantic units. Consequently, the neural machine translation of mental health information too often entails the transmission of negative social sentiments in the output, even when social prejudice against mental disorders is actually absent from the original

English materials. Our study has examined this understudied tendency in neural machine translation. We argue that this examination is appropriate and necessary as human communication technologies move rapidly toward more human-centric AI. Accordingly, we have developed Bayesian machine learning classifiers to assist with the probabilistic detection and prediction of socially biased neural machine translation outputs, using computational modeling and pairwise comparisons of original English and back-translations of neural machine translation outputs on anxiety disorders in Chinese, Hindi, and Spanish.

Via Google's Translate API, we collected and compared original English documents on anxiety disorders from U.S., UK, Canadian, and Australian health authorities and their back-translations from Chinese, Hindi, and Spanish. Through automatic, statistically informed feature optimization, RVM classifiers were developed. These models provided informative probabilistic predictions of the likelihood that an English text on anxiety disorders would be translated by Google into one of the three languages with subtle but strong negative connotations – again, because neural machine translation favors natural language translations.

The best-performing RVM (RVM_ best 64) contained 64 English linguistic features: 59 (semantic features) and 5 (LDR: DiSp9:0.8–0.9, DiSp10:0.9–1.0, DiWr8:0.7–0.9, DiWr9:0.8–0.9, DiWr10:0.9–1.0). This result suggests that, in spoken and written English words belonging to certain semantic classes, words with high dispersion of meaning are relatively likely to produce negative neural machine translation results for anxiety disorders. The best-performing RVM (both optimized and normalized) achieved a mean AUC of receiver operator characteristic (0.893), accuracy (0.892), sensitivity (0.864), and specificity (0.84). Its sensitivity (SE) and specificity (SP) were statistically higher than those of unoptimized, normalized classifiers RVM_153 (min-max normalized MMN) (SE: $p=0.0098$, SP: $p=0.007$); of automatically optimized and normalized classifiers: RVM_82 (MMN) (SE: $p=0.0095$, SP: $p=0.0083$), RVM_75 (SE: $p=0.0078$, SP: $p=0.0121$); and of an automatically optimized and statistically refined classifier: RVM_71 (MMN) (SE: $p=0.0103$, SP; $p=0.0095$); RVM_68 (MMN) (SE: $p=0.0095$, SP: $p=0.0080$); RMV_63 (ZSM) (SE: $p=0.0095$, SP: $p=0.0077$). The stability of RVM_ best 64 appeared in its mean AUC (0.82, SD=0.05) when the training data sizes were reduced from 600 to 150.

Content analysis indicates that negative neural machine translations of anxiety disorders were primarily associated with increased linguistic fluency and communicative naturalness in the target Chinese, Hindi, and Spanish texts. However, once again, these stylistically enhanced phrasal patterns reflect persistent social attitudes toward mental health disorders in the relevant languages and cultures. And again, this bias is to be expected: as in any form of artificial intelligence, neural machine translation is designed to accommodate and understand human wants, needs, and thinking patterns.

This study demonstrates that phrasal patterning in target cultures does indeed yield increased negativity toward mental disorders as a consequence of greater translation naturalness. In compensation, however, we demonstrate that machine learning tools for the promotion of mental health translation can indeed detect instances of the automatic generation and dissemination of negative, discriminatory translation. In this way, neural tools can also promote positive and supportive social understanding and acceptance of mental disorders. This study confirms that, while neural machine translation technology is inevitably and increasingly culturally skewed, it can nevertheless be harnessed to foster more tolerant global health cultures.

References

Best, S. 2017. "Is Google Translate Sexist? Users Report Biased Results When Translating Gender-Neutral Languages into English," The Daily Mail. Accessed January 28, 2020. www.dailymail.co.uk/sciencetech/article-5136607/Is-Google-Translate-SEXIST.html.

Chawla, N. V., K. W. Bowyer, L. O. Hall, and W. P. Kegelmeyer. 2002. "SMOTE: Synthetic Minority Over- Sampling Technique," *Journal of Artificial Intelligence Research*, 16, pages 321–357.

Downes, W. 1998. *Language and Society*, Volume 10, New York: Cambridge University Press.

Feng, Y., W. Xie, S. Gu, et al. 2020. "Modeling Fluency and Faithfulness for Diverse Neural Machine Translation," *Proceedings of the AAAI Conference on Artificial Intelligence*, 34 (01), pages 59–66. https://doi.org/10.1609/aaai.v34i01.5334.

Fishman, J. A. 2019. *The Sociology of Language: An Interdisciplinary Social Science Approach to Language in Society*. Rowley, MA: Newbury House.

Font, J. E. and M. R. Costa-jussà, 2019. "Equalizing Gender Bias in Neural Machine Translation with Word Embeddings Techniques," *Proceedings of the 1st Workshop on Gender Bias in Natural Language Processing*, pages 147–154.

Grechishnikova, D. 2021. "Transformer neural network for protein-specific de novo drug generation as a machine translation problem," *Sci Rep* 11, 321. https://doi.org/10.1038/s41598-020-79682-4.

Johnson, M., M. Schuster, Q. V. Le, et al. 2017. "Google's Multilingual Neural Machine Translation System: Enabling Zero-Shot Translation," *Transactions of the Association for Computational Linguistics*, 5, pages 339–351.

Koehn, Philipp. 2020. *Neural Machine Translation*, Cambridge: Cambridge University Press.

Martindale, M. J., M. Carpuat, K. Duh, and P. McNamee. 2019. "Identifying Fluently Inadequate Output in Neural and Statistical Machine Translation," *Proceedings of MT Summit XVII*, 1, Dublin, August 19–23.

Montgomery, M. 1995. *An Introduction to Language and Society.* London: Routledge.

Popel, M., M. Tomkova, J. Tomek, et al. 2020. "Transforming Machine Translation: A Deep Learning System Reaches News Translation Quality Comparable to Human Professionals," *Nat Commun*, 11, 4381. https://doi.org/10.1038/s41467-020-18073-9.

Prates, M. O. R., P. H. C. Avelar, and L. Lamb. 2019. Assessing Gender Bias in Machine Translation: A Case Study with Google Translate, https://arxiv.org/abs/1809.02208.

Ritchie, H. and M. Roser. 2018. Mental Health. Our World in Data. https://ourworldindata.org/mental-health.

Salles, A., M. Awad, L. Goldin, et al. 2019. "Estimating Implicit and Explicit Gender Bias Among Health Care Professionals and Surgeons," *JAMA Netw Open*, 2 (7): e196545. DOI: 10.1001/jamanetworkopen.2019.6545.

Saunders, D. and B. Byrne. 2020. Reducing Gender Bias in Neural Machine Translation as a Domain Adaptation Problem. ACL. arXiv:2004.04498

Thomas, L. and S. Wareing. 1999. Language, Society and Power. London: Routledge.

Tomalin, M., B. Byrne, S. Concannon, et al. 2021. "The Practical Ethics of Bias Reduction in Machine Translation: Why Domain Adaptation Is Better Than Data Debiasing," *Ethics Inf Technol.* https://doi.org/10.1007/s10676-021-09583-1.

Weng, R., H. Yu, X. Wei, and W. Luo. 2020. "Towards Enhancing Faithfulness for Neural Machine Translation," *Proceedings of the 2020 Conference on Empirical Methods in Natural Language Processing*, pages 2675–2684, November 16–20, Association for Computational Linguistics.

Yonghui W., M. Schuster, Z. Chen, et al. 2016. Google's Neural Machine Translation System: Bridging the Gap between Human and Machine Translation, https://arxiv.org/abs/1609.08144

Appendix 1 Examples of Back-Translations with Negative Connotations

Original	Back-Translation(from Chinese, Hindi, Spanish)
EN	CH
Those younger than 25 should be carefully watched for increased depression, agitation, irritability, *suicidality*, and *unusual* changes in behavior, especially at the beginning of treatment or when doses are changed.	People under 25 years of age should be carefully observed for depression, agitation, irritability, *suicide,* and *abnormal* behavior changes, especially at the beginning of treatment or when the dose is changed.

(cont.)

Original	Back-Translation(from Chinese, Hindi, Spanish)
EN	CH
People with Social Anxiety Disorder may feel *very uneasy* when talking with others, asking questions, going into a store, or ordering food in a restaurant.	People with social anxiety disorder may feel *very upset* when talking to others, asking questions, entering a store, or ordering food in a restaurant.
EN	CH
People with this *disorder* are afraid that others will judge them in a negative way and will lead to extreme embarrassment or rejection.	People with this *disease* are afraid that others will judge them in a negative way leading to extreme embarrassment or rejection.
EN	CH
Both males and females can *have* Social Anxiety Disorder.	Both men and women may *suffer* from social anxiety disorder.
EN	CH
Panic attacks are frequently mistaken for a medical event such as a *heart attack.*	Panic attacks are frequently mistaken for medical events such as a *heart disease.*
EN	CH
Family and other sources of social support can have a significant impact on the recovery process for *people* with panic disorder.	Family and other sources of social support can have a significant impact on the recovery process of *patients* with panic disorder.
EN	CH
Rather than denying their (people with social anxiety disorder) feelings, take the following steps to allow the person to feel seen and heard: *Remain supportive*	Rather than deny their (people with social anxiety disorder) feelings, take the following steps to make them feel seen and heard: *Stay supported*
EN	CH
The National Alliance on Mental Illness (NAMI) can help ***people with panic disorder*** and family members normalize the experience and help the individual know and realize, that they are not alone.	The National League for Mental Illness (NAMI) can help ***panic sufferers*** and family members normalize their experiences and help individuals understand and realize that they are not alone.

(cont.)

Original	Back-Translation(from Chinese, Hindi, Spanish)
EN	**SP**
For a person with panic disorder, social relationships can be an important way to cope with the symptoms of *the condition*.	For a person with panic disorder, social relationships can be an important way of coping with the symptoms of *the illness*.
EN	**SP**
A panic attack can be upsetting. It can sometimes be a *challenging* situation to deal with, but it is important to avoid seeming *judgmental* or upset.	A panic attack can be upsetting. It can sometimes be a *difficult* situation to deal with at times, but it is important to avoid coming across *critical* or upset.
EN	**Hindi**
The fear of Social Anxiety Disorder is extreme and is not the same *ordinary shyness* that many people sometimes feel.	The fear of Social Anxiety Disorder is extreme and is not the same *general shame* that many people sometimes feel.
EN	**Hindi**
Here are some possible symptoms of Social Anxiety Disorder: Anxiety or *panic* when interacting with others in social situation	Here are some possible symptoms of Social Anxiety Disorder: Anxiety or *nervousness* when interacting with others in social situation

Appendix 2 Description of Different Feature Sets

Feature Set Description	Abbrev.	Description of Items	Removed	Added
BNC Frequency Lists	Freq (20)	FrSp1:0–500, FrSp2:500–1000, FrSp3:1000–1500, FrSp4:1500–2000, FrSp5:2000–2500, FrSp6:2500–3000, FrSp7:3000–3500, FrSp8:3500–4000, FrSp9:4000–57010,		

(cont.)

Feature Set Description	Abbrev.	Description of Items	Removed	Added
		FrWr1:0–500, FrWr2:500–1000, FrWr3:1000–1500, FrWr4:1500–2000, FrWr5:2000–2500, FrWr6:2500–3000, FrWr7:3000–3500, FrWr8:3500–4000, FrWr9:4000–64420		
BNC Dispersion Lists	Disp (18)	DiSp1:0.0–0.1, DiSp2:0.1–0.2, DiSp3:0.2–0.3, DiSp4:0.3–0.4, DiSp5:0.4–0.5, DiSp6:0.5–0.6, DiSp7:0.6–0.7, DiSp8:0.7–0.8, DiSp9:0.8–0.9, DiSp10:0.9–1.0 DiWr1:0.0–0.1, DiWr2:0.1–0.2, DiWr3:0.2–0.3, DiWr4:0.3–0.4, DiWr5:0.4–0.5, DiWr6:0.5–0.6, DiWr7:0.6–0.7, DiWr8:0.7–0.9, DiWr9:0.8–0.9, DiWr10:0.9–1.0		
Original USAS List	USAS (115)	A1, A10, A11, A12, A13, A14, A15, A2, A3, A4, A5, A6, A7, A8, A9, B1, B2, B3, B4, B5, C1, E1, E2, E3, E4, E5, E6, F1, F2, F3, F4, G1, G2, G3, H1, H2, H3, H4, H5, I1, I2, I3, I4, K1, K2, K3, K4, K5, K6, L1, L2, L3, M1, M2, M3, M4, M5, M6, M7, M8, N1, N2, N3, N4, N5, N6, O1, O2, O3, O4, P1, Q1, Q2, Q3, Q4, S1, S2, S3, S4, S5, S6, S7, S8, S9, T1, T2, T3, T4, W1, W2, W3, W4, W5, X1, X2, X3, X4, X5, X6, X7, X8, X9, Y1, Y2, Z0, Z1, Z2, Z3, Z4, Z5, Z6, Z7, Z8, Z9, Z99		
Automatic selection RFE_SVM	Disp (9)	DiSp1:0.0–0.1, DiSp3:0.2–0.3, DiSp6:0.5–0.6, DiSp9:0.8–0.9, DiSp10:0.9–1.0, DiWr4:0.3–0.4, DiWr6:0.5–0.6, DiWr8:0.7–0.9, DiWr10:0.9–1.0		
Automatic selection RFE_SVM	Freq (7)	FrSp1:0–500, FrSp5:2000–2500, FrSp9:4000–57010, FrWr4:1500–2000, FrWr7:3000–3500, FrWr8:3500–4000, FrWr9:4000–64420		
Automatic selection RFE_SVM	USAS (66)	A12, A13, A14, A15, A3, A7, B1, B2, B3, B4, B5, E2, E3, E4, E5, E6, G2, H1, H2, H3, H4, H5, I1, I2, I3, K4, K5, K6, L1, L2, M2, M3, M5, M6, M8, N2, O1, O3, O4, Q1, Q2, Q3, Q4, S1, S2, S8, S9, T1, T3, T4, W1, W3, X1, X3, X4, X5, X6, X7, X8, X9, Z3, Z4, Z6, Z7, Z8, Z99		

(cont.)

Feature Set Description	Abbrev.	Description of Items	Removed	Added
Statistical & Automatic selection RFE_SVM	USAS (59)	A12, A13, A14, A15, A3, A7, B1, B2, B3, B4, B5, E2, E3, E4, E5, E6, G2, H1, H2, H4, H5, I1, I2, I3, K4, K6, L1, M2, M3, M5, M6, M8, N2, O1, O4, Q1, Q2, Q3, Q4, S1, S2, S8, S9, T1, T3, T4, X3, X4, X5, X6, X7, X8, X9, Z3, Z4, Z6, Z7, Z8, Z99	H3,K5,L2, O3, W1,W3,X1	
Statistical & Automatic selection RFE_SVM	Disp (5)	DiSp9:0.8–0.9, DiSp10:0.9–1.0, DiWr6:0.5–0.6, DiWr8:0.7–0.9, DiWr10:0.9–1.0	DiSp1:0.0–0.1, DiSp3:0.2–0.3, DiSp6:0.5–0.6, DiWr4:0.3–0.4	
Statistical & Automatic selection RFE_SVM	Disp (4)	DiSp9:0.8–0.9, DiSp10:0.9–1.0, DiWr8:0.7–0.9, DiWr10:0.9–1.0	DiWr6:0.5–0.6	
Statistical & Automatic selection RFE_SVM	Disp (6)	DiSp9:0.8–0.9, DiSp10:0.9–1.0, DiWr6:0.5–0.6, DiWr8:0.7–0.9, DiWr9:0.8–0.9, DiWr10:0.9–1.0		DiWr9:0.8–0.9
Statistical & Automatic selection RFE_SVM	Disp (best 5)	DiSp9:0.8–0.9, DiSp10:0.9–1.0, DiWr8:0.7–0.9, DiWr9:0.8–0.9, DiWr10:0.9–1.0	DiWr6:0.5–0.6	DiWr9:0.8–0.9

Appendix 3 Mann Whitney U Test of English Original and English Back-Translations of Chinese, Hindi, and Spanish Health Texts

	Mann Whitney U	Wilcoxon W	Z	Asymp. Sig. (2-tailed)
DiSp1:0.0–0.1	89648	181454	−0.78	0.435
DiSp2:0.1–0.2	91592	183398	0	1
DiSp3:0.2–0.3	90508	182314	−0.394	0.694
DiSp4:0.3–0.4	91592	183398	0	1
DiSp5:0.4–0.5	87469	179275	−2.233	0.026 **
DiSp6:0.5–0.6	88593	180399	−1.136	0.256 **
DiSp7:0.6–0.7	70673	162479	−5.817	0 **
DiSp8:0.7–0.8	58353.5	150159.5	−9.191	0 **
DiSp9:0.8–0.9	69068	160874	−6.228	0 **
DiSp10:0.9–1.0	76650	168456	−4.131	0 **
DiWr1:0.0–0.1	91592	183398	0	1
DiWr2:0.1–0.2	91592	183398	0	1
DiWr3:0.2–0.3	91592	183398	0	1

(cont.)

	Mann Whitney U	Wilcoxon W	Z	Asymp. Sig. (2-tailed)
DiWr4:0.3–0.4	90524.5	182330.5	−1.892	0.058
DiWr5:0.4–0.5	91592	183398	0	1
DiWr6:0.5–0.6	90736	182542	−2.004	0.045 *
DiWr7:0.6–0.7	91378	183184	−1	0.317
DiWr8:0.7–0.9	83319	175125	−2.829	0.005 **
DiWr9:0.8–0.9	77904.5	169710.5	−3.792	0 **
DiWr10:0.9–1.0	66993	158799	−6.801	0 **
FrSp1:0–500	63116.5	154922.5	−7.873	0 **
FrSp2:500–1000	76380.5	168186.5	−4.207	0 **
FrSp3:1000–1500	72000.5	163806.5	−5.424	0 **
FrSp4:1500–2000	73940.5	165746.5	−4.892	0 **
FrSp5:2000–2500	82849	174655	−2.425	0.015 **
FrSp6:2500–3000	84883	176689	−1.87	0.061
FrSp7:3000–3500	82505	174311	−2.54	0.011 **
FrSp8:3500–4000	87808	179614	−1.07	0.285
FrSp9:4000–57010	80821.5	172627.5	−2.982	0.003 **
FrWr1:0–500	66228	158034	−7.013	0 **
FrWr2:500–1000	69789.5	161595.5	−6.029	0 **
FrWr3:1000–1500	71272.5	163078.5	−5.621	0 **
FrWr4:1500–2000	76411.5	168217.5	−4.207	0 **
FrWr5:2000–2500	76381	168187	−4.304	0 **
FrWr6:2500–3000	77464.5	169270.5	−3.997	0 **
FrWr7:3000–3500	85839.5	177645.5	−1.628	0.104
FrWr8:3500–4000	86366.5	178172.5	−1.59	0.112
FrWr9:4000–64420	80821.5	172627.5	−2.982	0.003 **

Appendix 4 List of English Health Information Websites

https://au.reachout.com
https://familydoctor.org
https://foundrybc.ca
https://headspace.org.au
https://healthyfamilies.beyondblue.org.au
https://kidshealth.org
https://kidshelpphone.ca
https://medlineplus.gov
https://mindyourmind.ca
https://my.clevelandclinic.org
https://patient.info
https://psychcentral.com

https://riseabove.org.uk
www.anxietycanada.com
www.apa.org
www.betterhealth.vic.gov.au
www.beyondblue.org.au
www.blackdoginstitute.org.au
www.camh.ca
www.childline.org.uk
www.emedicinehealth.com
www.healthline.com
www.healthychildren.org
www.independentage.org
www.mayoclinic.org
www.medicinenet.com
www.menshealthforum.org.uk
www.mentalhealth.org.uk
www.msdmanuals.com/home
www.nami.org
www.papyrus-uk.org
www.postpartum.net
www.verywellmind.com
www.webmd.com
www.womenshealth.gov
https://youngmenshealthsite.org
https://youngminds.org.uk

5

Enhancing Speech Translation in Medical Emergencies with Pictographs

BabelDr

WITH CONTRIBUTIONS FROM PIERRETTE BOUILLON,
JOHANNA GERLACH, MAGALI NORRÉ AND HERVE
SPECHBACH

5.1 Introduction

In emergency care settings, there is a crucial need for automated translation tools. In Europe, this need has been fueled by the migratory crisis (Spechbach et al., 2019), but the same need obtains in countries such as the USA (Turner et al., 2019) and Australia (Ji et al., 2020), where the foreign-born population is increasing. Emergency services often have to deal with patients who have no language in common with staff; and this issue has been shown to negatively impact both healthcare quality and associated costs (Meischke et al., 2013). In particular, a lack of clear communication can interfere with the prompt and accurate delivery of care (Turner et al., 2019). Language barriers also increase the risk of erroneous diagnoses and serious consequences (Flores et al., 2003).

According to Kerremans et al. (2018), various bridging solutions are currently used by services addressing asylum seekers or mental healthcare. They cite the use of plain language and professional or *ad hoc* interpreters, but also the use of gestures, communication technologies, and visual supports such as images or pictographs. In particular, in emergency settings where interpreters are not always available, there is a growing interest in the use of translation tools to improve communication (Turner et al., 2019). Fixed-phrase translators (Seligman and Dillinger, 2013), also known as "phraselators", are often used in the medical field for safety and accuracy reasons, for example, "Culturally and Linguistically Diverse (CALD) Assist," "Canopy Speak," "Dr. Passport (Personal)," "MediBabble Translator," "Talk To Me," and "Universal Doctor Speaker" (Panayotou et al., 2019; Khander et al., 2018). These are based on a limited list of pre-translated sentences, which then can be presented to the patient in written or spoken form, using either text-to-speech or human audio recordings. Some of these fixed-phrase systems are now relatively sophisticated and speech-enabled, for example, "BabelDr" (Spechbach et al., 2019).

These enable doctors to speak freely, with the system linking the recognition result to the closest source-language match that is a clear and explicit variant of the original sentence. This intermediate result can be presented to the doctor for confirmation, and can also be used as the input for translation into the system's target languages (Mutal et al., 2019; Bouillon et al., 2021).

Machine translation is another alternative, but the quality is too often low for this type of discourse, due in part to many context-dependent phenomena (ellipsis, etc.). Literal translation is often problematic as well, since cultural differences may influence the way questions are asked (Halimi et al., 2021). Some recent studies have showed that both patients and doctors tend to prefer a fixed-phrase translator to generic machine translation such as Google Translate (Turner et al., 2019; Panayotou et al., 2019; Bouillon et al., 2017).

We focus here on the BabelDr system, a speech-enabled phraselator used to improve communication in emergency settings between doctors and allophone patients (Bouillon et al., 2021). The aim of the chapter is two-fold. First, we wish to assess if a bidirectional version of the phraselator allowing patients to answer doctors' questions by selecting pictures from open-source databases will improve user satisfaction. Second, we wish to evaluate pictograph usability in this context. Our hypotheses are that images will in fact help to improve patient satisfaction and that multiple factors influence pictograph usability. Factors of interest include not only the comprehensibility of the pictographs *per se*, but also how the images are presented to the user with respect to their number and ordering.

Visual supports have been already suggested for medical dialogue in research studies among patients with limited English proficiency (Somers, 2007) or hospitalized individuals with language or motor disabilities (Eadie et al., 2013; Bandeira et al., 2011), and some systems are already available for medical use (see Section 5.2). However, to the best of our knowledge, BabelDr is the first system which integrates speech and automatically links doctors' spoken questions to specific pictographs for the patient. Some studies have evaluated the effect of pictographs on user satisfaction, but not in the context of a diagnostic interview or with a CALD population.

Section 5.2 of the chapter provides an overview for the reader of the broader context of pictographs in the medical domain. In Section 5.3, we describe the bidirectional BabelDr system and our method for selecting images and integrating them into the system. We then summarize two user studies intended to answer our research questions. The first focuses on user satisfaction (Section 5.4.1) and the second on pictograph usability (Section 5.4.2). Finally, in Section 5.5, we draw conclusions and briefly describe our future work on this topic.

5.2 Pictographs in Medical Communication

Patients, especially those with limited health literacy skills, often have trouble understanding health information. Pictographs are one proposal for clarifying and elucidating that information. As emphasized by Katz et al., (2006), "research in psychology and marketing indicates that humans have a cognitive preference for picture-based, rather than text-based, information".

In clinical settings, pictographs have been developed mainly for communication of health information and tested for delivery of specific instructions (concerning medication, etc.). In this domain, the use of images has been shown to positively affect patient comprehension by improving attention, recall, satisfaction, and adherence (Houts et al., 2006; Katz et al., 2006). For example, Hill et al., (2016) and Zeng-Treitler et al., (2014) evaluated automated pictograph illustrations generated by the Glyph system for communicating patient instructions (e.g., "Call your doctor if you experience fainting, dizziness, or racing heart rate"). They found that participants who received pictograph-enhanced discharge instructions recalled more of their instructions than those who received standard discharge instructions. In addition, patients were more satisfied with the understandability of their instructions. In the same context, several studies also highlighted the importance of using pictures together with written or oral instructions to avoid misinterpretation of picture-only instructions. That is, combinations of formats are generally preferred to picture- or text-alone (Houts et al., 2006).

Clearly, pictographs are of potential value, and in fact several sets are available. However, only a few are open-source, which limits actual usability. Some sets were developed for specific purposes. For example, USP pictograms were specifically developed to help convey medication instructions, precautions, and/or warnings to patients and consumers. Similarly, "Visualization of Concepts in Medicine" (VCM) (Lamy et al., 2008) is an iconic language based on a small number of graphical primitives and combinatory rules for facilitating access to drug monographs by practitioners. SantéBD is a French database, accessible under certain conditions, that provides educational content in the form of images, comics, or texts using the method "Easy-to-Read-and-Understand" (FALC [Facile à Lire et à Comprendre]) is designed to aid individual comprehension in healthcare situations, but also to facilitate communication between doctors and patients during consultations (Figure 5.1). Similarly, "Widgit Health" (Vaz, 2013) offers a symbol board created to help medical staff to communicate quickly and easily in various domains, including coronavirus disease 2019 (COVID-19). Arassac and Sclera are two large open-source datasets (over 13,000 pictographs per set) designed for AAC

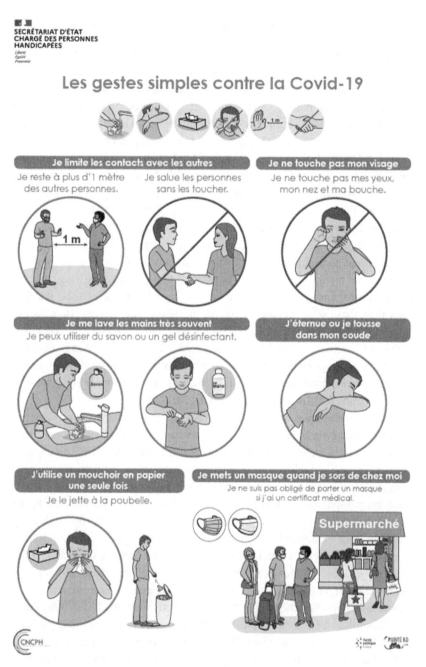

Figure 5.1 SantéBD

(Augmentative and Alternative Communication). They have been used in several contexts, including hospitals (Paolieri and Marful, 2018), and have been integrated into various online applications. In particular, the Sclera set was used by Vandeghinste and Schuurman (2014) in a text-to-pictograph translation system for people with disabilities, while the Arasaac set by Vaschalde et al., (2018) was used in a speech-to-pictograph system. Many other specific pictograph sets were designed for healthcare use, but are not accessible online (Cataix-Nègre, 2017; Beukelman and Mirenda, 1998).

Pictographs are unlikely to be universal (Sevens, 2018). Some medical research focused on the pictograph comprehensibility and crowdsourcing. Kim et al. (2009) concluded that "there is a large variance in the quality of the pictographs developed using the same design process". Yu et al. (2013) used Amazon Mechanical Turk (MTurk) workers to test a crowdsourcing approach in order to have 20 medical USP pictograms evaluated by 100 US "turkers." Their comprehensibility ranged between 45% and 98% (mean=72.5). Another study using a crowdsourced game called Doodle Health (Christensen et al., 2017) showed that it is possible to design a large set of medical images (596 drawings) and validate them by a larger community (114 volunteers made more than 1758 guesses). They obtained a score between 70% and 90%. According to the authors, this game had several limitations: not all participants had sufficient specialized knowledge to draw and/or recognize certain medical concepts, for example, the word "defibrillator". These studies show the importance of testing pictographs with a specific target group and task. In addition, most reports demonstrated an impact of the culture on comprehensibility. Yu et al. (2013) conclude that the "educational level is the only factor that affected participant performance". Kassam et al. (2004) similarly show that "basic education and time since immigration predicted interpretation accuracy better than first language or any other demographic characteristic".

Although the potential of pictographs for medical diagnosis is recognized (e.g., Somers, 2007), studies in this domain are very scarce (Alvarez, 2014). Existing medical phraselators generally do not contain pictographs (Wołk et al., 2017). Only a few medical pictographic fixed-phrase translators are available online, for example, "My Symptoms Translator" on Apple devices (Alvarez, 2014) or "Medipicto AP-HP" on Android and Iphone developed by the Hospitals of Paris; but these are quite limited and unsophisticated. "My Symptoms Translator" is aimed at reducing communication barriers and allowing patients to express their symptoms during medical emergencies. Pictographs represent types of pain, injuries, and medication. In the "Medipicto AP-HP" mobile application, the patient chooses pictographs labeled in his/her language to communicate with the caregiver, who can ask

questions by choosing pictographs translated into patient and caregiver languages from a predefined list. Wołk et al. (2017) also recently developed
a cross-lingual medical aid application with pictographs on mobile devices
(e.g., smartwatch) for communication between doctors, foreigners, and patients
with speech, hearing, or mental disabilities. However, none of these applications can be adapted for specific needs or pictograph sets, and this limitation
impedes use and evaluation. In the following sections, we describe BabelDr,
conceived as a platform for experimentation in the domain of medical
communication.

5.3 BabelDr and the Bidirectional Version

BabelDr is an online, speech-enabled phraselator for medical dialogue between
doctors and patients (Bouillon et al., 2021, Spechbach et al., 2019). BabelDr is
a project of the Faculty of Translation and Interpreting of the University of
Geneva in collaboration with Geneva University Hospitals (Geneva,
Switzerland). Several languages are available: Albanian, Arabic, Dari, (simple)
English, Farsi, Spanish, Tigrinya, and Swiss-French sign language (LSF-CH)
(Strasly et al., 2018).

The BabelDr interface was initially unidirectional and designed only for the
translation of doctor's questions. Patients answered non-verbally using gestures (e.g., head movements for "yes" and "no"), facial expressions, etc.
However, to allow doctors to ask open questions (likely to be faster, less
restrictive, and more engaging), we have now designed a bidirectional interface
(Figure 5.2) by manually associating BabelDr sentences with pictographs
representing a range of possible responses for patients, for example, "burn,"
"sore throat," and "headache" pictographs in response to the question "Can you
show me why you have come here?" ("*Pouvez-vous me montrer ce qui vous
amène ?*").

The bidirectional interface includes two different views, one for the doctor
and one for the patient. The doctors' view allows doctors to speak or to search
for questions in a list, using keywords. When the doctor confirms the speech
recognition result (based on the back-translation produced by the system
(Spechbach et al., 2019)) or selects a sentence in the list, the system switches
to the patient view and speaks the question for the patient in the target language.
If desired, the patient can replay the spoken translation (or the video for the
LSF-CH version). The patient view presents a selection of clickable response
pictographs corresponding to the question, among which the patient can select
his or her answer. To help patients use this interface, several animated visual

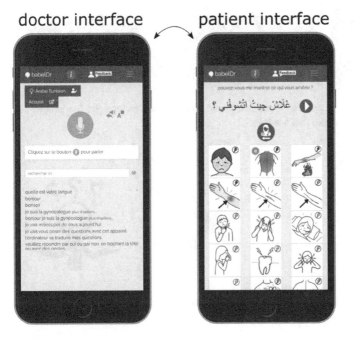

Figure 5.2 BabelDr bidirectional interface

hints are included. For example, the "Back" button is temporarily highlighted if
the patient does not click on it within a given time after selecting a response.
Once the patient has responded, the system switches back to the doctor view
and displays the selected response(s) in written form in French. If necessary, the
doctor can ask a new question to confirm the patient's answer. All questions and
answers are automatically recorded in a history of the dialogue that the doctor
can view at any time during the session or download as a pdf. The doctor can
also deactivate the bidirectional version if required.

The pictographs were selected from the two open-source sets, Arasaac and
Sclera, based on a previous study of comprehensibility in medical settings
(Norré et al., 2020, 2021). In Sclera, the pictographs are mainly black-and-
white and designed with few distracting details. As mentioned by Sevens
(2018), the "characters that are depicted on the pictographs do not present
a specific race, body type, age, or gender, thus referring to virtually any person
in the world," as compared with Arasaac pictographs, for which we had to
choose the gender of the character each time (Figure 5.3). The Arasaac pictographs provided by the Aragonese Portal of AAC are available in color and in

Figure 5.3 Examples of one Sclera and four Arasaac pictographs (no gender, female and male) for "headache"

Figure 5.4 Examples of Arasaac pictographs for "yes", "no" and "I don't understand" in BabelDr

black-and-white. They are often more detailed and there are sometimes several variations for the same concept.

In the previous study on comprehensibility, we concluded that neither set is superior for all question types (Norré et al., 2020, 2021). For closed questions, we used the Arasaac "yes" and "no" pictographs (Figure 5.4), which had obtained a higher comprehension score (78.3%) than those in Sclera (50%). In the medical context, the Sclera pictographs for "yes" and "no" are not appropriate, as they combine the representation of a yes/no movement and a happy/not happy face (mouth pulled down/up). If the doctor asks: "Do you have pain in the abdomen?" ("*Avez-vous mal au ventre ?*"), the happy face of the "yes" pictograph can be confusing. For all interactions (including introductory phrases such as "Hello, I am the doctor" or "I will take care of you today"), questions and patient instructions, we included the Arasaac "I don't understand" pictograph (Figure 5.4). We used Sclera pictographs for questions related to the pain description because they appear to be less problematic in our context.

We have noted various comprehension issues. In Arasaac, for instance, a given pictograph often represents several concepts. For example, a specific type of pain (burn, etc.) is always depicted on a certain part of the body (arm, etc.), so that the relevant pictograph conveys both "burn" and "arm". (Linguistically, the combination might be expressed in a prepositional phrase, e.g., "burn on the/your arm"). The problem is that, in response to open questions such as "Can you describe your pain?", patients might not choose that pictograph if they have a burn elsewhere than pictured (or, conversely, if their arm hurts, but it is not a burn). There are no pictographs representing a burn in all possible places (and in fact the medical coverage of this set is limited overall). In the Sclera set, the type of pain is represented by a grimacing and identical character with a specific symbol ("fire", "hammer") for the symptom always located in the stomach area (Figure 5.5).

Additionally, the first Arasaac pictographs always used the same symbol to categorize pictographs related to health (a red cross) or pain description (a red lightning bolt) (Figures 5.5 and 5.6). In the preliminary study, these were often shown to be sources of ambiguity. When we asked the participants what the "chest pain" pictograph meant, they often gave the interpretation "I have electricity in my chest" (Figure 5.6). Even so, we can hope that, in the medical context, patients might after all infer that the lightning probably means "pain" rather than "electricity".

In any case, to improve the coverage of patient responses in BabelDr, we created and adapted some Arasaac pictographs, for example, those that were

Figure 5.5 Examples of Sclera for pain description: "burning pain", "throbbing pain", and of Arasaac pictographs for "burn" and "cut"

Figure 5.6 Arasaac pictograph for "chest pain" and pictographs that we created or adapted for "Syria", "left ear" and "five glasses"

missing for some countries. The patient can choose from 61 countries; between a right ear and a left ear for the question "In which ear do you hear less well?"; and between one or more glasses/bottles of wine for the question "How many glasses of alcohol do you drink per day?", etc. (Figure 5.6).

One aim of BabelDr is to make its content easily expandable – first, to adapt to new health situations or demographics, but also to carry out experiments with various tool configurations for research purposes. An online interface allows developers to upload pictographs; define their corresponding (French) written forms, that is, the responses to be displayed for doctors; and finally link these pictographs to BabelDr questions, as shown in Figure 5.7. This interface enables easy integration of various sets of pictographs into the system, depending on needs, and enables direct evaluation of tasks, as proposed in these experiments. To aid linkage of the BabelDr sentences with pictographs, we manually categorized each BabelDr sentence according to the type of response expected by the doctor, for example, yes/no, pain description, cause and location of pain (e.g., activity, human body), time of day, ways to take medication, food, positions and movements, sports, countries and languages, colors, animals, professions, etc. Some pictographs were used for many questions. In total, BabelDr now includes approximately 395 unique pictographs that we sometimes had to rename to make them understandable in the context of the doctor's dialogue history. On average, each question is associated with twenty pictographs (not including yes/no questions with three possible responses or input fields with only one possible response). The maximum number of pictographs per question is sixty-one for questions related to countries (such as "Have you traveled recently?").

5.4 Usability of the Bidirectional Version of BabelDr

The usability of the bidirectional version of BabelDr was evaluated in two different studies. The first aimed at comparing patient satisfaction with the unidirectional and bidirectional versions, while the second focused on pictograph usability in the medical context.

5.4.1 Patient Satisfaction

5.4.1.1 Design

The first study aimed to compare patient satisfaction among foreign-speaking patients with the unidirectional as compared with the bidirectional version of BabelDr. The study was conducted online during the period of the COVID-19 epidemic in August and September 2020. In

Figure 5.7 BabelDr response editor

these user tests, twelve Arabic-speaking participants were asked to answer 50 medical questions with the two BabelDr interfaces via the Zoom video conferencing tool. Questions included 36% of the yes-no questions and 64% of the open questions about COVID-19 and the patient's history. Patients received task instructions via email. For the bidirectional part, they had to respond by clicking on one or more pictographs relevant to the context of the question. For the unidirectional part, they did not have access to pictographs, and thus had to find the best way to respond without speaking, for example, using gestures or facial expressions.

At the end of each user test, patients had to complete a satisfaction questionnaire, which consisted of a total of twenty items (ten for each type of interface). Items were derived from the System Usability Scale (SUS) questionnaire by Brooke (1996) and adapted to the functionalities of BabelDr. A 5-point Likert scale ("strongly disagree", "disagree", "neutral", "agree", and "strongly agree") was used to rate agreement with items. Patients were also asked to indicate which version they preferred.

Participants were recruited on social networks in groups linked to refugees in Belgium, charitable associations, or academic groups. In total, twelve people tested the system, including eleven males living in Belgium and one female in France. The inclusion condition for all participants was Arabic as mother tongue.

5.4.1.2 Results

During the entire experiment, patients selected more than 200 pictographs, of which 81 were unique. Figure 5.8 summarizes the results of the SUS test. Overall, the results of the satisfaction questionnaire were very positive (no one strongly disagreed with the various statements, such as "The system was easy to use"), with most participants agreeing or strongly agreeing with most statements, for both interfaces, unidirectional (without pictographs) and bidirectional (with pictographs).

We calculated averages of scores by item (0: no response, 1: strongly disagree, 2: disagree, 3: neutral, 4: agree, 5: strongly agree). To produce an overall score on a range of 0 to 100 for each system following the SUS approach, we summed the score contributions from the 10 items (see Table 5.1 for scores by item) and multiplied the result by two. The two systems are very close, achieving overall scores of 85.1 and 86.2 for unidirectional and bidirectional, respectively.

All patients found both versions of the system easy to use, with a slightly higher score for the bidirectional version (Q1), and felt the system enabled

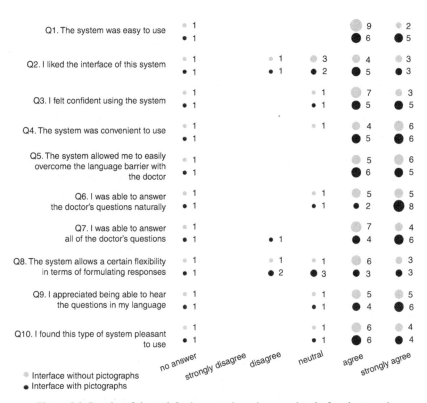

Figure 5.8 Results of the satisfaction questionnaire completed after the experiment for the interface without pictographs and the interface with pictographs. Numbers on the right side of the circles represent the number of patients (n=12)

them to easily overcome the language barrier with the doctor (Q5). They also felt more confident using the bidirectional version (Q3). The system was judged convenient to use (Q4), even though it was tested remotely via videoconference. The statements concerning appreciation of the interface (Q2) and flexibility for formulating responses (Q8) received slightly more mixed opinions than the others (Figure 5.8). Thus there seems to be room for improvement, even though the bidirectional interface allowed the clear majority (8 "strongly agree") to answer doctors' questions more naturally (Q6). Surprisingly, all patients ("strongly") agreed that they were able to answer all of the doctor's questions even with the unidirectional version (Q7), although in fact they actually did not respond to all the questions. We conclude that the results for the assessment of the text-to-speech (Q9) and the complete system (Q10) are similar for both interfaces.

Table 5.1 *Results (/5) of the satisfaction questionnaire for the unidirectional and bidirectional interfaces (n=11). Standard deviation is given in brackets.*

	Q1	Q2	Q3	Q4	Q5	Q6	Q7	Q8	Q9	Q10
Uni	4.2 (0.4)	3.8 (1.0)	4.2 (0.6)	4.5 (0.7)	4.5 (0.5)	4.4 (0.7)	4.4 (0.5)	4.0 (0.9)	4.4 (0.7)	4.3 (0.6)
Bidi	4.5 (0.5)	3.9 (0.9)	4.4 (0.7)	4.5 (0.5)	4.5 (0.5)	4.6 (0.7)	4.4 (0.9)	3.6 (1.1)	4.5 (0.7)	4.3 (0.6)

Of the twelve participants, almost all (n=10) preferred the bidirectional version, except one who preferred the interface without pictographs and one who did not answer. We received several comments highlighting the advantages of the bidirectional version: "It makes it easier for the person to answer and communicate" (translated from: "تسهل على الشخص الاجابة و التواصل"); "It makes it easier to clarify the problem, because we can show exactly where the pain is for example" (translated from: "*Parce que on peut montrer exactement où se trouve la douleur par exemple*"); "Photos make the expression easier in order to answer the questions better!" or "I found it better and useful for people". We received no comments about the interface without pictographs.

5.4.2 Pictograph Usability

5.4.2.1 Design

In the second study, we looked at the usability of the pictographs in the medical context, with a focus on: 1) their comprehensibility; and 2) for each question, how the number and order of pictographic response choices affect users' (a) ability to correctly find predefined responses and (b) response time. Our hypotheses are the following:

- responses to questions (including, for example, symptoms, actions, or pain descriptions) can be illustrated understandably using pictographs;
- including more response choices per question will lead to longer response times and/or more errors;
- the order in which the pictographic responses are presented will affect the selection.

For this experiment, we created a customized version of the bidirectional BabelDr system showing only the patient view. Participants were presented with a doctor's questions in French, accompanied by French audio produced by speech synthesis (and replayable at will), and the French written form of the "correct" response that should be chosen among the proposed response pictographs (e.g., headache). The French form was the official name of the pictographs (i.e., filenames in the Sclera and Arasaac sets). Participants were allowed to select only one response per question. The system logged the selected responses, as well as the response time for each question – the time between presentation of the question with its response choices and the validation of the response by the user. Figure 5.9 shows an example of the interface.

The study included six questions: three open questions repeated twice, with different correct responses. A closed question ("Do you understand what I am saying to you?") was used to introduce the test interface and response mechanism. This was followed by a question asking users to select from a list the languages with which they were familiar. These two questions were not counted in the results.

We used a between-subjects study design, in which each participant answered the same six question/response combinations in one of three different versions of the test. The versions were created by varying the number of response choices shown to the participant (five, ten, or fifteen) for each of the doctor's questions (Table 5.2), with each version including two questions with five choices, two with 10, and two with 15. In addition, the position (at the beginning, in the middle or at the end) of the correct response (in bold in Table 5.2) was automatically randomized for each participant.

The correct responses are presented in Figure 5.10. We used Arasaac (for Q1, Q3, Q4, Q6) and Sclera (Q2, Q5) pictographs in black-and-white. In addition,

Figure 5.9 Example of the evaluation interface showing the patient's view of the bidirectional version of BabelDr, with an additional text field (green background) to display the "correct" response to select, here "headache" ("mal de tête")

Table 5.2 *Question and response choices. The responses are given using the names of the Arasaac and Sclera pictographs*

	Can you show me what's going on? (Q1|Q4)	Can you describe your pain? (Q2|Q5)	Show me the movements that make the pain worse (Q3|Q6)
5 responses	**Fall, headache,** I don't know, injection, visit	Burning pain, I don't know, **nagging pain, pain radiating,** prickling pain	Eat, **go to sleep,** I don't know, **lean,** sit on the toilet
10 responses	5 Previous responses + blow the nose, cough, fever, shivery, sore throat	5 Previous responses + cramping pain, pain insensitively, pain numbness, pain pressure, throbbing pain	5 Previous responses + drink, get out of bed, sit on the chair, sleep, stand up from chair
15 responses	10 Previous responses + heart attack, hot, rehabilitation specialist, stomach ache, vomit	10 Previous responses + brief pain, little pain, pain always, pain sometimes, pressing pain	10 Previous responses + pick up, run, sport, urinate, work out

Figure 5.10 Correct pictographs for "headache" (Q1), "fall" (Q4), "nagging pain" (Q2), "pain radiating" (Q5), "lean" (Q3) and "go to sleep" (Q6)

the "I don't understand" pictograph was always presented as a response option, positioned after all the other pictographs.

The participants received a link, which brought them to one of the three versions of the test. No instructions were given regarding the device used to complete the task and users were free to use a desktop, mobile phone, or tablet. The user agent was also stored in the logs.

Forty-five participants were recruited among Master-level students at the Faculty of Translation at the University of Geneva. All have French as a working language, but not all are native French speakers. This roster allowed us to collect fifteen responses for each of the test versions.

5.4.2.2 Results

5.4.2.2.1 Comprehensibility of Pictographs Table 5.3 shows the number of correct pictograph selections for each question and the number of response choices. The proportion of correct responses by question varied between 2% and 91%, thus suggesting large differences in the difficulty of the questions and/ or complexity of the response pictographs. According to Goodman and Kruskal's lambda, there is an association between the question (Q1–Q6) and correctness (λ = 0.268). We observed that the pain description questions (Q2 and Q5) obtained far fewer correct responses, suggesting either that the corresponding pictographs are less comprehensible, or that the pain qualifiers used to provide the written form of the "correct" response are more complex or difficult to understand for non-native French speakers.

5.4.2.2.2 Impact of the Number and Order of Pictographic Response Choices Looking at the combined results for all questions (see last column of Table 5.3), we observe that when the number of presented response choices is increased, the proportion of correct responses decreases. Although this is not the case for all of the individual questions, this tendency does suggest that increasing the number of response choices makes it harder for users to find the correct one.

The second variable analyzed is response time. Table 5.4 shows the median response time by question after removal of outliers.[1] We observe that the response time strongly varies between questions, with median response times

Table 5.3 *Correct responses by question and number of available response choices*

Response choices	Q1	Q2	Q3	Q4	Q5	Q6	all
5	14 (93%)	1 (7%)	14 (93%)	15 (100%)	10 (67%)	13 (87%)	67 (74%)
10	14 (93%)	0 (0%)	11 (73%)	15 (100%)	8 (53%)	13 (87%)	61 (68%)
15	13 (87%)	0 (0%)	10 (67%)	11 (73%)	9 (60%)	14 (93%)	57 (63%)
combined	41 (91%)	1 (2%)	35 (78%)	41 (91%)	27 (60%)	40 (89%)	185 (69%)

---

[1] The median time per question was 11.800ms, with eight very high values where participants took more than one minute to answer a single question. As the experiment was not carried out under controlled conditions, participants may have been distracted by influences external to the task. We have therefore excluded these eight extreme values from our analysis.

Table 5.4 *Median response time by question*

Question	Q1	Q2	Q3	Q4	Q5	Q6
Median response time [ms]	11,760	20,127	16,386	6673	10,360	7920

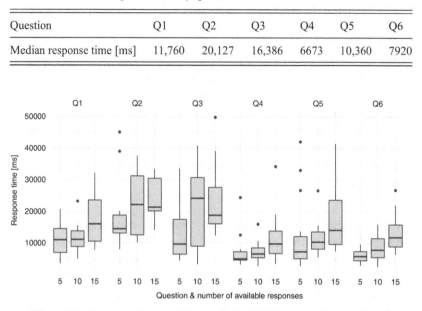

Figure 5.11 Response time in milliseconds for Q1-Q6, grouped by number of responses presented

ranging from 6 to 20 seconds. Moreover, response times are not normally distributed (Shapiro-Wilk test, p<0.01). A Kruskal-Wallis test showed that the question has a relatively strong, significant effect on the response time (X^2(5, N=262) =71.89; p<0.001; ε^2=0.275).

As illustrated in Figure 5.11, response times are also influenced by the number of response pictographs presented: for most questions, the response time increases with the number of pictographs among which the participant had to find the correct response. The computation of Kendall's Tau (τ=0.293) confirms that there is a medium-to-strong association between response time and the number of pictographs.

Regarding the order in which pictograph response choices are presented, in particular the position of the correct pictograph among the choices, we observed no impact on the correctness of the response according to Goodman and Kruskal's lambda (λ = 0.05). Response times appear equally unaffected, with median response times of 11,926, 11,152, and 10,410 milliseconds for correct pictographs positioned respectively at the beginning, middle, or end of the available choices. A Kruskal-Wallis test showed that the effect of the order on the response time is not significant (X^2(2, N=262)=0.192; p=0.908; ε^2=0.0007).

These results suggest that participants will look at all proposed options, even if they have already found a matching pictograph.

Finally, regarding the device used, seven of the forty-five participants completed the test on a mobile device, while the others used a desktop. The type of device did not have an impact on the correct selection of responses (Phi coefficient = -0.04).

5.5 Conclusion

To sum up, we assess the potential of using pictographs for medical dialogue and demonstrate the importance of evaluating their comprehensibility in a real context. We present two studies focused on the BabelDr system, a speech-enabled phraselator used to improve communication between doctors and allophone patients in emergency settings. The first study compared patient satisfaction with the bidirectional and unidirectional versions of BabelDr. Findings show that both versions are easy and convenient to use, even remotely, although most respondents prefer to use the interface with pictographs.

The second study aimed to evaluate the pictographs' usability in context. In a customized version of the bidirectional BabelDr system showing only the patient view, participants were presented with a doctor's question in French; a set of pictographic response choices; and the written form of the "correct" response that they should select. Results show that the pictographs are not equally comprehensible and that some – in particular, those used to describe pain types – present considerable difficulties, with as few as 2% of participants identifying the correct one. Regarding the number of pictographs presented, we observe that an increased number of response choices negatively affects participant's ability to select the correct answer and increases response time, thereby confirming our second hypothesis. Finally, regarding our third hypothesis, results do not show a notable impact of the order in which the pictographic responses are presented. Overall, this experiment has shown that multiple factors influence participants' ability to find a pictograph based on a written form, but that the comprehensibility of the individual pictographs is probably the most important.

These studies have some limitations. First, participants were not real patients in emergency situations, so factors such as stress or time constraints could not be considered. Second, we evaluated only a subset of the diagnostic questions available in BabelDr, with response pictographs extracted from only two open-source sets designed for AAC. A more extensive study using other pictograph sets, for example, domain-specific pictographs or illustrations aimed at different target audiences, would further our understanding of usability in this context. It would also be worthwhile to investigate whether the available pictographs cover all the symptoms and reasons for seeking consultation necessary for diagnosis in emergency settings.

Many studies have evaluated the usability of pictographs in the medical domain. However, to the best of our knowledge, our work contributes novel insights by focusing on the use of pictographs for diagnosis in a real-life system setting. Due to its flexible architecture, the BabelDr system is well suited to facilitate evaluation of various pictograph sets in a concrete and task-oriented manner. As an additional advantage of performing such evaluation directly in a medical translation tool, we can target varied language groups, such as the simulated CALD population of our first study.

5.6 Acknowledgments

This work is part of the PROPICTO project, funded by the Fonds National Suisse (N°197864) and the Agence Nationale de la Recherche (ANR-20-CE93-0005). The pictographs used are the property of the Government of Aragón, which distributes them under a Creative Commons License (BY-NC-SA), and have been created by Sergio Palao for Arasaac (http://arasaac.org). The other pictographs used are the property of Sclera vzw (www.sclera.be/), which distributes them under a Creative Commons License 2.0.

References

Alvarez, J. 2014. "Visual Design: A Step Towards Multicultural Health Care," *Arch Argent Pediatr*, 112 (1) pages 33–40.

Bandeira, F. M., Faria, F. P. D., and Araujo, E. B. D. 2011. "Quality Assessment of Inhospital Patients Unable to Speak Who Use Alternative and Extended Communication." In *Einstein*, São Paulo, 9, pages 477–482.

Beukelman, D. R., and Mirenda, P. 1998. *Augmentative and Alternative Communication*. Baltimore: Paul H. Brookes.

Bouillon, P., Gerlach, J., Mutal, J. D., Tsourakis, N., and Spechbach, H. 2021. "A Speech-Enabled Fixed-Phrase Translator for Healthcare Accessibility." In *Proceedings of the 1st Workshop on NLP for Positive Impact*. Association for Computational Linguistics.

Bouillon, P., Gerlach, J., Spechbach, H., Tsourakis, N., and Halimi, S. 2017. "BabelDr vs Google Translate: A user study at Geneva University Hospitals (HUG)." In *Proceedings of the 20th Annual Conference of the EAMT*, Prague, Czech Republic.

Boujon, V., Bouillon, P., Spechbach, H., Gerlach, J., and Strasly, I. 2018. "Can Speech-Enabled Phraselators Improve Healthcare Accessibility? A Case Study Comparing BabelDr with MediBabble for Anamnesis in Emergency Settings." In *Proceedings of the 1st Swiss Conference on Barrier-free Communication (BfC)*, Winterthur, Switzerland.

Brooke, J. 1996. "SUS: A Quick Dirty Usability Scale," *Usability Evaluation in Industry.* 189 (3), pages 189–194.

Cataix-Nègre, E. 2017. *Communiquer autrement. Accompagner les personnes avec des troubles de la parole ou du langage : Les communications alternatives.* De Boeck Superieur.

Christensen, C., D. Redd, E. Lake, et al. 2017. "Doodle Health: A Crowdsourcing Game for the Co-design and Testing of Pictographs to Reduce Disparities in Healthcare Communication." In *AMIA Annual Symposium Proceedings.* American Medical Informatics Association, 585–594.

Eadie, K., Carlyon, M. J., Stephens, J., and Wilson, M. D. 2013. "Communicating in the Pre-Hospital Emergency Environment," *Australian Health Review*, 37 (2) pages 140–146.

Flores, G., Laws, M. B., Mayo, S. J., et al. 2003. "Errors in Medical Interpretation and Their Potential Clinical Consequences in Pediatric Encounters," *Pediatrics*, 111 (1) pages 6–14.

Halimi, S.A, Azari, R., Bouillon, P., and Spechbach, H. 2021. "A Corpus-Based Analysis of Medical Communication: Euphemism As a Communication Strategy for Context-Specific Responses." In *Corpus Exploration of Lexis and Discourse in Translation.* Routledge, 1–25.

Hill, B., Perri-Moore, S., Kuang, J., et al. 2016. "Automated Pictographic Illustration of Discharge Instructions with Glyph: Impact on Patient Recall and Satisfaction," *Journal of the American Medical Informatics Association*, 23 (6), 1136–1142.

Houts, P. S., Doak, C. C., Doak, L. G., and Loscalzo, M. J. 2006. "The Role of Pictures in Improving Health Communication: A Review of Research on Attention, Comprehension, Recall, and Adherence," *Patient education and counseling*, 61 (2),173–190.

Ji, M., Sørensen, K., and Bouillon, P. 2020. "User-Oriented Healthcare Translation and Communication." In *The Oxford Handbook of Translation and Social Practices.* Oxford University Press.

Kassam, R., Vaillancourt, R., and Collins, John B. 2004. "Pictographic Instructions for Medications: Do Different Cultures Interpret Them Accurately?" *International Journal of Pharmacy Practice*, 12(4),199–209.

Katz, M. G., Kripalani, S., and Weiss, B. D. 2006. "Use of Pictorial Aids in Medication Instructions: A Review of the Literature," *American Journal of Health-System Pharmacy*, 63(23), 2391–2397.

Khander, A., Farag, S., and Chen, K. T. 2018. "Identification and Evaluation of Medical Translator Mobile Applications Using an Adapted APPLICATIONS Scoring System," *Telemedicine and e-Health*, 24(8), 594–603.

Kerremans, K., De Ryck, L. P., De Tobel, V., et al. 2018. "Bridging the Communication Gap in Multilingual Service Encounters: A Brussels Case Study," *The European Legacy*, 23(7–8), 757–772.

Kim, H., Nakamura, C., and Zeng-Treitler, Q. 2009. "Assessment of Pictographs Developed Through a Participatory Design Process Using an Online Survey Tool," *Journal of Medical Internet Research*, 11(1), e5.

Lamy, J. B., Duclos, C., Bar-Hen, A., Ouvrard, P., and Venot, A. 2008. "An Iconic Language for the Graphical Representation of Medical Concepts," *BMC Medical Informatics and Decision Making*, 8(1), 16.

Meischke, H. W., Calhoun, R. E., Yip, M. P., Tu, S. P., and Painter, I. S. 2013. "The Effect of Language Barriers on Dispatching EMS Response," *Prehospital Emergency Care*, 17(4), 475.

Mutal, J. D., Bouillon, P., Gerlach, J., Estrella, P., and Spechbach, H. 2019. "Monolingual Backtranslation in a Medical Speech Translation System For Diagnostic Interviews: A NMT Approach." In *Proceedings of Machine Translation Summit XVII: Translator, Project and User Tracks*, 196–203.

Norré, M., Bouillon, P., Gerlach, J., and Spechbach, H. 2021. "Evaluating the Comprehension of Arasaac and Sclera Pictographs for the BabelDr Patient Response Interface." In *Proceedings of the 3rd Swiss Conference on Barrier-free Communication (BfC)*. ZHAW.

Norré, M., Bouillon, P., Gerlach, J., and Spechbach, H. 2020. Évaluation de la compréhension de pictogrammes Arasaac et Sclera pour améliorer l'accessibilité du système de traduction médicale BabelDr. Handicap 2020: Technologies pour l'autonomie et l'inclusion, 177–182.

Panayiotou, A., Gardner, A., Williams, S., et al. 2019. "Language Translation Apps in Health Care Settings: Expert Opinion," *JMIR Mhealth Uhealth*, 7(4):e11316.

Paolieri, D., and Marful, A. 2018. "Norms for a Pictographic System: The Aragonese Portal of Augmentative/Alternative Communication (ARASAAC) System," *Frontiers in Psychology*, 2538.

Seligman, M., and Dillinger, M. 2013. "Automatic Speech Translation for Healthcare: Some Internet and Interface Aspects." In *Proceedings of 10th International Conference on Terminology and Artificial Intelligence (TIA-13)*, Paris, France.

Sevens, L. 2018. *Words Divide, Pictographs Unite: Pictograph Communication Technologies for People with an Intellectual Disability*. Thesis, Katholieke Universiteit Leuven, Belgium.

Somers, H. 2007. "Theoretical and Methodological Issues Regarding the Use of Language Technologies for Patients with Limited English Proficiency." In *Proceedings of the 11th International Conference on Theoretical and Methodological Issues in Machine Translation (TMI-07)*, Skövde, 206–213.

Spechbach, H., Gerlach, J., Karker, S. M., et al. 2019. "A Speech-Enabled Fixed-Phrase Translator for Emergency Settings: Crossover Study," *JMIR Medical Informatics*, 7 (2), e13167.

Strasly, I., Sebaï, T., Rigot, E., et al. 2018. "Le projet BabelDr : rendre les informations médicales accessibles en Langue des Signes de Suisse Romande (LSF-SR)." In *Proceedings of the 2nd Swiss Conference on Barrier-free Communication*, Geneva, Switzerland, 92–96.

Turner, A. M., Choi, Y. K., Dew, K., et al. 2019. "Evaluating the Usefulness of Translation Technologies for Emergency Response Communication: A Scenario-Based Study," *JMIR Public Health and Surveillance*, 5(1), e11171.

Vandeghinste, V., and Schuurman, I. 2014. "Linking Pictographs to Synsets: Sclera2Cornetto." In *Proceedings of the Ninth International Conference on Language Resources and Evaluation (LREC 14)*. ELRA, Paris, 3404–3410.

Vaschalde, C., Trial, P., Esperança-Rodier, E., Schwab, D., and Lecouteux, B. 2018. "Automatic Pictogram Generation from Speech to Help the Implementation of a Mediated Communication." In *Proceedings of the 2nd Swiss Conference on Barrier-free Communication*, Geneva, Switzerland, 97–101.

Vaz, I. 2013. "Visual Symbols in Healthcare Settings for Children with Learning Disabilities and Autism Spectrum Disorder." *British Journal of Nursing*, 22 (3),156–159.

Wołk, K., Wołk, A., and Glinkowski, W. 2017. "A Cross-Lingual Mobile Medical Communication System Prototype for Foreigners and Subjects with Speech, Hearing, and Mental Disabilities Based on Pictograms," *Computational and Mathematical Methods in Medicine*. DOI: 10.1155/2017/4306416.

Yu, B., Willis, M., Sun, P., and Wang, J. 2013. "Crowdsourcing Participatory Evaluation of Medical Pictograms Using Amazon Mechanical Turk," *Journal of Medical Internet Research*, 15(6), e2513.

Zeng-Treitler, Q., Perri, S., Nakamura, C., et al. 2014. "Evaluation of a Pictograph Enhancement System for Patient Instruction: A Recall Study," *Journal of the American Medical Informatics Association*, *21*(6), 1026–1031.

6

Healthcare Accessibility for the Deaf

The BabelDr Case Study

WITH CONTRIBUTIONS FROM IRENE STRASLY, PIERRETTE
BOUILLON, BASTIEN DAVID[1]
AND HERVE SPECHBACH[2]

[1] *University of Geneva, Faculty of Translation
and Interpreting, Geneva, Switzerland*
[2] *Geneva University Hospitals, Emergency Unit, Geneva,
Switzerland*

Access to healthcare profoundly impacts the health and quality of life of Deaf people. Automatic translation tools are crucial in improving communication between Deaf patients and their healthcare providers. The aim of this chapter is to present the pipeline used to create the Swiss-French Sign Language (LSF-CH) version of BabelDr, a speech-enabled fixed-phrase translator that was initially conceived to improve communication in emergency settings between doctors and allophone patients (Bouillon et al, 2021). In order to do so, we start off by explaining how we ported BabelDr in LSF-CH using both human and avatar videos. We first describe the creation of a reference corpus consisting of video translations done by human translators, then we present a second corpus of videos generated with a virtual human. Finally, we relate the findings of a questionnaire on Deaf users' perspective on the use of signing avatars in the medical context. We showed that, although respondents prefer human videos, the use of automatic technologies associated with virtual characters is not without interest to the target audience and can be useful to them in the medical context.

6.1 Introduction

According to the Swiss Federal Statistical Office, 9 percent of the population speaks a language not among the four national languages. Moreover, one-third of this 9 percent understands none of the national languages. If these people are ill and require treatment, language barriers can pose considerable obstacles to their care, from both clinical and ethical viewpoints. Clearly, this issue hugely impacts equal access to healthcare (Flores et al., 2003; Wasserman et al., 2014). One way to provide quality healthcare to all and to facilitate communication between doctors and patients is through the use of translation technologies – more specifically, by using fixed-phrase translators, now widely used in the medical field (see Chapter 5). Although ideal tools would provide the flexibility of full machine translation systems, various studies show that the fixed-phrase translation systems currently available can offer good alternatives to full machine translation for such safety-critical domains (Bouillon et al., 2017; Turner et al., 2019).

BabelDr is a flexible speech-enabled phraselator aimed at language barrier-related problems in emergency settings (Bouillon et al., 2021). BableDr is now in use for immigrants speaking non-national languages; however, the application is also under development at present for the local Deaf linguistic minority. We refer here to Deaf patients who live in the French-speaking area of Switzerland and use Swiss-French Sign Language (LSF-CH) as their mother tongue or preferred language. Deaf LSF-CH users identify as members of a minority community with its own language and culture (Padden and Humphries, 1988; Preston, 1995). The use of the capital D in "Deaf" refers to their cultural identity.

Research in past years has shown that access to healthcare impacts the health and quality of life of Deaf people. Although the need for enhanced access to healthcare services has been highlighted (Emond et al., 2015; Kuenburg et al., 2016), the issue remains quite challenging, even in high-income countries (Pollard et al., 2014; Smeijers and Pfau, 2009). Much like ethnic minority groups, Deaf people encounter severe barriers when trying to communicate in a healthcare context. The associated miscommunication between patients and their healthcare providers can lead to potential misunderstandings of diagnosis and treatment (Scheier, 2009) and to a lack of trust. In England, a report by the Royal National Institute for Deaf People recounts the experiences of various Deaf people using health services. Sixty-six percent of British Sign Language users find communication with staff difficult; thirty percent avoid visiting their family doctor for communication reasons; and 33 percent remain unsure about instructions or about the correct treatment following consultations with family doctors (Abou-Abdallah and Lamyman, 2021; Middleton et al., 2010). Similar results have been shown in the Netherlands, where a study found that 39 percent of Deaf patients who took part in the survey rated their communication with healthcare practitioners as moderate or bad (Smeijers and Pfau, 2009), and in the USA where Deaf patients report great difficulties in communication with their physicians (Ralston, Zazove and Gorenflo, 1996). In Switzerland, studies carried out by Tatjana Binggeli in 2015 and by Odile Cantero in 2016 also highlight similar barriers (Binggeli, 2015; Cantero, 2016). While additional projects have addressed the healthcare needs of Deaf people in Switzerland, communication barriers still remain today (Strasly, in preparation).

Improvements are certainly achievable. For instance, provision of specific training in cultural competency by knowledgeable community representatives could make healthcare professionals more aware of their communication preferences. In recent years, rapid advances in the use and performance of information technology have also greatly benefited Deaf people, and have the potential to make healthcare more accessible to this community and thus enable them to receive adequate and equal care. The aim of this chapter is to focus on the development of speech-enabled fixed-phrase translators for sign languages and, more specifically, to present the pipeline used to create the LSF-CH version of the BabelDr system. While phraselators such as MediBabble (medibabble.com) and Universal Doctor (universaldoctor.com) are commonly used in medicine (Khander et al., 2018; Panayiotou et al., 2019), they rarely integrate sign language. Development of such a pipeline is therefore a necessary step toward collection of corpora and creation of useful translation tools.

In the following sections, we first give an outline of the current legal framework regarding the right to health and access to healthcare in Switzerland in order to elucidate the legal background favorable to our project's emergence. A brief overview of the core principles of the "right to health" follows. We then describe existing sign language projects aimed at improving doctor-patient communication. While some translation tools do exist, they are always limited to very specific coverage, are often unsophisticated, and provide no general solutions for production of sign language resources and translation into sign language. We then explain how we ported BabelDr for LSF-CH using both human and avatar videos. Finally, we present the results of a questionnaire about Deaf users' perspective on the use of signing avatars in the medical context.

6.2 Legal Framework in Switzerland

Currently, there are no precise or official statistics concerning the number of profoundly Deaf individuals in Switzerland. Current estimates are based on the following formula, established by the World Health Organization (WHO) and used worldwide: number of Deaf signing people = 0.001 percent of the total population, i.e., 1 per 1000 inhabitants. Based upon this formula, and upon the numbers of (1) memberships of Deaf people in clubs and associations and (2) users of interpreting services, Deaf sign language users in all of Switzerland currently number approximately 10,000 people (Braem and Rathmann, 2010). Three different sign languages are used: Swiss-German Sign Language (DSGS) is used in the German-speaking area of Switzerland; LSF-CH in western Switzerland; and Swiss-Italian Sign Language (LIS-SI) in the Italian-speaking region.

Each region formerly had its own association of Deaf people. These were then federated in 2006 under an umbrella organization, the Swiss Federation of the Deaf, which strives to achieve equal rights for the Deaf and hard-of-hearing throughout the country. Per its new strategic plan for 2021–25, the Federation will undertake four key areas of action, as voted by members in October 2020: (1) inclusion in the labor market; (2) participation in direct democracy; (3) access to the healthcare system; and (4) inclusive education (SGB-FSS, 2021). Concerning access to the healthcare system, discrimination against Deaf people is not due to a lack of legislation (Binggeli and Hohenstein, 2020). In fact, Switzerland has signed international treaties and has enacted national and cantonal legislation that promotes the highest health standards for its population. Instead, the challenges probably stem from the country's federal makeup (Marks-Sultan et al., 2016). There are twenty-six cantons in the Swiss Confederation, each with its own constitution, legislature, executive, and judiciary. Where health is concerned, Switzerland has a two-tier system built on the federal constitution and cantonal legislation, giving cantons the largest share of responsibilities. Cantons implement regulations in areas where the Federal State has adopted laws, but can also adopt their own health policies, laws, and regulations.

6.2.1 Overview of the Core Principles of the Right to Health

The right to health means that States must establish ethically and culturally suitable policies that address local needs, as well as plans for measures and resources for promotion of national health according to their individual capacities. Two principles that are key to this right are non-discrimination and equality. States must recognize and provide for groups having specific needs and generally facing health-related challenges. And since Deaf people are particularly vulnerable in terms of health, access to care is a major topic of discussion in the local Deaf community.

At the international level, the right to health was first recognized in the Preamble of the Constitution of the WHO in 1946 (WHO, 1948). Because this treaty is binding for Switzerland as a Member State, the country should ensure maximum health for its population by protecting and promoting appropriate measures. According to WHO (WHO, 1948, Preambule, §2), health is "a state of complete physical, mental and social well-being and not merely the absence of disease or infirmity". The right to health is also recognized in the Universal Declaration of Human Rights of 1948, in Article 25, which states that "[e]veryone has the right to a standard of living adequate for the health and well-being of himself and of his family, including food, clothing, housing and medical care [...]". States must take active measures to assure suitable quality of life for all their citizens. Adequate health is also defined in Article 12 of the International Covenant on Economic, Social and Cultural Rights (ICESC, 1976) as " ... the right of everyone to the enjoyment of the highest attainable standard of physical and mental health." This treaty was ratified by Switzerland in 1992.

At a national level, the 1999 Swiss Constitution is the most significant legal document. It views the right to health as a duty of the State (articles 41 and 118) and prohibits discrimination on the basis of origin, race, sex, age, language, social situation, way of life, religious, philosophical or political beliefs, or psychological and mental deficiencies (article 8). On January 1, 2004, the Disability Equality Act came into force at the federal level, stating that all disabled persons have the same right to barrier-free access to social services (article 2). However, French-speaking Switzerland currently lacks sign language interpreters. Thus the Deaf community's access to health services can be enhanced by tools that can effectively bridge the gap between the need for language services in healthcare contexts and their actual availability.

The United Nations has developed three key documents that frame the understanding and promotion of accessibility: the World Programme of Action concerning Disabled Persons; the United Nations Standard Rules on the Equalization of Opportunities for Persons with Disabilities; and the Convention on the Rights of Persons with Disabilities. These require governments and the international community to ensure equal rights and opportunities for persons with disabilities. Particular attention is paid to access – first, to information and communication, and second, to public services such as healthcare. Of the three documents listed above, the Convention on the Rights of Persons with Disabilities (UNCRPD) (United Nations, 2006) is particularly important. In this document, which entered into force in 2008, the international community undertook a political and legal commitment to include people with disabilities in all aspects of society. Article 25 of the UNCRPD states that "persons with disabilities have the right to enjoy the highest attainable standard of health and that States Parties have to take all appropriate measures to ensure access for persons with disabilities to health services." Switzerland ratified the UNCRPD on 15 April 2014, thus making the same commitment.

As we rely more on technologies, the impetus increases to build tools functional for Deaf sign language users to enhance their equal access to healthcare. Well-designed tools should have the potential to improve users' quality of life and independence. Accordingly, we have reviewed the legal framework and the potential impact of technology on Deaf people's access to healthcare to explain our decision to create a version of BabelDr for LSF-CH. We go on now to a general review of existing tools developed for hospitals, followed by a description of the BabelDr application for LSF-CH.

6.3 Sign Language Translation Tools for Hospitals

With increased mobility worldwide, an increasing number of patients require translation services in healthcare settings. In order to respond to this demand, many medical translation applications for mobile phones have been developed (Khander et al., 2018). However, resources for sign languages are still lacking, despite progress in machine translation and in automatic sign language processing, both in sign language recognition and sign language animation (Bragg et al., 2019; Ebling, 2017; Papastratis et al., 2021; Sáfár and Glauert, 2012).

Sites do exist that provide resources and popular explanations related to medical terminology for Deaf communities, such as Pisourd[1] in Switzerland or World Health Sign[2] (Spanish/Italian project). One famous project for the collection of medical terminology was developed in Australian Sign Language (Auslan): the Medical Signbank project[3]. In view of a perceived lack of health and medicine vocabulary, this project conducted linguistic research among Auslan users. The collected signs were made available on the Signbank site. Interpreters and the Deaf community could then provide feedback concerning them (Johnston and Napier, 2010).

Some text-to-sign phraselators using human-recorded videos also exist, but the number of sentences they translate is limited, and translation is often into American Sign Language (ASL) only. Moreover, the methodology used to produce sign language videos is often unclear, and information is often lacking concerning extension of the systems to other content or sharing of resources. In Europe, TraducMed[4], a French tool first used for the medical care of migrants, offers text-to-sign translation in LSF, to be used in medical practices or hospitals. More recently, at the Department of General Practice of the University Medical Center Göttingen, a multilingual application informing

---

[1] pisourd.ch/ [2] worldhealthsign.com/index.html [3] auslan.org.au/about/medicalsignbank/
[4] traducmed.fr/application/traduction/accordeon/langue/100

about COVID-19 vaccinations has been developed, aimed at vaccination candidates with limited proficiency in the local language. There are thirty-nine target languages, including a German Sign Language (DGS) module equipped with a set of videos (Noack et al., 2022).

Hybrid medical tools have also been developed for the medical sector that combine human-recorded videos and avatar generation. For example, in Romania, the Carol Davila University of Medicine and Pharmacy in Bucharest and the Faculty of Sociology in Pitesti, in collaboration with teachers of Romanian Sign Language (LSR), implemented a corpus of video recordings in LSR related to oral health. The corpus could also be augmented through online editing using the JASigning animated avatar (Chiriac et al., 2016). The team then worked on a comparative study of the two characters – human and avatar – with consideration of their advantages and disadvantages (Chiriac et al., 2015). A recent tool for medical use was built in the Netherlands (Roelofsen et al., 2021), where the research group conceived a modular text-to-sign system that allows healthcare professionals interactively translate from written Dutch or English into Dutch Sign Language (NGT). The doctor enters a sentence or series of words in the search bar. He/she then chooses the closest match found within a database of written sentences. The system then shows prepared signed videos, some using recordings of human interpreters and some using a synthetic sign language module employing the JASigning virtual avatar. The team selected the human-recorded or the avatar videos according to the complexity or topic of the questions. (For example, videos with human interpreters were used when questions on ethical issues were asked.) (Figure 6.1).

There are also tools that use sign language recognition to allow patients to answer. HospiSign, a Turkish interactive translation platform, was developed to assist Deaf patients in the hospital reception area on a daily basis (Süzgün et al., 2015). At the reception terminal, the HospiSign interface displays a written

Figure 6.1 Prototype of SignLab, Dutch Medical Application: human recording (left); avatar generation (right)

question with its corresponding video[5]. The lower part of the screen displays various possible answers. The Deaf patient or his or her caregiver reproduces the corresponding signs. (Sign recognition is handled by a Microsoft Kinect v2 sensor, which has been configured to follow and recognize the hand movements of users when they respond (Süzgün et al., 2015, p. 82).) He or she then moves on to the next question. Once all the questions have been answered, a summary report is provided to the doctor.

The last decade has seen growing interest in sign language translation systems that seek to empower Deaf people in hospital settings. However, prototypes remain limited to very specific domains. They offer only text interaction and provide no generic tools for developing sign language resources (Albrecht et al., 2015). It is sometimes unclear what methodology has been used to translate written sentences into sign language, and videos are rarely shared with the research community. And for LSF-CH in particular, there is no specific open-source tool for the medical sector apart from the above-mentioned Pisourd website. Clearly, then, new tools are sorely needed that can address the needs of Deaf patients and their caregivers to increase access to hospitals. In the following section, we present our approach to creation of speech-to-sign fixed-phrase translators with the BabelDr platform and to production of sharable resources in LSF.

6.4 BabelDr for Swiss-French Sign Language

In contrast with other fixed-phrase translators, BabelDr aims for easy portability to new domains and coverage: it should be possible to continually add new content. Adapting BabelDr to sign language therefore requires flexible solutions. Human videos recorded by sign language interpreters/translators are known to be ideal, but they pose many technical problems. In particular, they cannot be generated productively and cannot be changed once recorded. We therefore decided to combine human and avatar videos, as suggested by Roelofsen et al. (2021).

The translation of BabelDr content was carried out in two steps. First, a reference corpus consisting of video translations with human translators was created for a subset of sentences, in order to develop reference translations for many terms and typical structures. The first set of recorded videos was then annotated and used to develop a larger corpus of videos generated with a virtual human (an avatar). In the following sections, we explain (1) the methodology

---

[5] The Turkish Sign Language (TID) videos are from the medical corpus of the larger BosphorusSign corpus. (Camgöz et al., 2016)

used to film the human translations and (2) how the avatar version was generated and integrated into BabelDr to develop a flexible speech-to-sign translator.

6.4.1 Recording Translations with Deaf Experts

We used a community participatory approach to translate a first set of sentences from written French into LSF-CH. The team working on the translation is comprised of a Deaf nurse and two Deaf sign language specialists (both working as sign language teachers and translators). Also in the exchange group is a doctor currently doing a specialization in Switzerland who – together with a translation researcher (a co-author of this work) – organizes sign language courses in hospitals in French-speaking Switzerland. As of March 2022, 2,661 medical questions have been translated and validated (1,552 for the hospital reception unit, 1,063 in the field of abdominal pain, and 46 specific to COVID-19).

Three main challenges were encountered by the translation work group. 1) The translation of medical jargon. The use of specific terminology in the medical context is well known to be a source of serious misunderstandings in medicine (e.g., Ong et al., 1995). Translation problems are frequent even for widely used languages (Major, 2012). In the Deaf community, the problem is compounded: specific medical terms are rarely used (see also Major et al. 2013) and often there is no sign that would be universally accepted by the community – as in the case of "spleen" or "bile ducts". 2) The translation of proper names, such as the names of medication like Dafalgan®, for which there is no specific sign. Translators consider that using the manual alphabet to translate these names would cause excessive eye strain for Deaf people watching the video.3) The recording medium. Videos require a switch to a two-dimensional presentation, which is especially challenging when sentences must be partially signed on the signer's back.

Solutions that our translation work group found for these challenges were: 1) the use of paraphrases when a word was unambiguous and its meaning could be paraphrased with general concepts considered easily understandable by the patients; 2) the use of subtitles when the meaning of a word was ambiguous and a short paraphrasis was not possible; 3) the use of images to clarify the meaning of a word (e.g., the image of a specific part of the body to ensure that the Deaf patient understands the intended location, or the image of a specific medicine). Table 6.1 displays a few sentences and the strategies employed to translate specific terminology.

To record our translations in real time, we used the LiteDevTools online platform developed at the University of Geneva (https://regulus.unige.ch/litedevtools/client/#/login), designed to facilitate the recording of oral/video translations (Strasly et al., 2018).

Table 6.1 *Sample sentences from the BabelDr corpus and the translation strategies applied for specific terminology*

Sample sentences		Strategies employed to translate
are you allergic to **aspirin**?	Subtitle	
are you allergic to **codeine**?		
have you taken **anticoagulants** today?	Paraphrasis	AGAINST-BLOOD-MASS
have you stopped taking **antiarrhythmics**?		MEDECINE-FOR-HEART-RHYTHM-STABILITY
have you taken any treatment for **osteoporosis** today?		BONE-INSIDE-BRITTLE
do you also have pain in the **upper left side** of your back?	Image	
do your **shoulder blades** also hurt?		

6.4.2 Virtual Avatar Generation

One way to generate virtual animation is to rely heavily on humans throughout the whole production process, exploiting motion capture and/ or animation by hand. This technique can make the final rendering quite realistic. Another way is to use automatic sign language processing (Ebling et al., 2017). For BabelDr, we opted for translation via a fully synthesized avatar developed by the School of Computing Sciences at the University of East Anglia (United Kingdom) – the JASigning avatar. The system's main version (Ebling and Glauert, 2013) is freely available for research purposes and provides several virtual characters. It was developed in the context of the European Union-funded ViSiCAST (Bangham, 2000), eSIGN (Zwitserlood et al., 2005) and DictaSign (Efthimiou et al., 2012) projects. In the context of BabelDr, the avatar Françoise was selected for its realism, ethnic neutrality, and expressiveness.

The JASigning avatar is based upon a notation system called G-SiGML (Gestural Signing Gesture Markup Language), which enables the transcription of sign language gestures (Elliott et al., 2004). The application uses XML to encode the features of individual signs using the Hamburg Notation System for Sign Languages (HNS) (Prillwitz et al., 1989). HNS describes the physical form of the signs (Figure 6.2) and has been developed to support transcription of the hands' activity: handshape, orientation, location, and movement (Table 6.2). G-SiGML also allows researchers to represent non-manual features: facial expressions, body expressions, and gesture mouthing.

Table 6.2 *HNS symbols for NURSE in LSF-CH, based on (Smith, 2013)*

	Dominant hand (right hand)		Non-dominant hand (left hand)	
	Symbol	Description	Symbol	Description
Handshape	⟳	The hand forms a closed fist with the thumb extended.	○	The hand forms a closed fist.
Orientation	⟨ ◊	The extension of the index finger is oriented to the signer's left and the orientation of the palm to the left and down the axis of rotation.	⌐◌	The extension of the index finger is directed toward the front of the body, to the right of the signer and the orientation of the palm downwards.
Location	⊟▪(Ⴟ ₁）	The right thumb touches the signer's right shoulder.	⊟	The hand is located in front of the lower abdomen.
Movement	ᴎ\ ↓ ↖→ ₒ	The hand moves down, forward, up slightly on the outside left of the signer and then moves to the right.	⊘	No movement is made.

NURSE

: [⟳↙○][⟨◊↙⌐◌][▪⊟(Ⴟ₁）↙⊟][ᴎ\ ↓ ↖→ ₒ ↙⊘]

Figure 6.2 HNS description of NURSE in LSF-CH: gloss (top); image with cross movement represented by arrows (middle); HamNoSys (HNS) notation (bottom)

To facilitate the production of the G-SiGML code, we developed the SigLa platform[6]. Its aim is to generate G-SiGML from two main resources: 1) a lexicon that associates individual signs (named with glosses) with their HNS representation; and 2) a synchronous context-free grammar that productively maps source sentences into their corresponding sign tables.

Sign tables (Table 6.3, below) are intermediate representations of signed utterances (Rayner, 2016). They specify a sequence of glosses (the manual signs defined via HNS) and associate them with non-manual features. The tables consist of eight rows that represent the parallel channels of signed output. The first row, GLOSS, specifies the sequence of glosses. The second row, APERTURE, refers to the degree of openness of the eyes, for example, ClosedLeft or Small. The third row, BODY, describes the movement of the body, for example, RotateLeft or TiltRight. The fourth row, EYEBROWS, describes the movement of the eyebrows, for example, Up or LeftUp. The fifth row, GAZE, indicates where the signer is looking, for example, Down or LeftUp. The sixth row, HEAD, describes the movement of the head, for example, TurnRight or TiltedBack. The seventh row, SHOULDERS, refers to the movement of the shoulders, for example, RaiseLeft, HunchBothForward. The eighth and last row, MOUTHING, describes the movement of the lips, cheeks, tongue, or teeth. The associated grammar describes the link between these sign tables and generated sentences, using variables (terminal and non-terminal symbols) as described in Rayner, 2016.

Once the lexicon and the synchronous grammar are ready, they can be uploaded to the SigLa platform and compiled. The SigLa platform then produces the G-SiGML code for sentences as generated by the grammar, or for specific rules only. During generation, each element of the sign

Table 6.3 *Sign Table 6.for the sentence "I am a cardiologist"*

Gloss	BE_1SG	DOCTOR	SPECIALIST	HEART
Aperture	Wide	Wide	Wide	Wide
Body	Straight	Straight	Straight	TiltBack
Eyebrows	Neutral	Neutral	Up	Neutral
Gaze	Neutral	Right	Neutral	Down
Head	Neutral	TurnRight	Neutral	Neutral
Shoulders	Neutral	Neutral	Neutral	Neutral
Mouthing	null	medsa	spesialis	kO:

---

[6] https://ftitim2.unige.ch:8041/

table is mapped to the corresponding G-SiGML element. SigLa also aims to facilitate rule development: while storing all necessary resources and enabling the grammar developer to produce the signed animation for a sentence, it also enables modification of the corresponding grammar rule if necessary. Table 6.4 shows the resulting G-SiGML representation of the sign NURSE in LSF-CH.

6.4.3 Speech2sign Version of BabelDr

When new sentences are added in the BabelDr application, their G-SiGML code is generated with the SigLa platform. They are imported into BabelDr with the metadata and stored with other translation resources (SL human videos and written translations in other languages) so that they can be played directly in real time with JASigning in the BabelDr application. The two versions of BabelDr (with human videos and avatar generation) are accessible online[7], along with non-signed languages. Figure 6.3 shows the doctor and patient views for both versions.

As of March 2022, the glossary consists of 608 HamNoSys entries: 370 nouns, 82 verbs/actions, 57 adjectives, 36 adverbs, 19 transfer signs[8], 15 pronouns, 8 prepositions, 5 forms of punctuations, 3 interjections, and 3 conjunctions. The grammar consists of 438 rules with 121 non- terminal and 381 terminal symbols, and can generate G-SiGML code for 1,234,828 sentences. For compliance with the FAIR principles (Findable, Accessible, Interoperable, and Reusable), the parallel corpus of human and avatar videos is now fully available on the Yareta Swiss repository in .webm and .mp4 formats (for human recordings) and G-SiGML files (for the avatar-based version).[9]

6.5 Qualitative Evaluation on the Perception of Avatars and Human Videos

How do Deaf people in French-speaking European countries perceive the use of human and avatar videos in the BabelDr context? To find out, we created an online questionnaire (Bouillon et al., 2021). The survey, launched in four

---

[7] https://babeldr.unige.ch/

[8] Specific signs used to explain by demonstration. There are several different sorts of transfer, such as size and shape transfer, situation transfer, character transfer, and so on (Cuxac, 1996; Tournadre and Hamm, 2018).

[9] DOI Repository: 10.26037/yareta:aldcuemsybbcjpnzqwn74knf24

Table 6.4 *G-SiGML code for the gloss NURSE in LSF-CH*

Manual features

```
<split_handconfig>
        <handconfig handshape="fist" thumbpos="out" />
        <handconfig handshape="fist" />
</split_handconfig>
<split_handconfig>
        <handconfig extfidir="l" palmor="dl" />
        <handconfig extfidir="or" palmor="d" />
</split_handconfig>
<split_location>
        <location_bodyarm contact="touch"
        location="shoulders" side="left_at">
        <location_hand digits="1" />
        </location_bodyarm>
        <location_bodyarm location="stomach" />
</split_location>
<split_motion>
        <seq_motion>
          <directedmotion direction="do"
          second_direction="d" />
          <directedmotion direction="ul" size="small" />
          <directedmotion direction="r" />
        </seq_motion>
        <nomotion />
</split_motion>
```
Non-manual features
```
<mouthing_tier>                                          a.firmiE
        <mouth_picture picture="a:firmiE" speed="1.2" />
</mouthing_tier>
<body_tier>
        <body_movement movement="RR" />
</body_tier>
<head_tier>
        <head_movement movement="SL" />
</head_tier>
<facialexpr_tier>
        <eye_lids movement="WB" />
</facialexpr_tier>
```

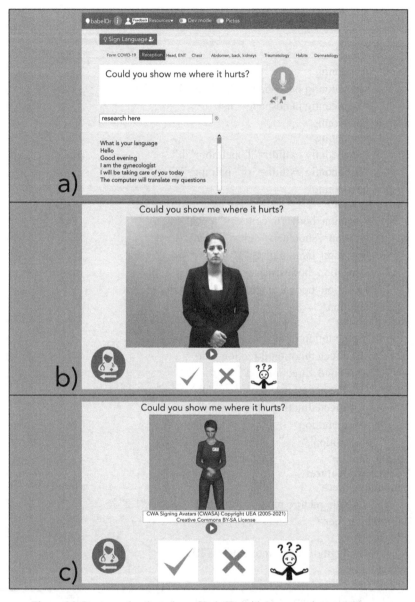

Figure 6.3 Doctor and patient view of BabelDr with human and avatar videos

languages (LSF, LSF-CH, French Belgian Sign Language [LSFB] and written French) was implemented through LimeSurvey, an accessible online survey platform. A "snowball" sampling method was used to recruit respondents, who were given six weeks to participate. Thirty-two questions were divided into six sections on the following themes: 1) background of the videos; 2) additional images added to clarify content; 3) subtitles; 4) screen format and size; 5) advertisements and logos displayed on the screen; and 6) perception of the use of three-dimensional avatars.

The questionnaire, written in French, was made accessible through videos in LSF, LSFB and LSF-CH, all made by Deaf professionals who are native speakers of these sign languages. Each theme was introduced by a short video summarizing the topic covered. Responses were limited to "yes/no" or multiple-choice (Haug et al., 2015). The questionnaire is available on the Research outputs tab of the Swiss Centre for Barrier-free Communication[10].

We focus here on results concerning the appreciation of virtual characters. Four questions were asked:

	Question	Answer
Qu. 1	Do you consider that videos with avatars can be useful?	Yes/No question
Qu. 2	In this medical context, would you prefer videos with filmed humans or virtual characters?	Multiple-choice questions "Filmed humans"; "Virtual character"
Qu. 3	To better understand the signer, which video would you prefer?	Multiple-choice questions
Qu. 4	Do you have anything to add?	Text zone

Past studies have determined that Deaf people may have problems in understanding the signs performed by an avatar (Huenerfauth et al., 2008; Kipp et al., 2011). While our current work may also have demonstrated a certain preference for traditional human interpretation (Question 2: 64 percent; N=16/28), we also find that the use of automatic technologies associated with virtual characters is not without interest for the target audience. Considering the abstention rate (Question 1: 9.7 percent; N=3/31) and the negative rate (Question 1: 12.9 percent; N=4/31), our study shows that in fact most Deaf respondents (Question 1: 77.4 percent; N=24/31) do find the video information provided by a virtual character useful in the medical context (Figure 6.4).

Concerning the display of avatars on the screen, a major number of respondents [Question 3: 64 percent; N=18/28] prefer the signer to be shown front-on

---

[10] https://bfc.unige.ch/en/research-outputs/resources/

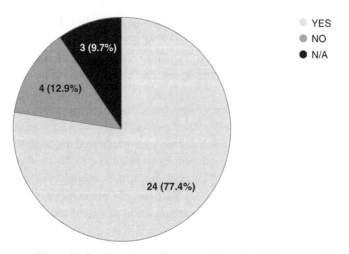

Figure 6.4 Results of our online survey. "Question 1. Do you consider that videos with avatars can be useful?" (N=31)

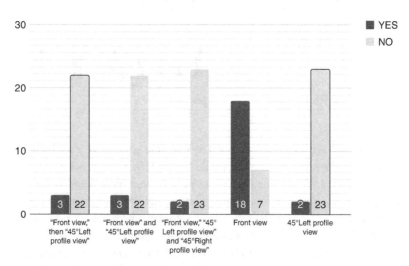

Figure 6.5 Results of our online survey. "Question 3. To better understand the signer, which video would you prefer?" (N=28)

only. The options proposing multiple perspectives on the same screen or a 45° left/right perspective were almost unanimously rejected (Figure 6.5).

Respondents could also leave personal comments if they wished. One of our participants was particularly conscious of the possibility of customizing avatars (i.e., with respect to physical appearance, age, sex and origin), so that no patients need feel uneasy or excluded:

> (...) *l'avatar est intéressant, car on peut choisir enfant, homme, femme, blanc, noir, etc. selon l'éthique auquel certains peuvent s'identifier sans aucune discrimination.*
> *(...) the avatar is interesting because we can choose a child, a man, a woman, white, black, etc. according to the ethics* [ethnicity would be the correct word here, but in French our Deaf respondent wrote "ethics"] *of people and the group they identify with without discrimination* [our translation]

Some of our respondents provided suggestions for improving the avatar. In particular, they suggested that we emphasize some movements in order to make sentences more understandable. For example, they suggested adding shrugs of the shoulders, frowning eyebrows, and a more intense look in order to make the avatar more understandable:

> *Pour toute interrogation, on hausse les épaules quand il s'agit des questions.*
> *(...) je trouve qu'il manque des expressions faciales pour montrer que c'est une question.*
> *Every time we ask a question, we shrug our shoulders (...) I find facial expressions are missing to show that we are asking a question* [our translation].

6.6 Conclusions and Future Work

This chapter examines the difficulties faced by Deaf people in gaining access to healthcare. In contrast to the few other existing translation tools for the Deaf, the BabeldDr project aims to create a pipeline for productive development of quality sign language resources and to make those resources available to doctors for diagnosis via a flexible speech-enabled fixed-phrase translator, or phraselator. To produce the signed videos used in BabelDr, we have developed innovative platforms directly linked with BabelDr, including LiteDevTool and SigLa. Our results include several corpora, including (1) a reference corpus of human LSF videos for medical questions and instructions and (2) a large artificial corpus of SiGML representations.

An initial questionnaire for Deaf people concerning their perception of avatars showed that 77 percent of respondents found the information conveyed by the avatars useful in this context, although they preferred human videos. Even if avatars are far from perfect, this technology seems promising for emergency situations and for the production of sign language video corpora.

This research is pioneering in our field. To our knowledge, it is the first automatic speech translation system with sign language used in hospitals for diagnosis. The system will soon be evaluated on diagnostic tasks with the Deaf population. That evaluation will also allow us to validate the quality of the human and avatar videos and to compare patients' satisfaction level related to the diagnostic task. In another study, we showed that Arabic and Albanian patients have less confidence in their doctor when a speech translation system uses speech synthesis instead of human recording for translated output (Gerlach et al., 2023). It would be interesting to replicate that study for Deaf patients with human and avatar videos.

The SigLa platform will soon be made available to researchers. Experiments will be conducted to involve Deaf people in the development of the SigLa grammar and the validation of the SiGml code. We also intend to evaluate the effort needed to port the grammar to another Swiss sign language, for example, to Italian sign language or another closely related sign language, for example, LSFB. To facilitate the translation of medical sentences into real-human videos, we plan to employ Deaf people currently studying in a new training program developed at our Faculty, a Diploma in Advanced Studies (DAS) for Deaf translators.

6.7 Acknowledgments

The authors would like to thank the translation work group, especially Tanya Sebaï, Adrien Pelletier, Sonia Tedjani, Evelyne Rigot and Valentin Marti; Jonathan Mutal for the development of the SigLa platform and to thank Johanna Gerlach for her comments on this chapter.

References

Abou-Abdallah, M., and A. Lamyman. 2021. Exploring Communication Difficulties with Deaf Patients. *Clinical Medicine*, 21 (4) pages e380–e383. DOI: 10.7861/clinmed.2021-0111; PMCID: PMC8313197; PMID: 35192482

Albrecht, U.-V., T. Jungnickel, and U. von Jan. 2015. ISignIT – Communication App and Concept for the Deaf and Hard of Hearing. In J. Mantas, A. Hasman, and M. S. Househ (Eds.), *Enabling Health Informatics Applications, Studies in Health Technology and Informatics* (Vol. 213, pages 283–286). Presented at the 13th International Conference, ICIMTH 2015, Athens, Greece, July 9 – July 11, 2015, IOS Press. DOI: 10.3233/978-1-61499-538-8-283; PMID: 26153016

Bangham, J. A. 2000. Signing for the Deaf Using Virtual Humans. *IEE Seminar on Speech and Language Processing for Disabled and Elderly People* (Vol. 2000, pages 4–4). Presented at the IEE Seminar on Speech and Language Processing for Disabled and Elderly People, London, UK: IEE. DOI: 10.1049/ic:20000134

Binggeli, T. 2015. "Für eine Welt ohne Barrieren". *Besteht in der Schweiz ein barrierefreier Zugang zum Informationserwerb sowie zur Inanspruchnahme von medizinischen Dienstleistungen für Menschen mit Hörbehinderung?* UFL Private Universität im Fürstentum Lichtenstein, Lichtenstein.

Binggeli, T., and C. Hohenstein. 2020. Deaf Patients' Access to Health Services in Switzerland: An Interview with Dr. Tatjana Binggeli, Medical Scientist and President of the Swiss Federation of the Deaf SGB-FSS. In C. Hohenstein and M. Lévy-Tödter (Eds.), *Multilingual Healthcare*, FOM-Edition (pages 333–347). Wiesbaden: Springer Fachmedien Wiesbaden. DOI: 10.1007/978-3-658-27120-6_13

Bouillon, P., B. David, I. Strasly, and H. Spechbach. 2021. A Speech Translation System for Medical Dialogue in Sign Language: Questionnaire on User Perspective of Videos and the Use of Avatar Technology. *Barrier-free Communication* (pages 46–54). Presented at the 3rd Swiss Conference, BFC 2020, Wintherthur (online), June 29–July 4, 2020, Winterthur, Switzerland: ZHAW Zürcher Hochschule für Angewandte Wissenschaften.

Bouillon, P., J. Gerlach, H. Spechbach, N. Tsourakis, and S. Halimi. 2017. BabelDr vs Google Translate: A User Study at Geneva University Hospitals (HUG). 20th Annual Conference of the European Association for Machine Translation (EAMT) (pages 747–752). *Presented at the 20th Annual Conference of the European Association for Machine Translation (EAMT)*, Prague, Czech Republic.

Braem, P. B., and C. Rathmann. 2010. Transmission of Sign Languages in Northern Europe. In D. Brentari (Ed.), *Cambridge Language Surveys: Sign Languages* (1st ed., pages 19–45). Cambridge University Press. DOI: 10.1017/CBO9780511712203.003

Bragg, D., O. Koller, M. Bellard, et al. 2019. Sign Language Recognition, Generation, and Translation : An Interdisciplinary Perspective. Presented at the 21st International ACM SIGACCESS Conference on Computers and Accessibility (ASSETS'19), Pittsburgh, PA, USA, October 28–October 30, 2019: ACM. DOI: 10.1145/3308561.3353774

Camgöz, N. C., A. A. Kındıroğlu, S. Karabüklü, et al. 2016. BosphorusSign : A Turkish Sign Language Recognition Corpus in Health and Finance Domains. *Proceedings of the Tenth International Conference on Language Resources and Evaluation (LREC 2016)* (pages 1383–1388). Portorož, Slovenia: European Language Resources Association (ELRA).

Cantero, O. 2016. *Accès aux soins et communication : Vers une passerelle entre la communauté sourde et les soignants de Suisse romande.* University of Lausanne, Lausanne, Switzerland.

Chiriac, I. A., Stoicu- L. Tivadar, and E. Podoleanu. 2015. Comparing Video and Avatar Technology for a Health Education Application for Deaf People. In R. Cornet, L. Stoicu-Tivadar, A. Hörbst, C. L. Parra Calderón, S. K. Andersen, and M. Hercigonja-Szekeres (Eds.), *Digital Healthcare Empowering Europeans*, Studies in Health Technology and Informatics (Vol. 210, pages 516–520). Presented at the 26th Medical Informatics in Europe Conference (MIE2015), Madrid, Spain, May 27 – May 29, 2015, Amsterdam: IOS Press. DOI: 10.3233/978-1-61499-512-8-516; PMID: 25991201

Chiriac, I. A., Stoicu- L. Tivadar, and E. Podoleanu. 2016. Romanian Sign Language Oral Health Corpus in Video and Animated Avatar Technology. In V. E. Balas, L. C. Jain, and B. Kovačević (Eds.), *Soft Computing Applications (SOFA 2014). Advances in Intelligent Systems and Computing* (Vol. 356, pages 279–293). Cham: Springer International Publishing. DOI: 10.1007/978-3-319-18296-4_24

Cuxac, C. 1996. *Fonctions et structures de l'iconicité des langues des signes : Analyse descriptive d'un idiolecte parisien de la langue des signes française*, (Thèse de doctorat en Linguistique). University Paris 5.

Ebling, S., and J. Glauert. 2013. Exploiting the Full Potential of JASigning to Build an Avatar Signing Train Announcements. *Proceedings of the Third International Symposium on Sign Language Translation and Avatar Technology (SLTAT)*. Chicago. DOI: 10.5167/uzh-85716

Ebling, S., S. Johnson, R. Wolfe, et al. 2017. Evaluation of Animated Swiss German Sign Language Fingerspelling Sequences and Signs. In M. Antona and C. Stephanidis (Eds.), *Universal Access in Human–Computer Interaction. Designing Novel Interactions* (pages 3–13). Cham: Springer International Publishing. DOI: 10.1007/978-3-319-58703-5_1

Efthimiou, E., S.-E. Fotinea, T. Hanke, et al. 2012. The Dicta-Sign Wiki: Enabling Web Communication for the Deaf. In K. Miesenberger, A. Karshmer, P. Penaz, and W. Zagler (Eds.), *Computers Helping People with Special Needs* (Vol. 7383, pages 205–212). Berlin-Heidelberg: Springer. DOI: 10.1007/978-3-642-31534-3_32

Elliott, R., J. Glauert, V. Jennings, and R. Kennaway. 2004. An Overview of the SiGML Notation and SiGMLSigning Software System. In O. Streiter and C. Vettori (Eds.), (pages 98–104). *Presented at the Sign Language Processing Satellite Workshop of the Fourth International Conference on Language Resources and Evaluation (LREC 2004)*, Lisbon, Portugal, May 24, 25, 29–30, 2004.

Emond, A., M. Ridd, H. Sutherland, et al. 2015. Access to Primary Care Affects the Health of Deaf People. *British Journal of General Practice, 65* (631), pages 95–96. DOI: 10.3399/bjgp15X683629; PMCID: PMC4325446; PMID: 25624302

Flores, G., M. B. Laws, S. J. Mayo, et al. 2003. Errors in Medical Interpretation and Their Potential Clinical Consequences in Pediatric Encounters. *Pediatrics*, 111 (1), pages 6–14. DOI: 10.1542/peds.111.1.6; PMID: 12509547

Gerlach, J., P. Bouillon, R. Troqe, I. S. Halimi Mallem, & H. Spechbach. 2023. Patient acceptance of translation technology for medical dialogues in emergency situations. In Translating Crises (pages 253–272). Bloomsbury Academic. https://doi.org/10.5040/9781350240117.ch-15

Haug, T., R. Herman, and B. Woll. 2015. Constructing an Online Test Framework, Using the Example of a Sign Language Receptive Skills Test. *Deafness and Education International, 17* (1), pages 3–7. DOI: 10.1179/1557069X14Y.0000000035

Huenerfauth, M., L. Zhao, E. Gu, and J. Allbeck. 2008. Evaluation of American Sign Language Generation by Native ASL Signers. *ACM Transactions on Accessible Computing*, 1 (1), pages 1–27. doi : 10.1145/1361203.1361206

ICESC. 1976. *International Covenant on Economic, Social and Cultural Rights*. New York, NY, USA: United Nations; UN document A/6316.

Johnston, T., and J. Napier. 2010. Medical Signbank: Bringing Deaf People and Linguists Together in the Process of Language Development. *Sign Language Studies, 10* (2), pages 258–275.

Khander, A., S. Farag and K. T. Chen. 2018. Identification and Evaluation of Medical Translator Mobile Applications Using an Adapted APPLICATIONS Scoring System. *Telemedicine and e-Health, 24* (8), pages 594–603. DOI: 10.1089/tmj.2017.0150; PMID: 29271702

Kipp, M., A. Heloir, and Q. Nguyen. 2011. Sign Language Avatars: Animation and Comprehensibility. In Hannes Högni Vilhjálmsson, S. Kopp, S. Marsella, and K. R. Thórisson (Eds.), *Intelligent Virtual Agents*, Lecture Notes in Computer Science (Vol. 6895, pages 113–126). Presented at the 10th International Conference, IVA 2011,

Reykjavik, Iceland, September 15 – September 17, 2011, Berlin, Heidelberg: Springer. DOI: 10.1007/978-3-642-23974-8_13

Kuenburg, A., P. Fellinger, and J. Fellinger. 2016. Health Care Access Among Deaf People. *Journal of Deaf Studies and Deaf Education, 21* (1), pages 1–10. DOI: 10.1093/deafed/env042; PMID: 26405210

Major, G. 2012. *Not Just "How the Doctor Talks": Healthcare Interpreting as Relational Practice* (Unpublished Doctoral Thesis). Macquarie University, Sydney, Australia.

Major, G., J. Napier, L. Ferrara, and T. Johnston (2013). Exploring Lexical Gaps in Australian Sign Language for the Purposes of Health Communication. *Communication and Medicine, 9*(1), 37–47. DOI: https://doi.org/10.1558/cam.v9i1.37; PMID: 23763235

Marks-Sultan, G., S. Kurt, D. Leyvraz, and D. Sprumont. 2016. The Legal and Ethical Aspects of the Right to Health of Migrants in Switzerland. *Public Health Reviews, 37* (1) page 15. DOI: 10.1186/s40985-016-0027-2

Middleton, A., A. Niruban, G. Girling, and P. K. Myint. 2010. Communicating in a Healthcare Setting with People Who Have Hearing Loss. *British Medical Journal*, 341 (7775), pages 726–729. DOI: 10.1136/bmj.c4672; PMID: 20880905

Noack, E. M., J. Schäning, and F. Müller. 2022. A Multilingual App for Providing Information to SARS-CoV-2 Vaccination Candidates with Limited Language Proficiency: Development and Pilot. *Vaccines, 10* (3), pages 360. DOI: 10.3390/vaccines10030360; PMCID: PMC8955787; PMID: 35334992

Ong, L. M. L., de J. C. J. M. Haes, A. M. Hoos, and F. B. Lammes. 1995. Doctor–Patient Communication: A Review of the Literature. *Social Science and Medicine, 40* (7), pages 903–918. DOI: 10.1016/0277-9536(94)00155-m; PMID: 7792630

Padden, C., and T. Humphries. 1988. *Deaf in America: Voices from a Culture*. Cambridge, Mass.: Harvard University Press.

Panayiotou, A., A. Gardner, S. Williams, et al. 2019. Language Translation Apps in Health Care Settings: Expert Opinion. *JMIR mHealth and uHealth, 7* (4) page e11316. DOI: 10.2196/11316; PMCID: PMC6477569; PMID: 30964446

Papastratis, I., C. Chatzikonstantinou, D. Konstantinidis, D. Konstantinidis, et al. 2021. Artificial Intelligence Technologies for Sign Language. *Sensors*, 21, 5843. DOI: 10.3390/s21175843.

Pollard, R. Q., W. R. Betts, J. K. Carroll, et al. 2014. Integrating Primary Care and Behavioral Health with Four Special Populations: Children with Special Needs, People with Serious Mental Illness, Refugees, and Deaf People. *American Psychologist, 69* (4), pages 377–387. DOI: 10.1037/a0036220; PMID: 24820687

Preston, P. 1995. Mother Father Deaf: The Heritage of Difference. *Social Science and Medicine*, 40 (11), pages 1461–1467. DOI: 10.1016/0277-9536(94)00357-y; PMID: 7667651

Prillwitz, S., R. Leven, H. Zienert, et al. 1989. Hamburg Notation System for Sign Language. *An Introduction Guide. International Studies on Sign Language and the Communication of the Deaf, 5*. Hamburg (Allemagne): Institute of German Sign Language and Communication of the Deaf. University of Hamburg.

Ralston, E., P. Zazove, & D. W. Gorenflo. 1996. Physicians' attitudes and beliefs about deaf patients. *The Journal of the American Board of Family Practice*, 9(3), 167–173.

Rayner, M. 2016. *Using the Regulus Lite Speech2Sign Platform*. Using the Regulus Lite Speech2Sign Platform.

Roelofsen, F., L. Esselink, S. Mende-Gillings, & A. Smeijers. 2021. Sign Language Translation in a Healthcare Setting. In R. Mitkov, V. Sosoni, J. C. Giguère, E. Murgolo, & E. Deysel (Eds.), *Sign Language Translation in a Healthcare Setting* (p. 110–124). Presented at the TRanslation and Interpreting Technology ONline (TRITON 2021), July 5–July 7, 2021, Shoumen: INCOMA Ltd. DOI : 10.26615/978-954-452-071-7_013

Sáfár, E., & J. Glauert. 2012. Computer Modelling. In R. Pfau, M. Steinbach, & B. Woll (Eds.), *Sign Language : An International Handbook*, Handbooks of Linguistics and Communication Science. Berlin: De Gruyter Mouton, pages 1075–1101.

Scheier, D. B. 2009. Barriers to Health Care for People with Hearing Loss: A Review of the Literature. *The Journal of the New York State Nurses' Association*, *40* (1), pages 4–10. PMID: 19835226

SGB-FSS. 2021). *Stratégie 2021-2025*. Fédération Suisse des Sourds.

Smeijers, A., and R. Pfau. 2009. Towards a Treatment for Treatment: On Communication between General Practitioners and Their Deaf Patients. *The Sign Language Translator and Interpreter, Amsterdam Center for Language and Communication (ACLC)*, *3* (1), pages 1–14.

Smith, R. (Ed.). 2013. *HamNoSys 4.0: User guide*. Blanchardstown: Institute of Technology.

Strasly, I. (upcoming). *Accessibilité et langue des signes en Suisse romande : Le projet BabelDr et l'accès à la santé*. Université de Genève, Faculté de traduction et d'interprétation, Geneva, Switzerland.

Strasly, I., T. Sebaï, E. Rigot, et al. 2018. Le projet BabelDr : Rendre les informations médicales accessibles en Langue des Signes de Suisse Romande (LSF-SR). *Proceedings of the 2nd Swiss Conference on Barrier-free Communication: Accessibility in educational settings (BFC 2018)* (pages 92–96). Presented at the Accessibility in educational settings (BFC 2018), Geneva (Switzerland).

Süzgün, M. M., H. Özdemir, N. C. Camgöz, et al. 2015. HospiSign: An Interactive Sign Language Platform for Hearing Impaired. *Journal of Naval Science and Engineering*, *11* (3), pages 75–92.

Tournadre, N., and M. Hamm. 2018. Une approche typologique de la langue des signes française. *TIPA. Travaux interdisciplinaires sur la parole et le langage*, (34). doi : 10.4000/tipa.2568

Turner, A. M., Y. K. Choi, K. Dew, et al. 2019. Evaluating the Usefulness of Translation Technologies for Emergency Response Communication: A Scenario-Based Study. *JMIR Public Health and Surveillance*, *5* (1), pages e11171. DOI: 10.2196/11171; PMCID: PMC6369422; PMID: 30688652

United Nations. 2006. Convention on the Rights of Persons with Disabilities. A/RES/61/106.

Wasserman, M., M. R. Renfrew, A. R. Green, et al. 2014. Identifying and Preventing Medical Errors in Patients with Limited English Proficiency: Key Findings and Tools for the Field. *Journal for Healthcare Quality*, *36* (3), pages 5–16. DOI: 10.1111/jhq.12065; PMCID: PMC5111827; PMID: 24629098

WHO. 1948. *Constitution of the World Health Organization. International Health Conference*, New York, June 19–22, 1946, (pages 1–18). New York, NY.

Zwitserlood, I., M. Verlinden, J. Ros, and S. van der Schoot. 2005. *Synthetic Signing for the Deaf: Esign*. Proceedings of the conference and workshop on assistive technologies for vision and hearing impairment.

7

Health Websites for All
A Localisation-Oriented Accessibility Evaluation
WITH CONTRIBUTIONS FROM LUCÍA MORADO VÁZQUEZ AND
SILVIA RODRÍGUEZ VÁZQUEZ

7.1 Introduction

Back in 2015, the international community committed, within the framework of the United Nations Sustainable Development Goals, to ensure healthy lives and promote well-being for all, and at all ages, by 2030 (United Nations, 2015). To measure progress toward this ambitious but necessary goal, we can assess the ease with which individuals can access healthcare. Some decades ago, the primary sources that people relied upon to seek medical services were mainly health professionals (e.g., doctors or pharmacists), or family and friends. At present, however, the web has become a ubiquitous health knowledge center that allows us to seek needed information quickly and privately. Now that people increasingly depend on the Internet to make informed health decisions – for example, to diagnose or treat given conditions, or to obtain lifesaving information in a crisis, as during the COVID-19 pandemic – it is essential to ensure access to web health content for all potential users.

The need becomes even more acute for people with disabilities (PwD), as they are more likely than others to use the Internet for health-related activities (Scanlan, 2021). Guaranteeing effective access to healthcare for PwD is a key action point under the recently published Strategy for the Rights of Persons with Disabilities 2021–2030 (European Union, 2021). However, evidence suggests that PwD report unmet needs for medical-related services four times more often than persons without disabilities (ibid.), and that their satisfaction rates with their medical care in general are lower than those of their non-disabled peers (Gibson and O'Connor, 2010). In times of crisis, these challenges can be exacerbated and make this population group more vulnerable, particularly during the response and recovery stages (Rodríguez Vázquez, 2023). In fact, after the COVID-19 outbreak, the United Nations (2020) acknowledged that PwD are at greater risk of discrimination in accessing healthcare and lifesaving procedures in emergency contexts. And yet, despite all this clear evidence of need, prior work indicates that key health websites, such as that of the World Health Organization, have failed to serve the information needs of all citizens during the health crisis (Fernández-Díaz et al., 2020).

If health websites are to achieve their ultimate informative goal and serve the needs of diverse communities – whether functionally, culturally, or linguistically (Rodríguez Vázquez and Torres-del-Rey, 2020) – their content must also be available in a language they can understand. The suggestion has been made that provision of multilingual health counseling and information services could efficiently (i) reduce short-term costs to health insurers of searches for health information and (ii) improve patient empowerment (Schmidt et al., 2021). However, we contend that this provision should also be seen as a form of accessibility in itself. We also believe that health websites offering information in several languages – especially those from concerned institutions in multilingual countries – must ensure that an acceptable and comparable level of accessibility is achieved across all language versions, per the Web Content Accessibility Guidelines (WCAG) 2.1 (Kirkpatrick et al., 2018).

In the present chapter, we will first review the existing literature on the topic of accessibility and localization of health websites (Section 7.2). Then we will present the methodology and the results of a study aiming to evaluate a selection of official multilingual health websites for accessibility compliance, with a particular focus on two language-oriented WCAG success criteria: 2.4.2, Page Titled and 3.1.1, Language of Page (Sections 7.3 and 7.4). The chapter will conclude with a discussion of the study's findings, of the challenges that can emerge from a localization-oriented accessibility evaluation, and of several ideas for continuing this line of research (Section 7.5).

7.2 Related Work

7.2.1 Accessibility of Health Websites

Health websites have been the focus of several studies investigating various aspects of information accessibility, including many issues surrounding availability, accessibility, and affordability of information.[1] For instance, some researchers have placed emphasis on studying the reliability and trustworthiness of health content online (Hamzehei et al., 2018), while others have assessed the availability and quality of information about specific conditions,

---

[1] UNESCO's Information for All Programme (IFAP), https://en.unesco.org/programme/ifap. Last access: March 25, 2022.

such as cancer (Lawrentschuk et al., 2012), benign prostatic hyperplasia (Chen et al., 2014), or female urinary incontinence (Saraswat et al., 2016), among others.

Considerable literature has also been published on the compliance of health websites with the accessibility guidelines created by the World Wide Web Consortium (W3C), ranging from the first WCAG 1.0 version (Chisholm et al., 1999) to the most recent WCAG 2.1 (Kirkpatrick et al., 2018).[2] Most studies we identified involved the classic web accessibility (WA) audits and error reports, in the form of proactive or reactive evaluation studies (Vigo 2009). The former usually support an iterative accessible development process by helping content producers identify lists of problems to fix and are therefore formative (Brajnik 2008). This was the approach adopted by Acosta-Vargas et al. (2018) for a web platform that enables home support as a patient recovers after an arthroplasty. By following the Website Accessibility Conformance Evaluation Methodology (WCAG-EM) 1.0 (Velleman and Abou-Zahra, 2014) and including both automatic and manual testing, the authors identified key issues that could be corrected at a later stage, thus improving the platform's overall accessibility.

Most of the other retrieved studies, however, opted for a reactive evaluation (Brajnik, 2008): the tests were carried out after the websites had been released, simply to assess or validate their accessibility levels. Not surprisingly, results across studies were similar, regardless of the method used – whether automatic testing was applied alone (the most popular choice) or in combination with human evaluation. When health websites in Italy (Mancini et al., 2005) and Canada (O'Grady, 2005) were automatically checked for compliance against WCAG 1.0, over 60 percent of the sampled sites failed to comply with the minimum accessibility requirements. Similarly, Zeng and Parmanto (2004) discovered that, although government and education health websites obtained better accessibility scores than the other web portals in their corpus of 108 worldwide sites (corporate, e-commerce, and community health websites), none were in fact fully accessible.

Low levels of accessibility compliance were also found in more recent studies that took the WCAG 2.1 as a baseline. These include, to name but a few, studies by Rahmatizadeh and Valizadeh-Haghi (2018) on medical university websites in Iran; Acosta-Vargas et al. (2018) in a corpus of twenty-two hospital websites chosen by following standard Webometrics rating criteria; and Alajarmeh (2021), who assessed public health websites of the top

---

[2] At the time of writing, versions 2.2 (Adams et al., 2021) and 3.0 (Spellman et al., 2021a) of the WCAG still had a working draft status.

twenty-five countries affected by the COVID-19 pandemic in 2020. Studies focusing on the needs of a particular group of users yielded similar conclusions. Of the 139 websites containing medical information addressing blind and visually impaired (BVI) laymen or patients explored by Lüchtenberg et al. (2008), only 18 percent (15 sites) achieved level A or AA. Similarly, findings from a study conducted by Yi (2020) with 25 BVI on the accessibility of ten government and public agency health websites in Korea revealed that all of them presented barriers for the relevant participants. Lastly and notably, some scholars have also looked into other accessibility-related variables that could enhance the end-user experience on medical information sites. For instance, in a usability experiment with American Sign Language (ASL) users, Kushalnagar et al. (2015) showed that making health websites accessible in ASL is insufficient, as the sites must also be user-friendly and easy to navigate. Finally, another interesting study by Youngblood (2020) on the mobile readiness of twenty-five of the top health information website homepages demonstrated that, while the overwhelming majority of the sites were at least partially mobile-ready, paradoxically enough, many of the sites violated critical accessibility guidelines.

Our contribution to the current literature is two-fold. First, by adopting a localization approach to WA evaluation, we make what we believe is the first attempt to systematically check accessibility features across two different language versions in multilingual health-related websites. Although most of the studies mentioned in the present section included in their test samples websites with content in several languages (e.g., Berland et al. (2001), Acosta-Vargas et al. (2018) and Alajarmeh (2021), to name but a few), all the accessibility assessments they conducted were language-independent. Second, although prior work has investigated the compliance of health websites with success criterion (SC) 2.4.2 and SC 3.1.1, checks were mostly limited to verifying that the lang attribute was present and whether or not the title attribute in the head element was empty. As we will explain in Section 7.3, our study will analyze both success criteria in context, thus reducing the risk of bias in the results due to false positives.

7.2.2 Localization of Health Websites

In Jiménez-Crespo's terms (2019: 354), industry's and society's prototypical understanding of web localization could be summarized as follows: such localization concerns the translation of interactive hypertexts, but entails a specific set of technological and management processes, such as web content management systems and other web-specific technologies, which are not shared with other translation practices. In addition, web localization requires human intervention; that is, "an instant translation of [web content] using any [Machine Translation] widget in websites without any post-editing or human intervention might not be considered in the industry as an exemplar of the prototype" (Jiménez-Crespo, 2019: 355). Most importantly, "web localization operates exclusively on digital web genres" (Jiménez-Crespo, 2019: 355) – that is, genres used only online.[3]

Considering Jiménez-Crespo's (2013: 95–100) proposal concerning the web genre category, we could define health websites as composing an informational web genre, aiming to both provide information (its expositive function) and to modify user behavior (its exhortative function). For example, a health website may contain descriptive information about a given condition but also recommendations related to its treatment or general health habits. For our work, we understand that these portals can be institutional, nonprofit, or community association websites, targeting either health professionals or lay users.

Existing research recognizes the "medical information website"[4] as the genre with the highest volume of translation around the word (Jiménez-Crespo and Tercedor Sánchez 2017: 412), considering it as a modern version of the classic patient health information leaflet. Surprisingly, nonetheless, it has received scant attention in the localization literature. The very few studies related to health website localization that do exist are based on a web corpus of sites from the United States (US) – an intriguing finding in itself, given that the US is not officially a multilingual country. Perhaps one reason for this decision is precisely the vulnerability of speakers of (official or non-official) minority languages with respect to information access. As Piller (2020: 14) rightfully puts it:

> For too long, state approaches to speakers of minority languages – whether indigenous or migrant – have ranged from benign neglect to forced assimilation. In order to gain access to the state and its institutions – education, health, welfare or the law – everyone was expected to speak the language of the state – English in the US, French in France, Mandarin in China, and so on. As a result of such monolingual approaches, Spanish speakers in the US, Arabic speakers in France, or dialect speakers in China have worse education, employment and health outcomes than their compatriots speaking the state language.

For the purposes of the present chapter, we will refer to three studies in particular. The first focused on the textual and structural analysis of nonprofit

---

[3] Jiménez-Crespo (2019: 355) also explains that websites can include other genres in their hyperlinked structured (e.g., a legal notice or a recipe), but indicates that only translating that content alone cannot be considered a web localization task per se.

[4] Term used by Jiménez-Crespo and Tercedor Sánchez (2017) as a synonym for "health website."

US websites across language versions (English and Spanish), including websites of healthcare organizations, in order to study content loss (Jiménez-Crespo, 2012). According to Jiménez-Crespo (2012), the United States offers more non-profits with a wider range of social services than any other Western nation. Upon examining the corpus, the author reported, as a key finding, that the overall probability that sections of the source website would not be localized were 44.18 percent, implying that, on average, almost half the sections of any source website will not be localized into Spanish. In a subsequent study, Jiménez-Crespo (2017) used the Translational Web Corpus of Medical Spanish (TWCoMS) – containing medical information websites addressing general audiences in the US and a comparable section of websites for Mexico and Spain – for a user evaluation study with twenty-five Spanish speakers living in the State of New Jersey. The goal was to assess users' preferences regarding reformulations and explicitations. His hypothesis was that medical texts translated from English into Spanish would be easier for end users to understand than their non-translated counterparts and thus preferred. However, the data collected in the human evaluation suggested otherwise: bilingual Spanish/English speakers living in the US preferred the most frequent reformulations explicitations in non-translated texts (Jiménez-Crespo, 2017). Their initial assumption was based on the results of a parallel study with the same corpus, in which US medical websites translated into Spanish displayed lower register and lexical specialization levels, with more frequent reformulation strategies than similar non-translated ones (Jiménez-Crespo and Tercedor Sánchez, 2017).

Notwithstanding the relevance of the aforementioned studies and their notable contribution to the web localization field, their focus was not on the needs of PwD. Similarly, accessibility compliance was not the main variable investigated, in contrast to our study and to the research that will be reviewed in the following section.

7.2.3 Multilingual Web Accessibility Studies

Truth be told, despite the inherent multilingual nature of the web, there is a general paucity of scientific literature specifically relating to the accessibility of localized websites. In the last ten years, continuous efforts have been devoted to the advancement of research on the knowledge and resources required to create multilingual web content for all.

Concretely, scholars have explored, on one hand, various process-related aspects, for example, ways in which existing technology can support the multiple stakeholders involved in the development of multilingual websites to render the sites accessible. These include, among others, studies involving the evaluation of how WA evaluation tools deal with language-related issues (Rodríguez Vázquez, 2016a) and mobile-related aspects (Morado Vázquez and Torres-del-Rey, 2023). Additional studies have also examined whether accessibility can be supported through the use computer-assisted translation (CAT) tools (Pacati and Rodríguez Vázquez, 2021), localization data exchange standards (Torres-del-Rey and Morado Vázquez, 2019), and controlled language checkers (Rodríguez Vázquez, 2015a) – and if so, how. On the other hand, product-oriented studies have investigated accessibility features in localized websites corresponding to specific WCAG guidelines (Kirkpatrick et al., 2018). Examples include the work of Rodríguez Vázquez (2016b) on the appropriateness of text alternatives for images (Guideline 1.1 Text Alternatives), or the observation exercise conducted by Rodríguez Vázquez et al. (2022) on the use of easy language in multilingual websites, which could be understood as a good practice to meet Guideline 3.1 Readable.

The web elements (the language and title of the page) that are central to the two WCAG success criteria, and which we will analyze in depth in our study (see Section 7.3), have been considered from various perspectives in prior work related to localization. For instance, in their proposal of a heuristic evaluation methodology to assess multilingual websites, Andreu-Valls and Marcos (2012) included the language of the page as an internationalization feature, while the verification of the page's title was recommended for SEO purposes, and thus not necessarily focusing upon these elements' added value for accessibility. Similarly, Jiménez-Crespo (2008) carried out a lexical analysis of the web page titles in an English-Spanish corpus of US corporate websites. He found that proper names were used in 25 percent of the cases. Interestingly enough, the terminology study also revealed the use of meaningless words, corresponding to website domain suffixes, such as "com" in the English subcorpus and "es" in the Spanish subcorpus. Although examination of the lang attribute was not among the goals of the study, it was reported as part of the corpus metadata: the author noted that around 30 percent of the pages in the localized web subcorpus had said attribute, only 25 percent of which actually had an appropriate language value.

The most recent multilingual WA studies focused on a varied range of web genres. Casalegno (2018) investigated the usability of two partially localized university websites for BVI people. During user testing, participants reported issues related to the inability of their screen readers (programs that automatically read aloud content visually represented on the screen) to correctly read the content of the pages, a problem stemming from the incorrect implementation of the lang attribute. This finding agreed with those reported by Rodríguez Vázquez (2015b) after a series of interviews with members of the BVI community about the challenges they usually faced when browsing multilingual websites. The two success criteria of our interest were also analyzed by Minacapilli (2018) and Pontus (2019) in multilingual airline and museum websites, respectively, within the framework of larger accessibility evaluation studies on compliance to language-related accessibility best practices. After combining automatic and human evaluation by a single inspector, they both concluded that the localized versions were less accessible than the original ones, both at a general level and in relation to compliance with SC 2.4.2 and SC 3.1.1.

Our ultimate goal is to explore whether these asymmetrical situations are found in health websites, and to recommend possible ameliorations that can promote universal access to multilingual health information for all. The study to be presented in the following sections differs from and complements prior work in that: (i) it proposes a localization-oriented accessibility evaluation of the two aforementioned success criteria in a new web genre: health websites; (ii) it includes a more in-depth and in-context analysis of both success criteria in two different language versions; and (iii) it involves a manual inspection step, conducted by more than one accessibility expert.

7.3 Methodology

As explained, our work aims to address the accessibility of health websites from a multilingual perspective. Concretely, we sought to answer the following main research question (RQ):

RQ1. Do multilingual websites provide the same level of access to health information in all their language versions?

For that purpose, we studied the home pages of a set of multilingual websites in English and Spanish providing health-related information (see Section 7.3.1) and automatically evaluated their accessibility (see Section 7.3.2). Taking into account the conclusions drawn in prior work with regard to the accessibility of the multilingual web, our main hypothesis was that, overall, the original web pages would feature a higher level of accessibility than their corresponding localized versions.

In addition, we aimed to explore the following secondary research questions:

RQ 1.1. Is the language of the original and localized web pages defined in such a way that it can be programmatically determined?

RQ 1.2. Are the titles of the original web pages more accessible than the localized ones?

To answer these questions, we examined two specific language-related accessibility features in our multilingual web sample: the Title of the page and the Language of the page, which respectively correspond to the success criteria 3.1.1 and 2.4.2 of the WCAG 2.1 (Kirkpatrick et al., 2018). Both criteria were analyzed through both automatic evaluation and manual inspection.

7.3.1 Data Selection

The multilingual websites included in our study were initially selected according to two main criteria: a) they should be sites that provide trustworthy health-related information, and b) they should be available in both English and Spanish.[5] Taking this into account, we decided to consult MedlinePlus, an online service of the US National Library of Medicine (NLM), whose mission "[...] is to present high-quality, relevant health and wellness information that is trusted and easy to understand, in both English and Spanish" (National Library of Medicine, 2022a). Considered the most visited health website in the world (Acosta-Vargas and Acosta-Vargas, 2021), it contains a directory of health-related organizations "[...] whose materials appear on MedlinePlus health topic pages" (National Library of Medicine, 2022b). This particular directory proved valuable and convenient in the context of our research, as it listed 705 organizations at the time of data collection (May 2021); yet many of those organizations' websites could not be integrated into our bilingual study because they were available only in English.

A third selection criterion was applied in relation to the level of localization of the sites in our sample: the localized version should include at least the home page and one of the main menus in the target language (Spanish in our case). Hence, we discarded all websites with a localization level ranging from 0 to 2, per the classification defined by Jiménez-Crespo (2013: 35–36), namely: a) websites that provide only isolated documents in Spanish (e.g., a PDF document about a specific event or topic); b) websites that include only a list of resources in Spanish; c) websites featuring only a short text or single page localized into Spanish, with all navigation menus in English; and d) websites localized through a third-party MT service without human post-editing (e.g. through a Google Translate plugin).

---

[5] According to the most recent data published in the Internet World Stats portal in March 2020, English and Spanish are the first and third most used languages on the Web, respectively (www .internetworldstats.com/stats7.htm, last access: February 7, 2022). In addition, English–Spanish is the main professional language combination of the researchers, which allowed them to conduct the necessary linguistic assessments during manual inspection.

Considering these criteria, our final web sample consisted of the home pages of seventy-four websites available in English and Spanish (see Annex A). As acknowledged in prior work (Acosta-Vargas et al., 2018; Alajarmeh, 2021), home pages are decisive for user experience, as they are the main entry point and, should problems arise, access to other pages within the same website could be compromised. Most of the sites (92 percent) were from US organizations[6] and only six (8 percent) were from international ones. We hypothesized that all the websites were originally created in English (either because it is the main official language in the US or as a preferred 'lingua franca') and later localized into Spanish; this assumption was also supported in that most of the Spanish versions were shorter than the English websites (indicating partial localization). The web sample was stored locally and analyzed between May and September 2021.

7.3.2 Testing Methods

Automatic testing is a popular accessibility evaluation method, as automated tools provide a quick and low-cost mechanism for gathering accessibility information. For our purposes, we chose Google Lighthouse,[7] an open-source web development tool that includes a specific accessibility audit module. We ran it in Chrome DevTools and assessed the 148 home pages of our web sample: seventy-four pages in English and seventy-four in Spanish. We decided to use this automated tool in our study because it fulfills the transparency principles described in Parvin et al (2021: 2):

a) It is clear which accessibility aspects are examined – see Google Developers (2019a). Among these, we find the aspects included in our study: the title and the language of the page.

b) The errors detected in the accessibility audits are properly categorized and presented. After conducting the accessibility analysis, the tool produces a clear report that can be downloaded in several formats for later reuse (Google Developers 2021). For each one of the accessibility audits performed by the tool, there are three possible values: not applicable, passed, or

---

[6] It is worth highlighting that compliance with the WCAG is formalized under law in the U.S. (Section 508 of the Rehabilitation Act), and it is applicable for at least federal government websites. In addition, according to the Bureau of Internet Accessibility, "the Americans with Disabilities Act (ADA) prohibits discrimination on the basis of disability in places of public accommodation, and websites are increasingly interpreted in legal cases as places of public accommodation. [Hence], the Department of Justice (DOJ) has reaffirmed that the ADA does apply to websites as well." Available at: www.boia.org/blog/is-there-a-legal-requirement-to-implement-wcag. Last access: February 7, 2022.

[7] Available at https://developers.google.com/web/tools/lighthouse. Last access: February 7, 2022.

failed.[8] This report also provides an overall accessibility score using a 100-point scale. We exploited both results in our study. Similarly, the tool lists a series of items that should be implemented manually because they cannot be tested automatically – for example, checking that the page has a logical tab order (Google Developers, 2022a).

c) It provides clear information on the procedure for calculating a weighted average of all the accessibility audits (Google Developers, 2019a) to derive the overall score. That is, the weight of the audits depends on their accessibility impact (ibid.).

Nevertheless, automatic evaluation tools entail limitations, and it is usually recommended that their use as a single testing method be avoided: they should be combined with human evaluation whenever possible (Abou-Zahra, 2008; Brajnik, 2008). Human evaluation can be carried out by accessibility experts or with the help of end users, who can be requested to assess the website(s) according to a given scenario. In the current study, we compared the results obtained through Google Lighthouse with those from the manual inspection conducted by the two researchers.

For the human evaluation of the two accessibility features selected, we extracted the language values and the titles of the 148 pages of our web sample and included them in an evaluation template created *ad hoc* for the purposes of our study. For research reliability purposes, once the first evaluator concluded the manual inspection of all pages in the web sample, the second reviewed all the error annotations. Minor discrepancies were then discussed and resolved.

7.3.3 Accessibility Features Studied

As mentioned, we checked our web sample against two success criteria of the WCAG 2.1 (Kirkpatrick et al., 2018): SC 3.1.1, Language of page, under the "Understandable" principle; and SC 2.4.2, Page Titled, under the "Operable" principle. Both success criteria are classified as level A, which is the minimum level of conformance defined in the WCAG 2.1 guidelines (Kirkpatrick et al., 2018: sec. 5.2.1). The WCAG 2.1 stablishes three levels of conformance: A, AA and AAA, and current national and international accessibility regulations and norms[9] tend to recommend that websites meet the success criteria

---

[8] This classification is similar to the one proposed by the WCAG-EM Report Tool (Abou-Zahra et al., 2021): Not present, Passed, and Failed. The WCAG-EM Report has two additional values for each aspect auditioned: "Not checked" (if the aspect has not been yet checked), and "Cannot tell" if an outcome cannot be provided after the audit.

[9] For example, see the Swiss eCH-0059 digital accessibility standard (Riesch et al., 2020).

classified as level A and AA. In the sections that follow, these two aspects will be explained in detail.

7.3.3.1 Language of the Page

In the WCAG 2.1 (Kirkpatrick et al., 2018), success criterion 3.1.1 (Language of Page) indicates that the "human language of each Web page can be programmatically determined." This aspect can help assistive technology to programmatically prepare the content to suit the user's needs: for example, the screen reader could automatically identify that the text is written in a specific language and pronounce it accordingly. In HTML (HyperText Markup Language), this information can be indicated by including the lang attribute in the <html> root element. There is a standardized list of language tags that is defined in the IETF's BCP 47 standard.[10] For example: <html lang="en"> indicates that the page is written in English, as "en" is the official value for English. It is also possible to include other subtag values, e.g., to indicate the region. For instance, <html lang="en-US"> refers to English from the United States. However, as Ishida (2014) recommends, the golden rule is to keep the value as short as possible whenever possible.

In our analysis, firstly, we followed the test rules defined in (Campbell et al., 2022: sec. Understanding Success Criterion 3.1.1: Language of Page) and, through Google Lighthouse, we checked:

1. If the web pages included the lang attribute in the <html> element.
2. If the value of that attribute followed the IETF's BCP 47 standard (Ishida, 2016).[11]

Secondly, we manually verified whether the value of that attribute matched the language of the page's content.[12] Finally, note that in HTML it is also possible to programmatically indicate that a specific section in a web page is written in a natural language different from the page's main language. The use of the attribute lang should be used for this purpose in the corresponding HTML element(s). This aspect, which is covered in the SC 3.1.2 of the WCAG 2.1 entitled "language of parts" (Kirkpatrick et al., 2018), was not examined in our analysis, but it would be interesting to cover it in future studies.

---

[10] www.rfc-editor.org/rfc/bcp/bcp47.txt. Last access: February 7, 2022.
[11] These two audits are also included in the list of WCAG 2 Test Rules of the WAI (2022).
[12] The tool can check whether the HTML has the lang attribute (Google Developers, 2019c), and whether the value of that attribute is valid, i.e., if it follows the IETF's BCP 47 standard (Google Developers, 2019d). Nevertheless, it does not check our third rule: whether the value of the lang attribute actually matches the language of the content of the page. We assessed this third compliance criterion manually.

7.3.3.2 Title of the Page

In a web page's HTML document, the title is located in the <title> element within the <head>. Usually it is visually represented at the top tab of a web browser. Under the SC 2.4.2 (Page Titled), the rule to be verified is that "Web pages have titles that describe topic or purpose" (Kirkpatrick et al., 2018). The title of the page is especially important for users of screen readers – again, programs that read aloud content visually represented on the screen. As explained in Deque Systems (2022), the title of the page will be the first element that these users will hear when visiting a page, and if this information is not descriptive and unique, they will have to explore the page to determine its content and purpose. Similarly, as Brajnik (2009) suggests, "if the title provides no information or does not change when pages are changed, it gives the wrong hint to the user who might not understand that the page has changed at all." The same applies if the page title is irrelevant or incorrectly translated.

The Web Accessibility Initiative (WAI) also provides a particular technique (G88) to help developers implement this criterion correctly.[13] In this technique, they prescribe the following rules to write descriptive page titles:

The title of each Web page should:

– Identify the subject of the Web page
– Make sense when read out of context, for example by a screen reader or in a site map or list of search results
– Be short

It may also be helpful for the title to

– Identify the site or other resource to which the Web page belongs
– Be unique within the site or other resource to which the Web page belongs"

(Accessibility Guidelines Working Group, 2022: sec.G88)

For our analysis, taking these recommendations into account, as well as those from other key stakeholders in the field of accessibility (Berners-Lee, 1992; Kirkpatrick et al., 2018; White et al., 2020; Google Developers, 2022b; WHATWG, 2022: sec.4.2.2) and considering the researchers' expertise on the subject, we decided to manually examine the titles of our web sample against the following compliance criteria:

1. The title is short, i.e., it does not contain more than sixty-four characters.[14]

---

[13] However, note that, at the time of writing, only two test rules were included in the list of WCAG 2 test rules (W3C Web Accessibility Initiative (WAI) 2022) in relation to the title of the page element, i.e., "HTML page title is descriptive" and "HTML page has non-empty title".

[14] As per Berners-Lee's (1992) recommendation. Other accessibility stakeholders (Mozilla and individual contributors, 2022) recommend a limit of 55–60 characters in the title of a page for

2. The title identifies the subject of the web page.
3. The title makes sense when read out of context.
4. The title does not include repetitions.[15]
5. The title does not include abbreviations without the expanded form.
6. The title does not include URL addresses.

When analyzing the localized versions, we observed that this particular subsample had its own language-related issues, so we decided to add three new criteria to our initial list. Hence, we additionally assessed the titles in the Spanish web pages against the following criteria:

7. The localized title differs from the original title.[16]
8. The text is in the target language.[17]
9. The title is not composed of text in both the original and the target languages.

Google Lighthouse can determine only if the <title> element is present or not (Google Developers, 2019b). Consequently, the nine criteria described above were assessed only through manual inspection.

As can be inferred from the list, some of these criteria depend heavily on human judgment and can be examined only in context. For instance, it is not possible to determine if the title accurately describes the subject of the page without reading the content of the page (criteria 2 and 3). Similarly, criterion 7 requires a comparison between the title of two different pages, while automating the verification of criteria 8 and 9 would imply the use of specialized natural language processing (NLP) tools. Other criteria can be subjectively analyzed on the isolated titles themselves; for example, to determine if an abbreviation was used without its expanded form (criterion 5). Certain criteria can even be automatically measured, such as determination of the title length, which we accomplished by automatically calculating the total number of characters in our evaluation template (criterion 1).[18]

It is worth highlighting here that several authors (White et al., 2020; Accessibility Guidelines Working Group, 2022: sec.G88; Google

---

search engine optimization (SEO) purposes, as search engines generally do not display more than that number of characters.

[15] The title should convey the subject of the page in the most efficient way: it needs to be succinct but also to avoid any redundant information. Hence, we considered that repeated content represented an error when evaluating this accessibility feature.

[16] The only exceptions that we applied to this criterion were in cases where the title was composed of the original English name of the organization, which also had not been translated into Spanish in the rest of the web page.

[17] The exception described in the previous note was also applied to this criterion.

[18] Using the LEN function in MS Excel. https://support.microsoft.com/en-us/office/len-lenb-functions-29236f94-cedc-429d-affd-b5e33d2c67cb. Last access: March 20, 2022.

Developers, 2022b; Mozilla and individual contributors, 2022) also recommend verifying that the titles of the web pages are unique within their websites. Nevertheless, we did not include this recommendation in the compliance criteria of our study because we focused on the home pages, and not on complete websites. In addition, we decided not to examine other recommendations and best practices which have SEO implications and/or that are more related to style preferences (e.g., "Brand your titles concisely" (Google Developers, 2022b)). Nonetheless, it would be pertinent to observe and assess them in future research.

7.4 Results

In order to answer our main research question, we collected and analyzed the overall accessibility scores of all the pages in our web sample, as provided by Google Lighthouse. These initial results indicated that the accessibility score of the 148 home pages thus analyzed was, on average, good[19] ($\bar{x}$ = 90, sd = 8.9). We did not find noteworthy differences between the results of the English (EN) home pages ($\bar{x}$ = 90.1, sd = 8.6) and the Spanish (ES) ones ($\bar{x}$ = 90, sd = 9.3). Therefore, if we were just to consider the results of the general automatic evaluation, we could conclude that the localized subsample (ES) seems to be as accessible as the original one (EN), thus tentatively disconfirming our initial hypothesis.

In a subsequent stage, we looked at the accessibility audits that were not met according to Google Lighthouse in each page, considered individually. Table 7.1 provides an overview of the errors detected by the tool, sorted from the most common to the least. The most recurrent errors were the following: "insufficient contrast ratio between the background and foreground colors," which was present in 84 (57 percent) of the pages analyzed; "links did not have a discernible name," present in 76 (51 percent) pages; "heading elements were not in a sequentially-descending order," present in 55 (37 percent) pages; and "images elements did not have the alt attribute," present in 40 (27 percent) pages. As we can see from the data in Table 7.1, according to Google Lighthouse's results, there are only minor differences between the EN and ES subsamples. A full discussion of these unmet criteria is beyond the scope of this study, but would certainly merit further consideration in future research.

---

[19] Google Lighthouse uses a traffic-light system to interpret the overall results in the reports: green represents scores from 90 to 100 (good), orange 50–89 (needs improvement) and red 0–49 (poor).

Table 7.1 *Accessibility errors (total number and %) in the study web sample according to Google Lighthouse*

Type of error	EN	ES	Total
Background and foreground colors do not have a sufficient contrast ratio	44 (59%)	40 (54%)	84 (57%)
Links do not have a discernible name	39 (53%)	37 (50%)	76 (51%)
Heading elements are not in a sequentially-descending order	29 (39%)	26 (35%)	55 (37%)
Image elements do not have [alt] attributes	22 (30%)	18 (24%)	40 (27%)
Buttons do not have an accessible name	12 (16%)	14 (19%)	26 (18%)
[user-scalable="no"] is used in the <meta name="viewport"> element or the [maximum-scale] attribute is less than 5	8 (11%)	8 (11%)	16 (11%)
[id] attributes on active, focusable elements are not unique	7 (9%)	5 (7%)	12 (8%)
Lists do not contain only <li> elements and script supporting elements (<script> and <template>)	7 (9%)	6 (8%)	13 (9%)
[aria-hidden="true"] elements contain focusable descendants	7 (9%)	9 (12%)	16 (11%)
ARIA IDs are not unique	7 (9%)	7 (9%)	14 (9%)
<frame> or <iframe> elements do not have a title	5 (7%)	4 (5%)	9 (6%)
ARIA input fields do not have accessible names	5 (7%)	3 (4%)	8 (5%)
<html> element does not have a [lang] attribute	**4 (5%)**	**5 (7%)**	**9 (6%)**
Some elements have a [tabindex] value greater than 0	3 (4%)	4 (5%)	7 (5%)
[role] values are not valid	3 (4%)	4 (5%)	7 (5%)
[role]s do not have all required [aria-*] attributes	3 (4%)	3 (4%)	(6) 4%
<object> elements do not have [alt] text	2 (3%)	3 (4%)	(5) 3%
List items (<li>) are not contained within <ul> or <ol> parent elements	2 (3%)	2 (3%)	(4) 3%
[role]s are not contained by their required parent element	2 (3%)	1 (1%)	(3) 2%
[aria-*] attributes do not have valid values	2 (3%)	2 (3%)	(4) 3%
button, link, and menuitem elements do not have accessible names	2 (3%)	3 (4%)	(5) 3%
Form elements do not have associated labels	1 (1%)	1 (1%)	(2) 1%
Elements with an ARIA [role] that require children to contain a specific [role] are missing some or all of those required children.	1 (1%)	2 (3%)	(3) 2%
The page does not contain a heading, skip link, or landmark region	0 (0%)	1 (1%)	(1) 1%

Note also that Google Lighthouse does not provide partially compliant results (Google Developers, 2019a), since it only provides a pass, fail, or non-applicable value for each of the forty-two accessibility audits that it performs. For example, if all of the image elements have alt attributes except for one, that page will entirely fail this specific accessibility audit. This approach, while effective, might not always reflect the impact of errors on the final user experience: for instance, omitting a text alternative for an image on the footer of the page might not have the same effect as omitting it for a content-rich image in the page's main body. This rationale is consistent with the most recent scoring proposal proposed by the W3C in the draft of the new WCAG 3.0 now in progress, which explores various scoring mechanisms beyond binary true/false tests (Spellman et al., 2021b: sec.5). Still, only empirical studies with end users would enable us to identify the real impact of partial violations of accessibility compliance.

7.4.1 Language of the Page

To study this accessibility feature in our web sample, we first analyzed the results from Google Lighthouse, and then compared them with those from the manual inspection. Overall, according to this automated tool, 139 out of the 148 (94 percent) pages defined the language of the page. The value of the lang attribute in those pages was also considered correct. In other words, as indicated in Table 7.1 (see the row with text in bold), nine pages were not compliant with this criterion according to Google Lighthouse, since they did not define the lang attribute in the root element. More specifically, four pages were from the EN subsample and five were from the ES one.

Figure 7.1 shows the percentage of pages per language that met the three compliance criteria defined in Section 7.3.3.1. In the case of the EN subsample, the results of the human and the automatic evaluation are identical: seventy out of the seventy-four pages (95 percent) featured the lang attribute with a valid value.

By contrast, the results from the manual inspection on the ES subsample do differ from the automated ones. Only forty-four of the seventy-four pages (59 percent) met this success criterion in the ES subsample (see Figure 7.1). The errors discovered during the human evaluation were related to the specific value used in the lang attribute, which did not match the language of the page (es). As previously explained, in the manual inspection, we not only checked the presence and validity of the lang attribute (criteria 1 and 2), but also examined whether the value of that attribute matched the language of the

Table 7.2 *Language values (total number) used in our web sample*

	en	en-US	en-GB	es	es-ES	es-US	es-MX
EN pages	51	18	1	-	-	-	-
ES pages	17	8	-	34	5	4	1

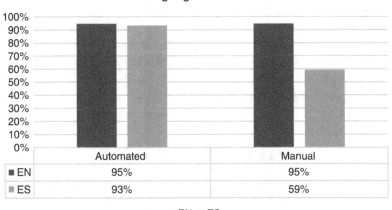

Figure 7.1 Pages (%) per language subsample complying with SC 3.1.1

pages from that subset (criterion 3). Table 7.2 displays the breakdown of the values found in the lang attributes. In the case of the Spanish subsample, seventeen pages defined the language of the page as English (en) and eight as English from the US (en-US). These results allow us to answer research question 1.1, since we could argue that the localized subsample of web pages was after all less accessible than the original one, as we initially hypothesized.

7.4.2 Title of the Page

The automatic tool identified no errors related to SC 2.4.2 because all the pages in our web sample had a <title> element. Nevertheless, as explained in Section 7.3.3.2, our manual inspection involved a more in-depth examination of the titles. We analyzed all the EN and ES titles independently against the criteria defined, annotating all the errors found in each title. We considered that the title was not valid if at least one of the criteria was not met. Similarly, note that there is only one title per page. Therefore, the data presented in this section refer not only to the percentage of titles in our sample that comply with SC 2.4.2., but also to the percentage of pages that passed this criterion.

The overall results of our manual inspection showed that less than half of the pages (62 of the 148, 42 percent) were compliant with all the criteria defined. Nonetheless, results differ across the two language subsamples, as can be observed in Figure 7.2. While less than half of the EN titles (34 out of 74, 46 percent) contained at least one error, more than half of the ES titles (52 out of 74, 70 percent)

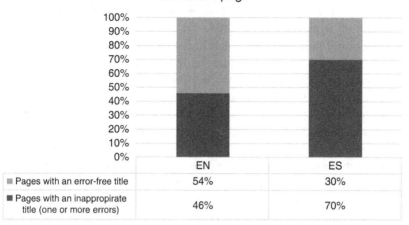

Figure 7.2 Pages (%) per language subsample complying with SC 2.4.2

contained one or more errors. This data seems to indicate that the titles of the localized versions (ES) were less accessible than the EN titles, thus allowing us to affirmatively answer research question 1.2 and support our initial hypothesis.

Tables 7.3 and 7.4 present an overview of the types of errors found in the titles, as well as examples taken from our web sample. The former shows the results from criteria 1–6, and the latter presents the results concerning criteria 7–9, which we checked only against the titles in the localized Spanish pages.

Importantly, in the ES subsample, 15 percent (11 out of 74) of the titles were left in English: they were either the same as their equivalent titles in the EN subsample, or had been changed but were still written in English. In the context of our study, those titles were considered erroneous since they were not written in Spanish, so they were not further analyzed against criteria 1 to 6. Hence, the data we present below account for that dissimilarity. In other words, they present the total number of occurrences as well as the percentage according to the total number of titles analyzed in each subsample, that is, 137 pages: seventy-four in the EN subsample and sixty-three in the ES subsample. Let us now summarize the results per criterion verified:

1. The title is short. We found that the titles of 38 of the 137 analyzed pages (28 percent) had more than 64 characters: 20 of the 74 titles in EN (27 percent) and 18 of the 63 analyzed titles (29 percent) in ES. As can be observed in the example provided in Table 7.3, that was the case of the home page of the American Kidney Fund in English, whose title was comprised of 137 characters.

2. The title identifies the subject of the web page. We found eight titles (6 percent) that did not meet this criterion: three in EN (4 percent) and five in ES (8 percent). For example, the title of the home page of the Life Options Rehabilitation Program in English was just "home."

3. The title makes sense when read out of context. The titles of ten pages (7 percent) violated this criterion. This error was more recurrent in the titles of the ES pages (N = 7, 11 percent) than in the EN pages (N = 3, 4 percent). When analyzing this criterion, we realized it was strongly related to the previous one (criterion 2). For instance, we interpreted that the previous example "home" did not identify the subject of the page, nor did it make sense when read out of context. In Table 7.3, we provide another example of a title that was not compliant with this criterion: the title of the National Organ and Tissue Donation Initiative in English was "Organ Donor | Organ Donor". Although a semantic relationship can be established between the title and the subject of the page, we considered that a user would not be able to identify that the title refers to that organization when read out of context.

4. The title does not include repetitions. Eight titles (6 percent) did not meet this criterion: three in EN (4 percent) and five in ES (8 percent). Table 7.3 includes three examples of titles with these unnecessary repetitions. The first one is

Table 7.3 *Overview of the errors (total number and %) found in the title of the pages, criteria 1–6*

Type of error	EN (74 pages/ titles)	ES (63 pages/ titles)	Example
1. Too long	20 (27%)	18 (29%)	The American Kidney Fund (AKF) fights kidney disease on all fronts as the nation's leading kidney nonprofit. – American Kidney Fund (AKF)
2. It does not identify the subject of the web page	3 (4%)	5 (8%)	home
3. It does not make sense when read out of context	3 (4%)	7 (11%)	Organ Donor	Organ Donor
4. Repetition	3 (4%)	5 (8%)	Medicare.gov: the official US government site for Medicare	Medicare
5. Abbreviation without expanded form	11 (15%)	12 (19%)	Home	NIDCD
6. URL	6 (8%)	8 (13%)		FEMA.gov

from the home page in EN of the American Kidney Fund; the second is the
from the home page in EN of the National Organ and Tissue Donation; and
the third is in the title of the home page of Medicare in EN.

5. The title does not include abbreviations without the expanded form. This
was one of the most common criterion violations found in our web sample,
as 23 pages (17 percent) had an abbreviation without the expanded form in
the title: 11 in EN (15 percent) and 12 in ES (19 percent). For example, the
title of the home page in EN of the National Institute on Deafness and Other
Communication Disorders was "Home | NIDCD." People unfamiliar with
this organization might not be able to decode the acronym by just reading
the title of the home page, especially when read out of context or through
assistive technology.

6. The title does not include URL addresses. We found fourteen titles (10 percent) that did not meet this criterion: six in EN (8 percent) and eight in ES
(13 percent). For example, the Federal Emergency Management Agency in
both the EN and ES home pages used the title "| FEMA.gov." Again, people
who know neither those organizations nor the URLs of the official websites
might be unable to identify the subject of the page with such a title.

All in all, the data suggests that there were more SC 2.4.1 violations in the
pages of the ES subsample than in the EN ones. The two most common errors
were: a) the excessive length of the titles, and b) the presence of abbreviations
without an expanded form. We now go on to describe in detail the three criteria
that were analyzed only in the ES subsample (see Table 7.4):

7. The localized title differs from the original title. Ten pages in our ES
subsample had the same title as in the EN page, but we considered that
only eight (11 percent) violated this principle. This dissimilarity was
due to the exception we made concerning the titles that included only

Table 7.4 *Overview of the errors (total number and %) found in the title of the
pages in the ES subsample, criteria 7–9*

Type of error	ES (74 pages/titles)	Example
7. Same as in EN	8 (11%)	Home – National Osteoporosis Foundation
8. Text in EN	11 (15%)	HOME – Spanish Office of Minority health
9. Combination of EN and ES	7 (9%)	En Español| Genetic and Rare Diseases Information Center (GARD) – an NCATS Program

the name of the organization. This was the reasoning in these particular cases:

a) If the name was in English and no official Spanish translation was proposed and used by the organization in the home page, the title was considered correct. We found two pages whose titles met this condition. We contend that not translating the name of the organization is completely valid, especially if it is treated as a proper noun.

b) If the name was in English within the title but it appeared in Spanish in the body of the localized web page, we marked it as an error. That was the case, for example, of the National Osteoporosis Foundation, that used in the ES home page the same title as in the EN page: "Home National Osteoporosis Foundation." However, in the main content of the ES version, users could find the corresponding name of the organization in ES: "Fundación Nacional de la Osteoporosis."

8. The text is in the target language. The titles of eleven pages (15 percent) from our ES subsample did not meet this criterion. We included in this category titles that were left in English and considered incorrect (i.e., the eight titles that did not meet criterion 7) and three additional titles that were different from the EN original title but were left in English. That was the case of the home page in ES of the Office of Minority Health: in the title "HOME – Spanish Office of Minority health," the text was different from that of the original EN page "Home Page – Office of Minority Health (OMH)," but still in the source language. In addition, the name of the organization in Spanish was included in the footer: "Oficina de Salud de Minorías."

9. The title is not composed of text in both the original and the target languages. Seven pages (9 percent) from our ES subsample violated this criterion because they included a combination of English and Spanish in their titles. This occurred, for example, on the website of the Genetic and Rare Diseases Information Center (GARD): "En Español | Genetic and Rare Diseases Information Center (GARD) – an NCATS Program."[20] Screen readers, when reading aloud, normally pronounce in only one language by default. A title like this one could be difficult to understand, since part of the sentence would be mispronounced. Further research with screen reader users would be needed to fully understand whether such bilingual strings actually represent a real accessibility obstacle.

---

[20] The original title in EN was "Genetic and Rare Diseases Information Center (GARD) – an NCATS Program | Providing information about rare or genetic diseases."

7.5 Discussion and Conclusions

Access to health information is crucial in today's society. This study set out to investigate the accessibility of health websites from a localization perspective. We gathered a web sample of seventy-four multilingual websites of health organizations mainly based in the US, assuming that EN was the source language and ES the target. Then we used automatic and human evaluation methods to check the home page of both language versions against two localization-related WCAG success criteria: 2.4.2, Page titled and 3.1.1, Language of the page.

The results provided by the automatic tool showed that the overall accessibility of the assessed web pages was generally high, and no noteworthy differences were observed between the two language versions. At first, this seemed to refute our initial hypothesis, as we expected the localized subsample to be less accessible than the original one. However, our manual inspection evaluation analysis revealed several underlying accessibility barriers with regard to the two success criteria analyzed in the target version. Our results are consistent with those of Jiménez-Crespo (2008), Minacapilli (2018), and Pontus (2019) with regard to the lower accessibility level observed in localized websites when compared to the original ones – first, with respect to general accessibility scores and secondly, in relation to the appropriateness of the page language definition and title.

The fact that some titles and language values were not modified in the localized pages suggests that these aspects might have been overlooked during localization. We hypothesize that this oversight could be due to some combination of the following factors:

a) *Lack of localization knowledge.* The localization process entails not only the translation of the textual content of the page, but also the modification of other technical and cultural aspects, such as the adaptation of the two accessibility features studied. Localization agents might have simply overlooked the need to modify the target page title or its language definition, whether unintentionally or due to lack of experience and know-how.

b) *Lack of accessibility knowledge.* We contend that accessibility assurance should be an inherent step in the localization process. Agents involved in the development of the examined web sample might have been unaware of accessibility guidelines and recommendations, and may therefore have overlooked implementation of the best practices we investigated. Thus we stress the importance of including accessibility study in the curricula of translators and localizers (Torres-del-Rey and Rodríguez Vázquez, 2016) or in the current localization data exchange standards (Torres-del-Rey and Morado Vázquez, 2019).

c) *Varied access to web authoring tool settings.* Localization workflows vary depending on the number of agents involved in the process, their professional profiles, and the available tools, among other aspects. Sometimes, when working directly on web authoring tools, translators or localizers have access only to the main content of the web page, and not to all the metadata that should be adapted, which might be hidden and/or protected. For example, in modern Content Management Systems, both the language and the title of a page are typically defined in a specific "properties" section, not on the page editor where the main content of the page can be modified. Inability to reach those particular sections due to lack of expertise or limited access rights could have contributed to the failure to make all the necessary changes in the ES versions. In other workflows, localizable content is extracted from the web authoring tool and brought into a localization data exchange file, such as XLIFF (Torres-del-Rey and Morado Vázquez, 2015). Again, depending on the tool settings, all localizable information might or might not be contained therein. In any case, we believe that well-trained localization specialists with accessibility knowledge would have been able to identify the issues related to SC 2.4.2 and SC 3.1.1 and to propose appropriate solutions.

7.5.1 Challenges in Localization-Oriented Accessibility Evaluation

Our study helped us identify a number of challenges related to the application of existing accessibility evaluation methods for the assessment of localized websites. With no claim to be exhaustive, we list some of them in this section, particularly in relation to the success criteria which were our focus.

7.5.1.1 Automated Audits

As mentioned in Section 7.3, and demonstrated through the results presented in Section 7.4, the automated tool used in this study was not able to check all the multilingual accessibility compliance criteria defined. Firstly, with respect to the language of the page, the tool was unable to identify the mismatch between the value of the lang attribute and the actual language of the web pages. While this error was absent in the EN subsample, manual inspection revealed that certain pages in the ES subsample did violate this criterion. Secondly, with regard to the title of the page, only its presence could be verified; the other nine defined criteria had to be assessed through manual inspection. These divergences between automated and human evaluation methods were also observed in prior work. For instance, Hanson and Richards (2013: 19), in a WA study combining automated and human evaluation, did indeed find that manual inspection revealed more errors than were detected by automated evaluation.

Our results reinforce the well-stablished idea that, when evaluating WA, it is paramount to complement the use of automated tools with manual inspection of the pages being studied (Abou-Zahra, 2008; Brajnik, 2008). However, this point becomes even more crucial for multilingual WA assessment. As we have already noted in previous studies (Rodríguez Vázquez, 2016b), there is still room for improvement in automated accessibility evaluation tools with regard to the verification of language-related aspects. Some of the additional audits that could be implemented to facilitate localization-oriented accessibility evaluation are:

1. Concerning the language of the page, the tool could feature an audit through which the human language used in the content of the page is recognized[21] and later compared with the value used in the lang attribute.
2. Regarding the title of the page, the tool could also integrate some of the compliance criteria we defined, so that it could: a) automatically measure the title's length (criterion 1); or b) by using regular expressions, detect repeated content (criterion 4), abbreviations without expanded form (criterion 5), or URL addresses (criterion 6). In addition, the technology used in existing CAT tools (such as quality assessment modules including spell checkers) could be integrated to check criteria 7, 8, and 9.

7.5.1.2 Definition of Compliance Criteria

For the purposes of our study, we defined and applied a specific list of language-oriented accessibility compliance criteria. Our ultimate goal was to complement other lists of criteria already defined in existing resources – for instance, in automated tools or in the test rule set of the W3C (W3C Web Accessibility Initiative, 2022) – in order to add localization-oriented value. In the process, however, we have also identified several challenges that deserve further consideration in future investigations.

The criteria selected to assess page titles were based mainly on official recommendations, as explained in Section 7.3.2.2. However, to the best of our knowledge, those recommendations do not stem from empirical research;

---

[21] This is done, for instance, in popular online Machine Translation tools, such as Google Translate: https://translate.google.com Last access: March 10, 2022.

hence the need to conduct more studies on their actual accessibility impact. Further, most of the existing recommendations are open for interpretation. For example, the recommendation for the length of titles is described by the WAI only as "short." To establish a length threshold in our study that would enable us to objectively measure this criterion's compliance, we used the 64-character limit recommended by Tim Berners-Lee (1992) in his Style Guide for online hypertext. However, it would be worthwhile to explore the possibility of defining a more flexible rule that would acknowledge that different languages might tolerate different limits.[22]

As a related matter, the geographical and cultural context of the sites' target audience should also be considered when verifying web page titles. For example, acronyms could be considered in titles if they are well known by the target audience and therefore do not pose accessibility barriers. With due recognition for the universal nature of the Web, in these particular cases, it would be ideal during human evaluation to include accessibility experts or end users living in the relevant geographical context to help decide on the best strategy. For health websites, this approach could be followed for local nonprofit or community association portals. For international websites, however, its validity should be scientifically measured.

All in all, we believe that web developers, localizers, and accessibility experts could benefit from a single resource that would assemble these and other recommendations for multilingual WA assessment. Our current list of nine criteria could serve as a starting point for building that cohesive resource, and could pave the way for future empirical studies in which the impact of the final list could be tested with real users.

7.5.1.3 Need for Accessibility Enablers with an Interdisciplinary Background

We firmly believe that localization professionals could play a leading role in making a website accessible, not only by ensuring the accessibility of the final localized web product but also by revealing and resolving compliance issues in the original version. Both of the researchers involved in the study presented here are web localization and accessibility experts. However, in a non-academic context, more human resources would probably have been needed to conduct a multilingual accessibility evaluation – at least a web developer and an accessibility expert per language version. These requirements could imply

---

[22] See, for instance, the data reported by the W3C in relation to text size in translation: www .w3.org/International/articles/article-text-size Last access: February 11, 2022.

more complex workflows and increased costs for websites with more than two language versions.

In this sense, advocacy for interdisciplinary training is essential. In the last decade, several members of the Cod.eX research group have put forward various proposals for the inclusion of accessibility in the curricula of translation and localization training programs (Torres-del-Rey and Rodríguez Vázquez, 2016; Torres-del-Rey 2019). Similarly, we have suggested integration of accessibility best practices and evaluation procedures in the quality assurance phase of the localization process (Rodríguez Vázquez and O'Brien, 2017; Torres-del-Rey and Morado Vázquez, 2019). It is true that, in an ideal scenario, accessibility should not be treated as an afterthought but as in integral step in web development and localization processes. However, accessibility audits performed before the launch of the localized web product would contribute to the detection and avoidance of the compliance violations that we observed in our study, among others. This strategy requires not only continuing technological progress, so that new types of audits concerning language-related accessibility features can be integrated, but also understanding of the need for accessibility enablers with interdisciplinary backgrounds.

7.5.2 Limitations and Future Work

As explained at the beginning of Section 7.5, the present study extends current knowledge of multilingual WA. However, we are aware that our findings resist generalization: our web sample was limited in terms of genre (health websites), language combination (English and Spanish), and geographical context (US and International organizations), among others. Moreover, our study focused upon only two aspects that can affect the accessibility of a web page. In order to obtain a comprehensive picture of the accessibility of multilingual health websites, a broader evaluation should be conducted – for instance, by (a) examining the quality of the multilingual health information included in the site; (b) verifying other success criteria; or (c) involving members of selected target population groups (e.g., migrants or screen reader users) in the human evaluation of the two accessibility features studied. For instance, it would be worth exploring whether the use of different user agents (including browsers and assistive technologies) impacts the acceptability of page titles, particularly concerning limitations in the number of characters (i.e., of title length) or the combined use of languages (i.e., of multilingual titles).

Apart from the ideas for future work already shared in previous sections, another potentially fruitful avenue for new research is the study of similar websites from other geographical contexts and with other language combinations. We have studied websites mainly from US organizations. Further studies could include, for example, multilingual websites from organizations based in Spanish-speaking countries, in order to explore whether similar accessibility violations are observed. Similarly, a follow-up study could examine our web sample in greater depth. For instance, it would be interesting to consider multiple Spanish variants, including "International Spanish" (Jiménez-Crespo, 2010) and to study the various localization strategies adopted, as per Yunker (2003), to deal with varied Spanish-speaking end users. We could also examine the websites of organizations based in the states with the highest concentration of Hispanics, as in prior work with US web corpora (Jiménez-Crespo, 2012), and could investigate whether the accessibility level of the localized Spanish pages is higher when compared with other sites in the sample.

In addition, further studies could examine the influence of web authoring tools in the establishment of certain accessibility best practices, including those we have analyzed: the language and title of web pages. As we have hypothesized, the lack of access to certain advanced features might impact the adaptation of those metadata elements. However, other factors might also condition the final content rendering. For example, to create the title of a given page, certain tools recommend combining the general name of the website with that of the page to be described.[23] As we have observed, for home pages, this procedure could yield redundant titles or repetitions.

In conclusion, we have attempted to demonstrate that localization specialists can play a central role in identifying and resolving accessibility issues to produce a more accessible multilingual web for all. Our findings and suggestions will, we hope, help others to explore new ways of studying multilingual accessibility and to better understand the causes of imbalances between original and localized website versions.

7.6 Acknowledgments

The preliminary results of our study were presented at the 7th International IATIS Conference. Barcelona, Spain, September 14–17, 2021. We would like to thank the organizers of our panel for the valuable feedback provided.

---

[23] See an example of this practice at https://documentation.concretecms.org/tutorials/how-to-change-the-default-site-name-page-title-formatting-in-5–7. Last access: February 11, 2022.

References

Abou-Zahra, S. 2008. "Web Accessibility Evaluation," in S. Harper and Y. Yesilada, eds., *Web Accessibility. A Foundation for Research*, Human-Computer Interaction Series, London: Springer-Verlag, pages 79–106.

Abou-Zahra, S., H. de Vries, and M. Hansma. 2021. *WCAG-EM Report Tool* [online], available: www.w3.org/WAI/eval/report-tool/#!/evaluation/audit.

Accessibility Guidelines Working Group. 2022. "Techniques for WCAG 2.1," available: www.w3.org/WAI/WCAG21/Techniques/#techniques.

Acosta-Vargas, P., T. Acosta, and S. Luján-Mora. 2018. "Framework for Accessibility Evaluation of Hospital Websites," in *2018 International Conference on EDemocracy EGovernment (ICEDEG)*, Presented at the 2018 International Conference on eDemocracy eGovernment (ICEDEG), 9–15, available: https://doi.org/10.1109/ICEDEG.2018.8372368.

Acosta-Vargas, P. and G. Acosta-Vargas. 2021. "(Dataset) The most visited health websites in the world," available: 10.17632/n468trh5my.1.

Acosta-Vargas, P., Y. Rybarczyk, J. Pérez, et al. 2018. "Towards Web Accessibility in Telerehabilitation Platforms," in *2018 IEEE Third Ecuador Technical Chapters Meeting (ETCM)*, Presented at the 2018 IEEE Third Ecuador Technical Chapters Meeting (ETCM), 1–6, available: https://doi.org/10.1109/ETCM.2018.8580272.

Adams, C., A. Campbell, R. B. Montgomery, M. Cooper, and A. Kirkpatrick (Eds.). 2021. "Web Content Accessibility Guidelines (WCAG) 2.2," available: www.w3.org/TR/WCAG22/.

Alajarmeh, N. 2021. "Evaluating the Accessibility of Public Health Websites: An Exploratory Cross-Country Study," Universal Access in the Information Society, available: https://doi.org/10.1007/s10209-020-00788-7.

Andreu-Vall, M. and M.-C. Marcos. 2012. "Evaluación de sitios web multilingües: metodología y herramienta heurística," *El profesional de la información*, 21 (3), pages 254–260.

Berland, G. K., M. N. Elliott, L. S. Morales, et al. 2001. "Health Information on the Internet: Accessibility, Quality, and Readability in English and Spanish," *JAMA*, 285 (20), pages 2612–2621.

Berners-Lee, T. 1992. The TITLE Element in HTML [online], available: www.w3.org/Provider/Style/TITLE.html.

Brajnik, G. 2008. "Beyond Conformance: The Role of Accessibility Evaluation Methods," in S. Hartmann, X. Zhou, and M. Kirchberg, eds., *Web Information Systems Engineering – WISE 2008 Workshops*, Lecture Notes in Computer Science, Springer Berlin Heidelberg, 63–80.

Brajnik, G. 2009. "Heuristic Evaluation Guided by Accessibility Barriers," available: https://users.dimi.uniud.it/~giorgio.brajnik/projects/bw/bw.html#nv_d7e1762.

Campbell, A., M. Cooper, and A. Kirkpatrick (Eds.). 2022. "Understanding WCAG 2.1," available: www.w3.org/WAI/WCAG21/Understanding/.

Casalegno, E. 2018. *Usability of Partially Localised Websites in Switzerland: A Study with Screen Reader Users*. Master Thesis,Université de Genève.

Chen, E. C., R. P. Manecksha, R. Abouassaly, et al. 2014. "A Multilingual Evaluation of Current Health Information on the Internet for the Treatments of Benign Prostatic

Hyperplasia," *Prostate International*, 2 (4), pages 161–168, available: https://doi.org/10.12954/PI.14058.

Chisholm, W., G. Vanderheiden, and I. Jacobs (Eds.). 1999. "Web Content Accessibility Guidelines 1.0," available: http://www.w3.org/TR/WCAG10/.

Deque Systems. 2022. Documents Must Contain a Title Element to Aid in Navigation Axe Rules | Deque University | Deque Systems [online], *Documents must contain a title element to aid in navigation Axe* Rules | *Deque University* | *Deque Systems*, available: https://dequeuniversity.com/rules/axe/3.2/document-title.

European Union. 2021. *Union of Equality: Strategy for the Rights of Persons with Disabilities 2021–2030* [online], Luxembourg: Publications Office of the European Union, available: https://ec.europa.eu/social/main.jsp?catId=738&langId=en&pubId=8376&furtherPubs=yes.

Fernández-Díaz, E., P. P. Iglesias-Sánchez, and C. Jambrino-Maldonado. 2020. "Exploring WHO Communication during the COVID 19 Pandemic through the WHO Website Based on W3C Guidelines: Accessible for All?" *International Journal of Environmental Research and Public Health*, 17 (16), page 5663, available: https://doi.org/10.3390/ijerph17165663.

Gibson, J. and R. O'Connor. 2010. "Access to Health Care for Disabled People: A Systematic Review," *Social Care and Neurodisability*, 1 (3), pages 21–31, available: https://doi.org/10.5042/scn.2010.0599.

Google Developers. 2019a. Lighthouse Accessibility Scoring [online], *web.dev*, available:https://web.dev/accessibility-scoring/.

Google Developers. 2019b. Document Doesn't Have a <title> Element [online], *web.dev*, available: https://web.dev/document-title/.

Google Developers. 2019c. <html> Element Does Not Have a [Lang] Attribute [online], *web.dev*, available: https://web.dev/html-has-lang/.

Google Developers. 2019d. [Lang] Attributes Do Not Have a Valid Value [online], *web.dev*, available: https://web.dev/valid-lang/.

Google Developers. 2021. Lighthouse | Tools for Web Developers [online], *Google Developers*, available: https://developers.google.com/web/tools/lighthouse.

Google Developers. 2022a. Accessibility Audits [online], *Accessibility audits*, available: https://web.dev/lighthouse-accessibility/.

Google Developers. 2022b. How to Write Title Tags for SEO [online], available: https://developers.google.com/search/docs/advanced/appearance/title-link?hl=fr.

Hamzehei, R., M. Ansari, S. Rahmatizadeh, and S. Valizadeh-Haghi. 2018. "Websites As a Tool for Public Health Education: Determining the Trustworthiness of Health Websites on Ebola Disease," *Online Journal of Public Health Informatics*, 10 (3), available: https://doi.org/10.5210/ojphi.v10i3.9544.

Hanson, V. L. and J. T. Richards. 2013. "Progress on Website Accessibility?" *ACM Transactions on the Web*, 7 (1): pages 1–2: 30, available: https://doi.org/10.1145/2435215.2435217.

Ishida, R. 2014. Language Tags in HTML and XML [online], available: www.w3.org/International/articles/language-tags/.

Ishida, R. 2016. "Choosing a Language Tag", available: www.w3.org/International/questions/qa-choosing-language-tags.

Jiménez-Crespo, M. Á. 2008. *El proceso de localización web: estudio contrastivo de un corpus comparable del género sitio web corporativo*, available: http://digibug.ugr.es /handle/10481/1908#.U9Yqv7HiNuQ.

Jiménez-Crespo, M. Á. 2010. *"Web Internationalization Strategies and Translation Quality: Researching the Case of 'International'* Spanish," *Localization Focus – The International Journal of Localization*, (8), pages 13–25.

Jiménez-Crespo, M. Á. 2012. "'Loss' or 'Lost' in Translation: A Contrastive Genre Study of Original and Localised Non-Profit US Websites," *JoSTrans – The Journal of Specialized Translation*, (17).

Jiménez-Crespo, M. Á. 2013. *Translation and Web Localization*, Oxon: Routledge.

Jiménez-Crespo, M. Á. 2017. *"Combining Corpus and Experimental Studies: Insights into the Reception of Translated Medical Texts,"* JoSTrans – The Journal of Specialised Translation*, (28), pages 2–22.

Jiménez-Crespo, M. Á. 2019. "Localization and Localization Research in Spanish-Speaking Contexts," in R. A. Valdeón and Á. Vidal Claramonte, eds., *The Routledge Handbook of Spanish Translation Studies*, Oxon: Routledge, pages 352–364.

Jiménez-Crespo, M. Á. and M. Tercedor Sánchez. 2017. "Lexical Variation, Register and Explicitation in Medical Translation: A Comparable Corpus Study of Medical Terminology in US Websites Translated into Spanish," *Translation and Interpreting Studies. The Journal of the American Translation and Interpreting Studies Association*, available: https://doi.org/10.1075/tis.12.3.03jim.

Kirkpatrick, A., J. O. Connor, A. Campbell, and M. Cooper. 2018. "Web Content Accessibility Guidelines (WCAG) 2.1," available: www.w3.org/TR/WCAG21/.

Kushalnagar, P., J. Naturale, R. Paludneviciene, et al. 2015. "Health Websites: Accessibility and Usability for American Sign Language Users," *Health Communication*, 30 (8), pages 830–837, available: https://doi.org/10.1080/10410236 .2013.853226.

Lawrentschuk, N., D. Sasges, R. Tasevski, et al. 2012. "Oncology Health Information Quality on the Internet: A Multilingual Evaluation," *Annals of Surgical Oncology*, 19 (3), pages 706–713, available: https://doi.org/10.1245/s10434-011-2137-x.

Lüchtenberg, M., C. Kuhli-Hattenbach, Y. Sinangin, C. Ohrloff, and R. Schalnus. 2008. "Accessibility of Health Information on the Internet to the Visually Impaired User," *Ophthalmologica*, 222 (3), pages 187–193, available: https://doi.org/10.1159 /000126082.

Mancini, C., M. Zedda, and A. Barbaro. 2005. "Health information in Italian public health websites: moving from inaccessibility to accessibility," *Health Information & Libraries Journal*, 22 (4), pages 276–285, available: https://doi.org/10.1111/j.1471 -1842.2005.00602.x.

Minacapilli, C. A. 2018. *A Heuristic Evaluation of Multilingual Lombardy: Museums' Web Sites*, Master Thesis, Université de Genève.

Morado Vázquez, L. and J. Torres-del-Rey. 2023. "Universal Access through Mobile Devices in Multilingual Websites on the COVID-19 Pandemic," in S. O'Brien, and F. Federici, eds., *Translating Crises: Beyond Words to Action*, London: Bloomsbury Academic, pages 273–296.

Mozilla and Individual Contributors. 2022. <title>: The Document Title Element – HTML: HyperText Markup Language | MDN [online], available: https://developer .mozilla.org/en-US/docs/Web/HTML/Element/title.

National Library of Medicine. 2022a. MedlinePlus: Learn about MedlinePlus [online], available: https://medlineplus.gov/about/general/aboutmedlineplus/.

National Library of Medicine. 2022b. Organizations: MedlinePlus [online], available: https://medlineplus.gov/organizations/all_organizations.html.

O'Grady, L. 2005. "Accessibility Compliance Rates of Consumer-Oriented Canadian health care Web sites," *Medical Informatics and the Internet in Medicine*, 30 (4), pages 287–295, available: https://doi.org/10.1080/14639230500367746.

Pacati, I. and S. Rodríguez Vázquez. 2021. "CAT Tools' Impact on the Achievement of Accessible HTML5 Documents: A Comparative Study," in S. Jekat, S. Puhl, L. Carrer and A. Lintner, eds., *Proceedings of the 3rd Swiss Conference on Barrier-Free Communication (BfC 2020)*, Winterthur: ZHAW Zurich University of Applied Sciences, pages 170–178, available: https://doi .org/10.21256/zhaw-300.

Parvin, P., V. Palumbo, M. Manca, and F. Paternò. 2021. "The Transparency of Automatic Accessibility Evaluation Tools," in *Proceedings of the 18th International Web for All Conference*, W4A '21, New York, NY: Association for Computing Machinery, 1–5, available: https://doi.org/10.1145/3430263.3452436.

Piller, I. 2020. "Covid-19 Forces Us to Take Linguistic Diversity Seriously," in G. Boomgaarden, ed., *12 Perspectives on the Pandemic: International Social Science Thought Leaders Reflect on Covid- 19*, Berlin: De Gruyter, pages 12–17.

Pontus, V. 2019. *Evaluating the Accessibility of Localised Websites: The Case of the Airline Industry in Switzerland*, Master Thesis,Université de Genève.

Rahmatizadeh, S. and S. Valizadeh-Haghi. 2018. "Monitoring for Accessibility in Medical University Websites: Meeting the Needs of People with Disabilities," *Journal of Accessibility and Design for All*, 8 (2), pages 102–124, available: https:// doi.org/10.17411/jacces.v8i2.150.

Riesch, M., A. Dungga, K. Weissenfeld, and A. Uebelbacher. 2020. *eCH-0059 – Accessibility Standard 3.0* [online], available: www.ech.ch/de/dokument/e2896a60-9489-4662-9ba9-be5ddb430f31.

Rodríguez Vázquez, S. 2015a. "A Controlled Language-Based Evaluation Approach to Ensure Image Accessibility during Web Localisation," *Translation Spaces*, 4 (2), pages 187–215.

Rodríguez Vázquez, S. 2015b. "Exploring Current Accessibility Challenges in the Multilingual Web for Visually-Impaired Users," in *The 24th International World Wide Web Conference (WWW) 2015 Companion Volume*, New York, NY: ACM Press, pages 871–873, available: https://doi.org/10.1145/2740908.2743010.

Rodríguez Vázquez, S. 2016a. "Measuring the Impact of Automated Evaluation Tools on Alternative Text Quality: A Web Translation Study," in *Proceedings of the 13th Web for All Conference*, W4A '16, New York: ACM.

Rodríguez Vázquez, S. 2016b. *Assuring Accessibility during Web Localisation: An Empirical Investigation on the Achievement of Appropriate Text Alternatives for Images*, PhD Thesis,Université de Genève.

Rodríguez Vázquez, S. 2023. "Accessible Crisis Communication for the Blind and the Visually- Impaired in Multilingual Settings," in S. O'Brien and F. Federici, eds., *Translating Crises: Beyond Words to Action*. London: Bloomsbury Academic, pages 215–236.

Rodríguez Vázquez, S. and S. O'Brien. 2017. "Bringing Accessibility into the Multilingual Web Production Chain," in M. Antona and C. Stephanidis, eds., *Universal Access in Human– Computer Interaction. Design and Development Approaches and Methods: 11th International Conference, UAHCI 2017, Held as Part of HCI International 2017, Vancouver, BC, Canada, July 9–14,2017, Proceedings, Part I*, Cham: Springer International Publishing, pages 238–257, available: https://doi.org/10.1007/978-3-319-58706-6_20.

Rodríguez Vázquez, S. and J. Torres-del-Rey. 2020. "Accessibility of Multilingual Information in Cascading Crises," in F. M. Federici and S. O'Brien, eds., *Translation in Cascading Crises*, Oxon: Routledge, pages 91–111.

Rodríguez Vázquez, S., J. Torres-del-Rey, and L. Morado Vázquez. 2022. "Easy Language Content on the Web: a Multilingual Perspective," in M. Sánchez Ramos, ed., *Investigaciones Recientes Sobre Traducción y Accesibilidad Digital*, Peter Lang, pages 147–180.

Saraswat, I., R. Abouassaly, P. Dwyer, D. M. Bolton, and N. Lawrentschuk. 2016. "Female Urinary Incontinence Health Information Quality on the Internet: A Multilingual Evaluation," *International Urogynecology Journal*, 27(1), pages 69–76, available: https://doi.org/10.1007/s00192-015-2742-5.

Scanlan, M. 2021. "Reassessing the disability divide: unequal access as the world is pushed online," *Universal Access in the Information Society*, available: https://doi .org/10.1007/s10209-021-00803-5.

Schmidt, H., E.-M. Wild, and J. Schreyögg. 2021. "Explaining Variation in Health Information Seeking Behaviour: Insights from a Multilingual Survey," *Health policy (Amsterdam, Netherlands)*, 125 (5), pages 618–626, available: https://doi.org/10 .1016/j.healthpol.2021.01.008.

Spellman, J., R. B. Montgomery, S. Lauriat, and M. Cooper (Eds.). 2021a. "Web Content Accessibility Guidelines (WCAG) 3.0," available: www.w3.org/TR/wcag-3.0/.

Spellman, J., R. B. Montgomery, S. Lauriat, and M. Cooper. 2021b. "Web Content Accessibility Guidelines WCAG 3.0," Working Draft 7 December 2021 [online], *W3C Recommendation*, available: www.w3.org/TR/wcag-3.0.

Torres-del-Rey, J. 2019. "The Proper Place of Localization in Translation Curricula: An Inclusive Social, Object-Driven, Semiotic-Communicative Approach," in D. B. Sawyer, F. Austermühl, and V. Enríquez Raído, eds., *The Evolving Curriculum in Interpreter and Translator Education: Stakeholder Perspectives and Voices*, Amsterdam, pages 153–176.

Torres-del-Rey, J. and L. Morado Vázquez. 2015. "XLIFF and the Translator: Why Does it Matter?" *Revista tradumàtica: traducció i tecnologies de la informació i la comunicació*, (13), 584–607.

Torres-del-Rey, J. and L. Morado Vázquez. 2019. "Transferring Web Accessibility through Localization and Internationalization Standards," *The Journal of Internationalization and Localization*, 6 (1) pages 1–24.

Torres-del-Rey, J. and S. Rodríguez Vázquez. 2016. "New Insights into Translation-Oriented, Technology-Intensive Localiser Education: Accessibility As an Opportunity," in *Proceedings of the 4th International Conference Technological Ecosystems for Enhancing Multiculturality (TEEM '16)*, New York: ACM Press, pages 971–978, available: https://doi.org/10.1145/3012430.3012634.

United Nations. 2015. "Transforming our world: the 2030 Agenda for Sustainable Development," available: www.un.org/ga/search/view_doc.asp?symbol=A/RES/70/1&Lang=E.

United Nations. 2020. "Policy Brief: A Disability-Inclusive Response to COVID-19," available: www.un.org/sites/un2.un.org/files/sg_policy_brief_on_persons_with_disabilities_final.pdf.

Velleman, E. and S. Abou-Zahra (Eds.). 2014. "Website Accessibility Conformance Evaluation Methodology (WCAG-EM) 1.0," available: http://www.w3.org/TR/WCAG-EM/.

Vigo, M. 2009. *Automatic Assessment of Contextual Web Accessibility from an Evaluation, Measurement and Adaptation Perspectives*. PhD Thesis,Universidad del País Vasco.

W3C Web Accessibility Initiative (WAI). 2022. All WCAG 2 Test Rules [online], *Web Accessibility Initiative (WAI)*, available: www.w3.org/WAI/standards-guidelines/act/rules/.

WHATWG. 2022. "HTML Standard," available: https://html.spec.whatwg.org/#the-title-element.

White, K., S. Abou-Zahra, and S. Lawton Henry. 2020. Writing for Web Accessibility – Tips for Getting Started [online], *Web Accessibility Initiative (WAI)*, available: www.w3.org/WAI/tips/writing/.

Yi, Y. J. 2020. "Web Accessibility of Healthcare Web Sites of Korean Government and Public Agencies: A User Test for Persons with Visual Impairment," *Universal Access in the Information Society*, 19 (1), pages 41–56, available: https://doi.org/10.1007/s10209-018-0625-5.

Youngblood, N. E. 2020. "Digital Inclusiveness of Health Information Websites," *Universal Access in the Information Society*, 19 (1), pages 69–80, available: https://doi.org/10.1007/s10209-018-0629-1.

Yunker, J. 2003. *Beyond Borders: Web Globalization Strategies*, San Francisco, CA: New Riders.

Zeng, X. and B. Parmanto. 2004. "Web Content Accessibility of Consumer Health Information Web Sites for People with Disabilities: A Cross Sectional Evaluation," *Journal of Medical Internet Research*, 6 (2), page e19, available: https://doi.org/10.2196/jmir.6.2.e19.

Appendix A Web Sample: List of Organizations and Web Pages

The pages included in the web sample were last accessed in September 2021 (see Table 7.5).

Table 7.5 *List of organizations and pages included in our web sample*

Organization	URL (English)	URL (Spanish)
International Federation of Red Cross and Red Crescent Societies	https://media.ifrc.org/ifrc/	https://media.ifrc.org/ifrc/?lang=es
KidsHealth (Nemours Foundation)	https://kidshealth.org/	https://kidshealth.org/ES/
Leukemia & Lymphoma Society	www.lls.org/	www.lls.org/lls-espanol/
Life Options Rehabilitation Program	https://lifeoptions.org/	https://lifeoptions.org/es/
Living Beyond Breast Cancer	www.lbbc.org/	https://es.lbbc.org/
Lupus Foundation of America	www.lupus.org/	www.lupus.org/es/resources
March of Dimes Birth Defects Foundation	www.marchofdimes.org/	https://nacersano.marchofdimes.org/
Medicare (Centers for Medicare & Medicaid Services)	www.medicare.gov/	https://es.medicare.gov/
MotherToBaby (Organization of Teratology Information Specialists)	https://mothertobaby.org/	https://mothertobaby.org/es/sitio-web-en-espanol/
National Alliance for Hispanic Health	www.healthyamericas.org/	www.nuestrasalud.org/
National Cancer Institute	www.cancer.gov/	www.cancer.gov/espanol
National Center for Farmworker Health	http://www.ncfh.org/	http://www.es.ncfh.org/
National Center for Missing and Exploited Children	www.missingkids.org/home	https://esp.missingkids.org/home
National Council on Aging	www.ncoa.org/	www.ncoa.org/page/bienvenidos-a-ncoa
National Institute for Occupational Safety and Health	www.cdc.gov/niosh/	www.cdc.gov/spanish/niosh/
National Institute of Arthritis and Musculoskeletal and Skin Diseases	www.niams.nih.gov/	www.niams.nih.gov/es/portal-en-espanol

Table 7.5 *(cont.)*

Organization	URL (English)	URL (Spanish)
National Institute of Biomedical Imaging and Bioengineering	www.nibib.nih.gov/	www.nibib.nih.gov/es/nibib-en-espanol
National Institute of Dental and Craniofacial Research	www.nidcr.nih.gov/	www.nidcr.nih.gov/espanol
National Institute of Environmental Health Sciences	www.niehs.nih.gov/	www.niehs.nih.gov/health/scied/teachers/educacion/
National Institute of Neurological Disorders and Stroke	www.ninds.nih.gov/	https://espanol.ninds.nih.gov/es
National Institute on Aging	www.nia.nih.gov/	www.nia.nih.gov/health/espanol/temas
National Institute on Deafness and Other Communication Disorders	www.nidcd.nih.gov/	www.nidcd.nih.gov/es/espanol
National Institute on Drug Abuse	www.drugabuse.gov/	www.drugabuse.gov/es
National Institutes of Health	www.nih.gov/	https://salud.nih.gov/
National Kidney Foundation	www.kidney.org/	www.kidney.org/espanol
National Organ and Tissue Donation Initiative (Health Resources and Services Administration)	www.organdonor.gov/	https://donaciondeorganos.gov/
National Osteoporosis Foundation	www.nof.org/	https://huesosanos.org/
National Pesticide Information Center	http://npic.orst.edu/	http://npic.orst.edu/index.es.html
Nemours Foundation	www.nemours.org/welcome.html	www.nemours.org/about/coronavirus-espanol.html
Office of Minority Health (Department of Health and Human Services, Office of Minority Health)	https://minorityhealth.hhs.gov/	https://minorityhealth.hhs.gov/espanol/
Pan American Health Organization	www.paho.org/en	www.paho.org/es
Parkinson's Foundation	www.parkinson.org/	www.parkinson.org/espanol
Patient Advocate Foundation	www.patientadvocate.org/#	www.patientadvocate.org/es/

Table 7.5 *(cont.)*

Organization	URL (English)	URL (Spanish)
PleasePrEPMe	https://pleaseprepme.org/	https://pleaseprepme.org/es
Postpartum Support International	www.postpartum.net/	www.postpartum.net/en-espanol/
Scoliosis Research Society	www.srs.org/	www.srs.org/espanol/ patient_and_family/
Stuttering Foundation of America	www.stutteringhelp.org/	www.tartamudez.org/
Susan G. Komen for the Cure	www.komen.org/	www.komen.org/espanol/
Tourette Association of America	https://tourette.org/	https://tourette.org/about-tourette/overview/espanol/
TrialNet	www.trialnet.org/	www.trialnet.org/es
Tuberous Sclerosis Alliance	www.tscalliance.org/	www.tscalliance.org/en-espanol/
Turner Syndrome Society of the United States	www.turnersyndrome.org/	https://es.turnersyndrome.org/
US Citizenship and Immigration Services	www.uscis.gov/	www.uscis.gov/es
UNESCO	https://en.unesco.org/	https://es.unesco.org/
UNICEF	www.unicef.org/	www.unicef.org/es
United States Pharmacopeial Convention	www.usp.org/	www.usp.org/espanol
University of Texas M. D. Anderson Cancer Center	www.mdanderson.org/	www.mdanderson.org/es/ why-choose-md-anderson.html
White House	www.whitehouse.gov/	www.whitehouse.gov/es/
World Health Organization	www.who.int/en/	www.who.int/es/home
World Organisation for Animal Health	www.oie.int/en/home/	www.oie.int/es/inicio/

Index